WILD LAW

"Even in an age that feels itself to be enlightened and humane, and condemns cruelty to animals, and claims to take 'the environment' seriously, the idea of Wild Law still seems, to many, to be bizarre. How can wild creatures, or landscapes, be granted the same kind of respect – the same rights – in law, as a human being? Yet, as Cormac Cullinan argues so powerfully, the morality of this is clear, and the logic of the case seems impeccable. Indeed we should be asking, can we claim to be fully civilized in the absence of such laws?"

—Colin Tudge, author of *The Secret Life of Trees*, *Feeding People is Easy* and *Consider the Birds: How They Live and Why They Matter*

"This book of Cormac Cullinan explains with great clarity how we can change our entire approach to governance so that we can continue life on a liveable planet. In its basic outlines this book is one of the finest contributions to the entire field of jurisprudence in recent times."

—Thomas Berry, author of *The Dream of the Earth*, *The Universe Story* and *The Great Work*

"*Wild Law* is a stimulating, eminently readable response to our governance crisis. The survival of our species and health of the Earth family depends on our ability to transform governance systems so that humans become part of the ecological matrix of biological and cultural diversity. This book is a milestone on that path."

—Dr Vandana Shiva, President of the Research Foundation for Science, Technology and Ecology, and author of *Staying Alive* and *Water Wars*

"The arrogance of the 'civilised' world has blinded it to the wisdom of the indigenous people for too long. Cormac Cullinan's call for the indigenous voices and the wisdom of thousands of years of human experience to be heard in the heart of our governance systems is both timely and powerful. This provocative and groundbreaking book is an important milestone in the process of finding a viable ecological role for contemporary human societies."

—Martin von Hildebrand, co-ordinator of COAMA, programme for indigenous people in Colombia, which received the Right Livelihood Award in 1999

"We desperately need some new thinking today about systems of global governance. We're stuck with the same obsolete, ignore-the-earth institutions that were brought into being after the 2nd World War, and they're now failing us ever more catastrophically. *Wild Law* shows just how radical we now need to be in creating new institutions that are genuinely 'fit for purpose' in the 21st Century."

—Jonathon Porritt, Director of Forum for the Future

"We urgently need to rethink our legal and political systems if we are to stop environmental destruction. The radical ideas in *Wild Law* will give both lawyers and grass-roots activists the tools they need to start the process."

—Michael Meacher, former UK Minister for the Environment

"Wild law is to law what quantum physics is to physics."

—Alessandro Pelizzon, co-founder of Earth Laws, the Australian network on Wild Law and Earth Jurisprudence

WILD LAW

A Manifesto for Earth Justice

SECOND EDITION

CORMAC CULLINAN

with a foreword by Thomas Berry

green books

This second edition published in 2011
by Green Books, Dartington Space, Dartington Space,
Totnes, Devon TQ9 6EN, UK
www.greenbooks.co.uk

in association with
EnAct International, Cape Town
www.enact-international.com

First edition published in August 2002 by Siber Ink,
PO Box 44754, Claremont 7735, South Africa

First UK edition published in November 2003 by Green Books
in association with the Gaia Foundation

Quotes on pages 23, 78, 89, 129, 131, 138, 142, 143, 144, 145 and 175 are sourced
from *Simply Living*, edited by Shirley Ann Jones, ISBN 1 57731 054 3;
published by New World Library, Novato, California (www.nwlib.com).

Design by Rick Lawrence, Samskara Design
samskara@onetel.net.uk

Cover image by Martos Hoffman
www.martoshoffmanimages.com

Text printed on 100% recycled paper

Printed by TJ International, Padstow, Cornwall, UK

ISBN 978 1 900322 90 4

Contents

Preface to the second edition   7
Preface to the first edition   11
Author's note   15
Foreword by Thomas Berry   16

Part 1   Rethinking governance
1   Anthills and aardvarks   25

Part 2   The world as we know it
2   The illusion of independence   35
3   The myth of the master species   50
4   Why law and jurisprudence matter   55
5   The conceit of law   62

Part 3   Earth governance
6   Respecting the Great Law   77
7   Remembering who we are   85
8   The question of rights   95
9   Elements of Earth governance   110

Part 4   The journey into wildness
10   Seeking Earth jurisprudence   121
11   The rhythms of life   131
12   The law of the land   138
13   A communion of communities   146
14   Transforming law and governance   157

Part 5   The terrain ahead
15   The mountain path   169

Postscript   The emergence of Wild Law   178

Appendix   Universal Declaration of the Rights of Mother Earth   192

References   196
Bibliography   200
Index   202

DEDICATION

To my parents Chatêlaine and Brendan, and to the hills,
forests and creatures of Townbush Valley, all of whom
instilled in me a love of Earth

to my sons Cian and Benjamin: may they know
the joy of being within the Earth Community

and in memory of Thomas Berry,
wise mentor and eloquent elder spokesman
for Earth and all her children

Preface to the
second edition

This book presents a vision of how we could change the systems that structure and order the industrialised societies that dominate the contemporary world. We need to do so in order to turn away from the catastrophically destructive path that we are currently pursuing and to find a viable role for our species in the Earth community – one that will increase rather than diminish the beauty, health and diversity of Earth. Making this transition before it is too late is difficult, but it is possible. Since human beings have no future on Earth unless we are able to do so, being deterred by the difficulties is tantamount to acquiescing to extinction.

As the gravity and extent of human-induced damage to the planet becomes increasingly apparent, more and more people are realising that we cannot solve the environmental challenges of the 21st century by merely tweaking existing systems of governance. This revised second edition (which incorporates a new postscript and the Universal Declaration of the Rights of Mother Earth proclaimed on 22 April 2010) has been published because over the last few years in many parts of the world there has been a rapid upsurge of interest in living and ordering society in a way that is consistent with nature instead of trying to dominate nature. To many people the idea that we should aim to live by the 'rules' of the community or Earth system within which we came into being still seems radical rather than self-evident. I believe that the only realistic prospect of securing the kind of future to which most of us aspire is to effect fundamental changes to how we regulate our societies, inspired by an Earth-centric perspective. Climate change and other environmental crises are a direct result of our failure to align human systems of governance with the fundamental rules of the Earth system of which we are a part. Humans will continue to violate ecological limits and upset fundamental ecological balances until we establish ways of regulating human conduct that ensure that we comply with the fundamental rules of the Earth community.

The first edition of *Wild Law* was published in South Africa, immediately before the World Summit on Sustainable Development (WSSD) convened in September 2002 in Johannesburg. The WSSD did not initiate any new strategies or approaches capable of halting and reversing the degradation of Earth by humans, nor has the international community of states adopted any since

2002. The inadequacies of the international governance system in the face of the most significant challenges of the 21st century were clearly visible in the failure of the 15th meeting of the conference of the parties to the United Nations Framework Convention on Climate Change (UNFCCC) held in Copenhagen in December 2009 to produce a consensus on how the global community should respond to climate change. Indeed the future of the UNFCCC process itself is now in jeopardy, and a new international agreement on climate change may not be in place before the Kyoto Protocol expires in 2012.

Meanwhile ongoing human 'development' has accelerated the degradation and destruction of almost every aspect of Earth to the extent that now we are confronted with the real possibility that we may already have triggered irreversible and runaway climate change. Some respected scientists, such as James Lovelock (originator of the Gaia theory), believe that Earth's climate system has already passed the point of no return and that Earth is now spinning inexorably towards a new equilibrium which will be inhospitable to human life.

Even if these scientists are wrong and human-induced climate change is not yet irreversible, we will not be able to avert the collapse of the industrial civilisations that dominate the contemporary world and to make the transition to ecologically sustainable societies unless we can simultaneously solve many other challenges that are less high-profile but equally fundamental. We will need to cope with declining production volumes of oil and other minerals, and to find ways of stemming and reversing the pollution and contamination of the biosphere, the loss of fertile soils, desertification, the depletion of freshwater and fish stocks, the destruction of forests and habitats for wild species, and accelerating levels of human consumption coupled with population growth. Eight years after *Wild Law* was first published, the Earth community is in far worse shape and the fundamental drivers of destruction seem more or less intact.

Many people who care deeply about Earth are sinking into despair and asking "Is there any point in striving to prolong the survival of the human race?" From the perspective of Earth as a whole, during the last few centuries or more, the human presence on Earth has been a malign one. The shadow of our rapacious greed and narcissism has fallen across the face of so many of Earth's communities, bringing devastation and death. We have failed to use the amazing abilities and the abundant nutrients and energy gifted to us by the Earth community to benefit the community as a whole as well as ourselves. Instead, most of the spiritual, cultural and technological achievements we celebrate have been achieved at the expense of that community. Perhaps we have run our course, and the final act of our species will be to use our amazing capacity to modify our environment in ways that hasten our own extinction?

These are serious questions. My answer is implicit in this new edition of *Wild Law*. Despite the rapidly worsening health of many human and ecological communities, I still believe in the power of the human spirit to shape the future and in the value of pursuing the greater good – whatever you may perceive that to be. My working hypothesis is that even if success is not assured (and when is it ever?) it is still worth defending what one loves and working for what one believes to be good. Striving for social justice, to protect the incredible beauty of Earth and to secure a future for the children of all of Earthkind seems to me to be worthwhile regardless of the prospects of success. I do not want to carry the shame of saying to our children "I knew but did nothing, believing it to be hopeless".

Experience has also taught me that life is consistently surprising and great events, like the implosion of the Soviet Union and the demise of apartheid, can happen unexpectedly and rapidly. Probably the most important reason for producing this new edition was the intuition that something mysterious is stirring in the world. A new current of change is eddying through the *Zeitgeist*, bringing with it a hunger for action, fundamental change and the reintegration of humankind into the Earth community that I have not felt before.

In January 2003 the celebrated writer Arundhati Roy ended a speech with the memorable words: "Another world is not only possible, she is on her way. On a quiet day, I can hear her breathing." For years whatever breath I have been able to discern has sounded more like the wheeze of the pollution-corrupted lungs of a monstrous future slouching towards its birth. But now I can hear something else, in snatches, like the distant sigh of a whale blowing, borne unexpectedly on the wind. It sounds like the loose, unhurried rhythm of a wild creature padding closer, difficult to hear and largely unnoticed in the corridors of power and noisy markets of commerce, but almost tangible in quiet places. Perhaps it is the stirrings of wildness in the collective consciousness; perhaps it is the re-emergence of the rejected and suppressed shadow of the industrial civilisations with their obsession for control, domination and uniformity. It may just be my imagination. Whatever it is, wild law is suddenly emerging all over the planet, sometimes spontaneously and sometimes seeded by this book. Not only that, but similar approaches in many other fields are gaining strength – in agriculture (permaculture and other forms of organic agriculture), architecture (earth and green buildings), engineering and design (biomimicry), education (a range of holistic, experiential and nature-oriented techniques), medicine (holistic understandings of health), and in psychology (ecopsychology).

The postscript to this edition describes how the ideas in this book have been spreading, but it is the recent acceleration in the application of these ideas that is most notable. For example, in September 2008 the people of Ecuador voted overwhelmingly in a referendum to adopt a constitution that recognises that Nature has legally enforceable rights to exist and to maintain its cycles, structures, functions and processes. The inclusion of these articles was achieved by co-operation between indigenous peoples who adhere to the ancient concept of Mother Earth (*Pachamama*) and believe that given clean soil, air and water and their communities they can live a fulfilling life in harmony with nature (*sumak kawsay*), and non-governmental organisations and leaders who were convinced by contemporary arguments for recognising rights for Nature. The whole process – from proposing the idea of including rights for nature in the Constitution of Ecuador to the adoption of the Constitution – took 18 months. Just over a year later, in April 2010, a conference of more than 35,000 people in Bolivia proclaimed a Universal Declaration of the Rights of Mother Earth (see Appendix). This was followed by the formation in September 2010 of a Global Alliance for the Rights of Mother Earth. In each case, the confluence of the right people, at the right place at the right time, was critical. However, there is a growing sense among all involved that rights for Nature is an idea whose time has come.

Ecuador has changed the debate forever. The question of whether or not it is possible to place wild law ideas at the heart of legal systems has been answered. Now the questions are: how do we implement these ideas everywhere, and how do we adapt the machinery of governance to make them effective?

Cormac Cullinan
Cape Town
January 2011

Preface to the
first edition

I had thought that the genesis of this book lay in discussions that a group of lawyers, ecopsychologists, wilderness experts, anthropologists and environmentalists had with Father Thomas Berry, the eminent social historian, 'geologian', author and poet, at the Airlie Centre in Virginia, USA, in April 2001. I was wrong. What I have to say is part of a story that starts much, much further back: a story that is inextricably interwoven with the story of my life.

Thomas Berry has pointed out that many legal and political systems actually legitimise and encourage the exploitation of Earth. He has for many years stressed the importance of redefining our ideas of law and governance in order to establish a sound basis for developing laws and political institutions that strengthen mutually beneficial relations between humans and the rest of the biosphere. The Airlie meeting was convened by the Gaia Foundation of London, to take up Thomas Berry's challenge to begin that process. After the Airlie meeting, many of us felt that it was essential that some of the emerging ideas that we had been discussing should be written down so that they could be disseminated, discussed and developed collaboratively by a wider range of people. The forthcoming Johannesburg Earth Summit seemed like the perfect means of transmitting and amplifying what we believe to be an exciting and important perspective to hundreds of thousands of like-minded people all over the world. As one of the few lawyers involved at that stage I agreed, with a mixture of excitement and trepidation, to write something that could be used for this purpose.

For a long time I wrestled with how to articulate and convey my emerging sense of this 'Earth jurisprudence'. Part of the difficulty was that I was very conscious that far wiser people than me have already written elegantly and profoundly about the central ideas and insights on which Earth jurisprudence is based, in other contexts. I was also painfully aware that the importance and breadth of the subject matter required years (perhaps lifetimes) of study and contemplation to do it justice. All I had was the scraps of time that could be spared from my roles as a legal practitioner, father and partner.

Eventually it dawned on me that I could not begin to communicate a true sense of what I really thought and felt about this subject without making myself visible within the story. I had been trying to discuss the insights of systems thinking and its implications for human self-governance in a conventional, detached and semi-academic manner. In so doing, I was perpetuating the mechanistic and flawed view of reality that I was criticising. The truth is that I am not a detached observer but a participant in the system—a dancer in the great dance of the universe. What I see is influenced by who, and where, I am. And so it seems to me that the only authentic way in which I can communicate what I want to tell you is by giving you some sense of the evolution of these ideas within my own consciousness.

By personalising this story, my intention is not to elevate the unremarkable details of my own life or to claim any brilliance or originality for my own thinking processes. Indeed, most of the ideas that you will find in this book have been expressed in different contexts and ways by many people over thousands of years. What I want to do is to give you some sense of the events and forces that shaped, and are shaping, my thinking about these issues, and to share my tentative conclusions. I am convinced that there is significance in the fact that you are, at this moment, holding this book in your hands. What has brought you to this point, and what will you become from here? I hope that by sharing something of my answers to these questions it may help to spark your own recognition of events in your life that may have led you to similar conclusions. After all, despite the variously tinted lenses through which we each view the world, we are all reading from the same universal 'text'.

There is also another reason. I often find it particularly hard to overcome my self-imposed divisions between my emotional and spiritual life on the one hand, and my intellectual and professional life on the other. In the moments when I am able to do so, I am reawakened with shock and pleasure to my own heightened abilities and effectiveness. I sincerely believe that if we and the next few generations are to meet the challenge of our age by successfully catalysing huge societal changes, we will have to bring our whole selves to the party. Anything less will not do. Accomplishing this "Great Work", as Thomas Berry calls it, will take far more than the cold, hair-splitting intellectualism and cynicism so beloved by many academics, professional experts and self-styled 'pragmatists'. It will take courage, intellectual honesty, passion and soul too.

This book is about issues at the core of who we are as individuals and as a species. It is also about how we must transform our societies if we are to turn away from the relentless destruction of life on Earth and the accompanying impoverishment of our inner selves that is so characteristic of most societies today. Although it is about the philosophy of law, or jurisprudence, I have not written it primarily for lawyers. In fact the jurisprudence discussed in this book would be unfamiliar to most contemporary lawyers. However I hope that some will read it, because few of our sub-species stop advising on what the law says for long enough to consider what it ought to say, much less to consider the purpose of our systems of governance. Consequently most of us have not noticed how misconceptions held by the dominant societies on

Earth about how the universe functions and our role in it, have shaped our ideas of law and governance. In particular, most of us have not consciously recognised that the jurisprudence of most of our societies is inadequate to meet the critical challenges that now face us.

Almost every day I notice signs that more and more people are longing for our species to cease its self-destructive war with Earth and with one another. Despite the hype around the brave new 'globalised' world that is supposed to bring all manner of blessings for our children, an unsettling stench is seeping out through the cracks in the information super-highway. Beneath the shiny surface of our super-, techno-, digitalised-, genetically engineered, globalised, wonder-societies, our planet and our humanity is decaying. Have you ever looked into the bright, clear eyes of a child and tried to explain why the whales are being killed and the forests burnt? Why playing naked in the sun is dangerous and some streams are poisonous? Why some frogs now have five legs and teenagers blow themselves up in the process of killing other children in the Middle East? Do you ever wonder why some of us work so furiously while others can't find work and why either way, a deep satisfaction and a sense of belonging is so elusive?

This book doesn't try to provide all the answers to these questions. However, it is an attempt to look one aspect of our 21st-century reality in the eye. The truth is that the dominant civilisations on the planet are behaving in a way that is leading our children and us into a bleak, unsustainable future that most of us do not want. It is a future that involves the casual destruction of ancient human cultures and biological communities, and the extinction of a shocking number of living beings that have co-evolved with us. Their passing involves not only the wanton destruction of millions of years of the Earth's experience and wisdom recorded in genetic structures and the complex webs of relationships within ecosystems; it also permanently diminishes the Earth Community and robs the survivors of the opportunity to co-evolve with them.

Recognising and acknowledging this is one thing. Creating a new future requires far more. We will need to galvanise our collective wills to act, engage empathically and use all our imaginative and other powers both to conceptualise the future that we want and to find ways of bringing it about. This book is about how we might begin to rethink how we constitute and regulate our societies so that we can regulate our species in a manner that reflects our responsibility for playing a mutually enhancing role within the wider community of life on this planet. This is a task that I believe is both critical and urgent. As Thomas Berry puts it in the final paragraph of *The Great Work*:

> But even as we make our transition into this new century we must note that moments of grace are transient moments. The transformation must take place within a brief period. Otherwise it is gone forever. In the immense story of the universe, that so many of these dangerous moments have been navigated suc-

cessfully is some indication that the universe is for us rather than against us. We need only summon these forces to our support in order to succeed. It is difficult to believe that the purposes of the universe or of the planet Earth will ultimately be thwarted, although the human challenge to these purposes must never be underestimated.

Even if you disagree with much in this book, I hope that it will, in some way, inspire you to transform the human communities of which you are a member. May we recognise ourselves once more as valuable members of the Earth Community to which we all belong. And may we have the wisdom, imagination and determination to learn how to govern ourselves accordingly.

My intellectual indebtedness to Thomas Berry is apparent in almost every chapter of this book. I would like to thank him for the many inspirational moments during our discussions at the Airlie Centre in Virginia and for his generous encouragement as I wrestled with writing this book. However I am most grateful to him for being such an inspirational presence. It was a rare privilege to meet not only a brilliant intellectual and philosopher with a passionate commitment to Earth and humanity, but also someone who did not neglect to appreciate the dogwoods in bloom, or the humour in life.

I might never have come across Thomas Berry's books, I would not have met him and this book would certainly not have been written, had it not been for the Gaia Foundation of London. Liz Hosken and Ed Posey in particular have taught me a great deal in the last few years, not only about some of the ideas and approaches discussed in this book, but also about having the courage to venture into unchartered territory without any guarantees. I would like to thank them and all at Gaia for their unfailing personal, intellectual and financial support, and Betty for having foretold this book.

I am also grateful to many others who shared their ideas and comments, many of which have been woven into this text. These include the participants in the meetings at the Airlie Centre in Virginia in April 2001, participants in the discussions on Earth jurisprudence at the Seventh World Wilderness Congress in November 2001, and those who gave me their responses to my earlier essay, 'Earth Jurisprudence: re-establishing integrity in law and society'. I would also like to thank my colleagues Terry Winstanley, Nicholas Smith, Belinda Bowling and Ludine Lee-Wright, for their help in improving the text, and Lindsay Norman and Madeline Lass who edited the text in difficult circumstances. I am particularly grateful to Simon Sephton of Siber Ink who was the driving force in ensuring that the firstedition of this book was published in time for the World Summit on Sustainable Development as originally planned.

Finally, I would like to thank my family for their sacrifices while I was labouring to give birth to this book.

Cormac Cullinan
July 2002

Author's note

The challenge facing each one of us is to take personal responsibility for orientating our lives and our communities towards a future that is ecologically, socially, and spiritually sustaining. However, we also need to act collectively to change the thinking and the social structures that are hindering us from making the transition—a transition that is necessary if we are to protect the integrity of the community of life on Earth, and reclaim the sense of purpose and belonging that comes from playing a valuable role within that community.

There is now an urgent need for a coherent, common vision for the future that is capable of uniting all who strive for environmental and social justice. We need a new, positive manifesto to enable us to create ecologically sustainable human societies on Earth. This is not something that can be achieved by simply thinking up another human-centred ideology. The necessary unity, and the liberation of the combined creativity of millions of like-minded people, will only be achieved by acknowledging that we are part of a greater whole, and must live and organise our societies in a manner that contributes to the health of the planetary whole. I hope that the ideas in this book will contribute one more strand to the web linking the emerging community for change.

I would like to thank everyone who has contributed to the publication of this new edition of *Wild Law*. I am particularly grateful to John Elford of Green Books for his meticulous editing, patience and dedication to quality. I would also like to thank those who have been carrying the ideas in these pages out into the world with such enthusiasm and passion.

Cormac Cullinan
January 2011

Foreword

Oswald Spengler, at the beginning of the 20th Century, just after World War I, wrote a book entitled *The Decline of the West*. It was a study of the origin, development, maturity and then the decline of the various civilisations that had arisen in the course of human history. Based on this survey of the past and a look at the contemporary world, he made the first clear statement that our Western civilisation, in reality, was in a state of decline.

The book sent a shock throughout Europe and America for, despite the devastation of World War I in the years 1914–1918, the scientific technologies developed at the end of the 19th Century had set in motion an amazing series of 'progressive' developments. 'Progress', by that time, had become, possibly, the central value word in the modern vocabulary of Western civilisation. With our new engineering capacities we could raise steel-frame buildings far into the sky. With our new electrical energy we could light up the entire horizon at night. With our automobiles and airplanes we could travel with an ease never known before. With our telephones we could communicate, like magic, over long distances. Our scientific research was giving us powers over the natural world that we had never dreamed of in previous centuries.

These accomplishments seemed sufficient evidence that a new and more brilliant phase of Western civilisation was coming into existence, not that the Western world was in its declining period. Yet Spengler could see what others could not see, that however wonderful the scientific and technological genius, this was external brilliance: the inner life, the cultural creativity was severely diminished, the soul was gone. No matter how much technology we developed, no matter how wondrous the automobiles and airplanes, the telephones and the radios, no matter how brilliant our universities, our medical schools, our engineering skills: the life-giving soul was no longer there.

We were into a phase of civilisation that was losing its capacity to provide any satisfying human fulfilment, a civilisation that had also become terribly destructive to the life systems of Earth on which we most depended. The soil, the rain, the air were being polluted. The forests, the meadows, the living creatures roaming the land were devastated. They could no longer evoke the sense of the sublime that was there in their original form.

This loss of soul, and the related loss of life-meaning, was recognised by American writers of this period, especially by Sinclair Lewis and F. Scott Fitzgerald in their description of the emptiness of contemporary American life. Later this awareness of the inner emptiness of life in Western civilisation was emphasised in Europe by the Existentialist writers Jean-Paul Sartre, Albert Camus and Samuel Beckett, also by such writers in America as Tennessee Williams and Arthur Miller.

To keep the civilisation (or the 'culture' in Spengler's terminology) alive, the typical response in the past was by increasing its organisational processes, by technological improvement, by new methods of plundering the natural world. So now, for these past few centuries, since the time of René Descartes (1596–1650), we have increased our assault on the natural world. We have cut the forests, ploughed the great Central Plains of the North American continent, we have blasted off the tops of the Appalachian Mountains to strip-mine for coal, we have paved over the land for highways and parking-lots, we have put great nets into the sea to sweep up shoals of cod in the North Atlantic waters. We have poured vast amounts of concrete into the 600-foot dams being built on the great rivers of the continent. All these industrial projects have made our 20th Century Western civilisation the technological and engineering marvel of the ages.

So too, in economics, we have organised the great entrepreneurial-commercial corporations into global coalitions to extend our control over natural resources and to increase production processes over the entire planet. These corporations have extended their control so extensively that they now provide the context in which the human populations of the planet find their livelihood. The people now discover themselves and their livelihood no longer in the dynamics of the land, but in the context of the corporation.

Because we have, apparently, been so successful in shaping the industrial phase of our Western civilisation, we even thought that the Western soul had been an obstacle in our way during previous centuries. We were now liberated from the judgements soul would impose upon us. We could now deal with all the world as mechanism to be controlled by advanced engineering projects and by the endless sequence of inventions we were making, inventions such as Thomas Edison had brought forth from his research institute founded in New Jersey in the 1870s.

This mechanistic world controlled by humans, for human advantage, saw the surrounding world as a vast assembly of natural resources put there for human use, not as manifestation of the sacred and sublime to be experienced in the wonder of its mountains and oceans, in the beauty of its meadows and birds and woodland creatures, in its healing of the loneliness of the human soul and the ills of the human body.

With the light pollution of our cities we lost the presence and power of the night sky with its moon and stars and mysterious planets. We could no longer feel ourselves enfolded in the great cosmic liturgy, a liturgy into which humans everywhere inserted themselves with their rituals to validate their own existence, which inspires the tribal peoples and has inspired the great civilisations that have existed in the past. These were the sources whence have come the great spiritual disciplines, the arts, the music and dance and works of literature, all of which have enabled the human soul to experience its most complete fulfilment.

Such is the context in which the honoured professions of religion, law, medicine, literature, science, and history have found their deepest meaning. All of these have been profoundly altered in this period. The amazing thing is that the story of this loss of soul has been told as immense gain, as liberation, as enlightenment, as a wondrous civilising achievement. A new freedom is experienced. The human mind could now develop the new economics, the new engineering, the new sciences. We could enter onto the transforming stage of industrial development, although this term 'development' should most often be written as 'development destruction', since development for humans in the industrial context was simultaneously devastation for the natural world. In the industrial world we seldom find development without a corresponding destruction. So far, in our great modern self-deception, we have been unwilling to associate these two words in the same phrase. That self-delusion is at the centre of the contemporary difficulties between humans and the Earth.

Yet this sense of the world without a sustaining inner principle or soul has been the context in which our sciences and our technologies of the natural world were able to develop. One immense benefit that resulted from this new situation was discovery of the evolutionary process whereby the universe and planet Earth came into being. At the same time we came to possess profound insights into both the microphase and macrophase functioning of the Earth. We did indeed gain in our capacity to deal with centuries-old diseases that humans were subject to with little understanding on our part and no capacity to remedy.

The pathos of the situation, however, is that we had abandoned our intimate presence to the Earth. In our new industrial world we knew more about the Earth and the universe than we had ever known previously and yet we no longer communed with the Earth in its original integrity. Our scientific understanding did not prevent us from devastating the forests, or from polluting the air and water and the land. Our intimate biological knowledge of the salmon who needed free access to the Columbia River each year to spawn the next generation could not prevent us from diminishing the spawning run from its original multitude to a trickle, and even eliminating some varieties of salmon by building the immense dams needed by our industrial civilisation.

Neither the needs of the natural world for survival nor the needs of humans for the wonder and inspiration of the natural world could restrain us from satisfying the prior needs of the industrial economy.

With the vast extent of our knowledge and the power of our technologies came an arrogant assurance that we could manage any difficulty associated with our actions. We would ourselves be the self-referent centre of the world. All the world was for humans, humans were for themselves. We had the research skills, we would soon have the education needed in the sciences and engineering. The religions were already detached from concerns over the destiny of the natural world. The one great need was for a legal structure that would authorise the assault on the natural world. This legal foundation found its primordial expression in the American Constitution, which exalted the property-owning citizen beyond anything known previously in the history of political establishments. The difficulty is not exactly with the rights granted to humans; the difficulty is that no rights and no protections were granted to any non-human mode of being.

From its beginning the American Constitution was clearly a document framed for the advancement of the human with no significant referent to any other power in heaven or on Earth. In the Bill of Rights, added as the first ten amendments, a detailed listing of the rights of individual persons was given. Humans had finally become self-validating, both as individuals and as a political community. This self-validation was invented and sustained by the union of the commercial-entrepreneurial powers with the legal-judicial powers to sustain the assault on the natural world.

A person might see the pathos of this self-validating situation, for the human had no power of bringing extinguished species back to life, no capacity for restoring the petroleum or any of the other natural resources that we were exhausting. Only a self-destructive arrogance would enable a society to assume the rights to devastate what nature could bring into being but which no power in heaven or on Earth, not even nature herself, could remedy once destruction had taken place.

It would be appropriate if the prologue of any founding Constitution enacted by humans would state in its opening lines a clear recognition that our own human existence and well-being are dependent on the well-being of the larger Earth Community out of which we were born and upon which we depend for our continued survival. This statement might be followed by a statement that care of this larger Earth Community is a primary obligation of the nation being founded.

Such a statement would be particularly appropriate in the assembly of nations known as the United Nations. As things are at present, each of the nations identifies itself as a 'sovereign' nation, that is, a people bonded together by a national covenant whereby it declares itself self-referent, that is, subject to no other earthly power in the conduct of its affairs. The United Nations is itself at present a bonding of such independent nations of the world pledged to maintain international peace and security and to provide a context of mutual assistance in economic and social development. There is no mention of any relationship with the natural world or with any other mode of being, not even of the planet we live on and out of which comes all that we are and all that we have.

After half a century when the nations have been functioning in these capacities, the political and military stress within and between nations remains a basic preoccupation of this world organisation. Yet a larger stress now looms over the horizon: the stress between the human community and the planet we live on. The industrial civilisation, with its dedication to the 'development of natural resources' has now spread over the entire Earth. No industrial nation is now self-sufficient in its basic needs for physical survival. Some of the less developed nations with large populations are particularly in difficulty. But even more important is the rate at which the resources of the Earth are being exhausted.

This work of Cormac Cullinan presents a new way of thinking about the intimate presence of the human community on the Earth. In his concept of the Great Jurisprudence he expresses the challenge that is before us. We have thought to reduce the Earth to our own human dimensions, to domesticate the Earth, to somehow insert the Earth into our own mechanistic pattern of functioning, to make the Earth obedient to ourselves rather than ourselves becoming responsive to the Earth. Obviously we are not succeeding.

But even while we set forth such stark alternatives we must be aware that we have spoken here of the deepest orientation of our human mode of presence to the natural world about us. We can never in the future do without the sciences and technologies in establishing a sustainable human way of life. Once we adjust our vision, once we set the basic patterns of dependence, once we accept that the norm and guide of our human mode of being is in the larger world about us, once we learn to live with, to foster and protect the wildness spoken of by Thoreau, once we honour the fierce green fire in the eyes of the living wolves rather than in the dying wolf encountered by Aldo Leopold, then we might be able to bring the assistance available to us from those remarkable insights of our modern technologies. What must be granted, however, is that merely diminishing the industrial attrition on the natural world, reusing, recycling, even using renewable resources such as wind power and solar energy—these do not satisfy the need that we are speaking of here.

It's time to replace our arrogance toward the Earth with a becoming humility, to replace our fear of the Earth with a grateful response to a benign and gracious mother; yet a severe and demanding mother, a mother who will at times starve us with famine, assault us with storms, drown us at sea, yet will provide us with a world of endless excitement and infinite meaning. She will give us the mystery and meaning of the starry sky at night, will awaken us with the glory of the dawn each day, will provide us with refreshing air to breathe, with uncontaminated soil for our cultivation, will spread out for us a vast array of flowers in her meadows. Her birds will sing to us at dawn and sunset and dazzle us as they soar so effortlessly through space.

There is a difference between such a world and the industrial world where we now live; a wild world indeed, but a world that is alive with an ever-renewing energy flowing spontaneously through its every component. We need legal structures and political establishments that will know that our way into the future is not through relentless industrial development but through the living forces that brought us into being and are the only forces that can sustain us in the coming centuries.

Thomas Berry
2003

Fr. Thomas Berry (1914–2009) was one the world's leading thinkers on human relationships with the natural world. Monk, philosopher, cultural historian and author, he considered himself to be a 'geologian' or earth scholar rather than a theologian. An eloquent and passionate spokesperson for the Earth, he has been described as "one of the most eminent cultural historians of our time" and by *Newsweek* as "the most provocative figure among the new breed of eco-theologians". He entered the Passionist order in 1934 and devoted his life to studying, reflecting and teaching. He had a doctoral degree in history, studied Chinese language and culture in China in the late 1940s, was an army chaplain in Europe in the 1950s, and then taught the cultural history of India and China at Seton Hall and Fordham Universities. He founded the History of Religions Program at Fordham University, New York, and the Riverdale Center of Religious Research. His works include *The Dream of the Earth*, *The Universe Story* (with scientist Brian Swimme), *The Great Work* and *Evening Thoughts* (edited by Mary Evelyn Tucker). He lived in the hill country of the Southern Appalachians, North Carolina, USA, until his death aged 94.

PART 1

Rethinking governance

We are planted here. Man is a plant that grows and branches and flowers on Earth.

Nahuatl-speaking descendant of the Aztecs, Mexico

Chapter 1

Anthills and aardvarks

THE ANTHILL

It was a clear African morning, with the freshness of overnight rain. Glossy Hadeda Ibises were preening themselves in the thorn trees and the earth was steaming softly in the warmth of the morning sun. As I walked back to my hotel in Lilongwe, Malawi, after a morning meeting, I noticed a small anthill next to the path. The rain had softened the protective outer dome and a passer-by had kicked off a cranium-sized section, exposing the cortex of cool, dark tunnels inside. The pale termites were working quickly and purposefully to repair the damage and to stop the rapidly warming sunlight streaming in. The workers moved back and forth, efficiently sealing the hole with spittle and earth. The soldier termites positioned themselves at strategic intervals so that they could protect the workers and prevent invaders gaining access to the nest.

I paused for a moment, struck by the organised efficiency with which they worked. Each termite knew exactly what it needed to do, and the actions of each tiny individual combined seamlessly to produce the outcome that the welfare of the community demanded. I remembered having been told that scientists were trying to puzzle out exactly how commands were relayed within the complex social structures of insects like ants and termites. Did the termite queen secrete special chemicals that were then passed on to each of the individuals, effectively giving them complex coded instructions as to what they were to do in any given circumstances? How was it that termites everywhere could build such marvellously complex structures with underground gardens, sophisticated ventilation systems, and a staggering degree of social organisation?

As I watched the tiny creatures moving about, it seemed to me highly improbable that they were either simply implementing instructions from the queen or deciding for themselves what to do. Each one might simply be responding to the external stimuli on the basis of internal 'programmes' or instincts. However, would this really explain their choreographed efficiency? Just how detailed could such internal codes be before they became too inflexible to deal with the immensely varied circumstances of life? It appeared to me that what I was observing was more like the functioning of a

single consciousness expressing itself through many creatures than many individuals co-ordinating their activities in some cunning way.

Then it occurred to me that each termite might be a tiny receiver, finely
tuned to a narrow bandwidth of the great symphony of the universe that gave
it the melody to which it should dance. Perhaps they did not need great brains
or complex instructions, because when they felt the juddering of a boot against
their home and light flooding in, each of them had the capacity to tap into a
greater source of termite lore? A kind of psychic website from which they
instinctively downloaded the knowledge of what they must do in order to
maintain the integrity of their community, and ultimately of their species and
of the ecosystem of which they are such an important part. In other words,
their actions were determined by the interaction between an information
source outside their bodies, and their own innate qualities, which allowed
them both to tap into termite-specific information and to act on it.

To this day I do not know what conclusions, if any, scientists have reached
regarding the functioning of termite communities, and whether or not my
musings were correct. Right or wrong, the image from that warm Malawi
morning has stayed with me. I have suspected ever since that building complex communities that are well functioning, harmonious, and resilient is
probably less about developing complex decision-making hierarchies and far
more about fine tuning our ability to 'hear' the universe, and to act accordingly. My guess is that more complex animals like humans probably have the
capacity to tune into a broader band of information than termites, and we
certainly have a greater capacity to choose how to respond to what we
'receive'. Of course, any such enhanced capacity will not help if we choose not
to tune in, or respond to, our environment.

A HYPOTHESIS GROWS

As I continued doing environmental law and policy work in various countries
during the 1990s, I became more interested in what made laws more or less
effective instruments for governing social behaviour. I became convinced that,
in my field at least, if laws are to be effective they need to recognise the inherent nature of the subject matter with which they are concerned. This means
that a governance system must to some extent reflect, or at least correspond
with, the qualities of that which it is seeking to regulate. For example, if we
observe that one of the qualities of the environment is that it is constantly
changing, we need environmental laws and governance structures that are flexible and adaptable. Equally, the pervasive nature of the environment requires
that the environmental governance system must have a very broad scope.

I gradually formed a working hypothesis in my mind that the prospects
of a governance system being successful could be increased by designing it in

a way that took account of the attributes of what was being governed. Over time I began unconsciously to embroider this rudimentary hypothesis with scraps of ideas picked up from here and there. One such idea was the conscious recognition that the way in which most governance systems rely on economic considerations and the functioning of markets to guide human behaviour is often highly inappropriate. Making certain decisions in this way virtually guarantees that from a long-term perspective, bad or sub-optimal decisions will result. This is so even if market distortions are corrected by full cost accounting that, for example, ensures that the costs of pollution are borne by the polluter and incorporated into the prices of commodities.

For example, reading *The Human Body Shop* by Andrew Kimbrell, and observing his predictions about the commercialisation of every aspect of the human body come true, year by year, reinforced my belief that the market is no place to make ethical decisions about the use of the human body. These decisions go to the heart of who we are as humans, and require careful consideration and wisdom. Furthermore, it is not simply a matter of deciding *what* should be done. *Why* and *how* something is done are vitally important. Paying blood donors may be fully justifiable on the grounds of efficiency and cost-effectiveness. However, as Kimbrell's book makes vividly clear, commercialising blood leads, quite literally, to bleeding dry the poorest and most vulnerable members of society. On the other hand, as was so graphically illustrated by the response of New Yorkers to the tragedy of 11 September 2001, the selfless ritual of giving blood to benefit unknown people who need it, can connect people and strengthen communities in a profound way.

While working on wildlife legislation in Namibia I was struck by how our unquestioning adoption of myopically human-centred laws often leads to results that are perverse and obstruct healthy relations between humans and other species. In Namibia (as in many countries) farmers who want to own wild game animals like rhinos, oryx and kudu on their land must fence them in with game-proof fences. In this way the law creates an incentive for farmers in this arid country to game-fence huge areas, which in turn prevents the natural migration of the herds in search of water and grazing. Worse still, there is no legal obligation on farmers to provide water or fodder, or to open the fences in times of drought. Some farmers simply keep all the water and fodder for their cattle and let the game die.

The same law encourages humans to slaughter innocent termite-eating aardvarks on sight by defining them as 'problem animals'. The 'problem' that condemns the aardvark to rogue status is that resourceful jackals use aardvark burrows to get under jackal-proof fences and into sheep farms. These laws would be unthinkable if these native inhabitants were not defined as objects that could be destroyed at the whim of human landlords.

My basic hypothesis—that there should be a correlation between the regulatory system and what was being regulated — was further encouraged by conversations with a friend in London who is a retired professor. He liked theorising about the development of new forms of business organisations in the information economy. One day he mentioned to me that he was reading up on embryology (the study of how embryos develop) to gain inspiration and insight into how new forms of business organisation might grow. At first this approach seemed rather a long shot to me, but I was attracted by the idea of consciously drawing on the rich library of experience offered by nature. Although the basic idea of being inspired by nature recurs in human history in different forms, I was initially rather wary of applying this approach to governance systems. I was well aware that the diversity of nature and our limited knowledge of it allows ample scope for everyone from fascists to nihilists and beyond to claim that nature supports their theories. Like many people with a background in the humanities rather than the sciences, I thought that any suggestion that we should, for example, draw lessons for the regulation of human societies from termite colonies, was likely to be misinterpreted as a new and crankier form of social Darwinism. These theories often involve projecting our ideas onto nature, like Moses Rusden's 1679 work, *A Further Discovery of Bees*, which claimed that bees were organised into social hierarchies with a king, dukes and plebeians.

It was only much later, when I read *The Universe Story* by Brian Swimme and Thomas Berry, that I realised why studying nature's patterns and methods is likely to be productive. The reason, of course, is that we are part of nature and not separate from it. It therefore stands to reason that those patterns that have evolved and which have stood the tests of the millennia, are likely to have inherent qualities that are consistent with the basic principles of the Earth system. Furthermore, as I discuss in Chapter Six, since we are part of nature, being conscious of the need to adapt human governance systems to human nature is likely to be helpful. Obviously there is a lot of room for error if we seek to cut patterns from one context and paste them down in another. Nonetheless, my guess is that if we consciously draw inspiration from the rich diversity of natural patterns, structures and processes, the probability of success will increase.

This is now increasingly recognised, and many different disciplines are engaged in consciously drawing inspiration from nature in designing anything from cities to industrial processes. For example, even the simple observation that in natural systems one organism's waste is another's food and that materials and energy are endlessly recycled, has profound implications for the redesign of our industrial processes. Almost all human processing systems are linear. They take in vast quantities of materials and energy at one end, transform it into something of transient use to humans and then return it all to Earth as (virtually) unusable waste.

As far as I know, public institutions in modern western cultures have not consciously drawn on nature when designing or reforming human regulatory systems. There are probably several reasons for this, including the fact that most lawyers and legislators do not know enough about natural regulatory systems, and in any case do not believe that they are relevant to humans.

However, my primary concern in this book is not with the redesign of legislation. One of the most important things that I learned from Thomas Berry was that reforming our governance systems will require us to entirely reconceptualise our *idea* of law from a biocentric or Earth-centred perspective. Reforming national legislation and entering into new international agreements will be insufficient unless these are done on the basis of a new understanding that the essential *purpose* of human governance systems should be to support people to play a mutually enhancing role within the community of life on Earth. This requires us first to recognise that at the moment the governance systems of most countries and of the international 'community' actually facilitate and legitimise the exploitation and destruction of Earth by humans. One of the implications of this, I believe, is that excellent initiatives such as the development of an 'Earth Charter', or the movement to popularise the groundbreaking 'World Charter for Nature' adopted by the General Assembly of the United Nations in 1982,[1] cannot succeed in isolation. Although these documents embody many of the values advocated in this book, they still exist within a governance context that is fundamentally opposed to prioritising these values.

In this book, I follow in the footsteps of Thomas Berry and argue that in order to change completely the purpose of our governance systems, we must develop coherent new theories or philosophies of governance ('Earth jurisprudence') to supplant the old. This Earth jurisprudence is needed to guide the realignment of human governance systems with the fundamental principles of how the universe functions (which I refer to in Chapter Six as the 'Great Jurisprudence'). Giving effect to Earth jurisprudence and bringing about systemic changes in human governance systems will also require the conscious fostering of wild law.

WALKING ON THE WILD SIDE

I know that 'wild law' sounds like nonsense—a contradiction in terms. Law, after all, is intended to bind, constrain, regularise and civilise. Law's rules, backed up by force, are designed to clip, prune and train the wilderness of human behaviour into the manicured lawns and shrubbery of the civilised garden. 'Wild', on the other hand, is synonymous with unkempt, barbarous, unrefined, uncivilised, unrestrained, wayward, disorderly, irregular, out of control, unconventional, undisciplined, passionate, violent, uncultivated, and riotous. In fact, the 'Wild West' of North America was described as 'wild' specifically because of the general lawlessness that prevailed there.

It is precisely the rigidity of this false dichotomy between the 'wild' and 'law', between 'nature' and 'civilisation', that we need to overcome. Like the Chinese symbol for Yin and Yang, both are part of the whole, and it is the dynamic balance that is important, not the triumph of one over the other. We need to find the wild Yin spot in the heart of the Yang of law, and also to perceive the core of law within the wilderness of Yin. Governing in a manner that stamps out wildness and promotes the dull conformity of monoculture is not desirable. Much of what is best in us is contained within our wild hearts. Wildness is associated with creativity and passion, with that part of us that is most connected with nature. It can also be understood as a metaphor for the life force that flows through us all and drives the evolutionary process. In this sense it has an eternal, sacred quality that both defines us and connects us most intimately with this planet.

In wildness is the preservation of the world.

Henry David Thoreau

Wildness is a quality that can only be experienced by straying off the orthodox path of civilisation as we know it. As we know, it is to be found most obviously in the wilderness, those special places where wildness rules. However, we would do well to remember that in many cultures the wilderness is also strongly associated with wisdom. It is the place to which people go in times of transition or confusion, and it is the place from which new insights emerge.

As will become apparent, particularly from Chapters Seven and Eleven, wild time, wild places and what used to be called 'wild people' are all important for wild law. If all this sounds like gobbledegook, bear with me a while longer and I will try to give you a clearer idea of what I mean.

WILD LAW

Firstly, the term 'wild law' cannot easily be snared within the strictures of a conventional legal definition. It is perhaps better understood as an approach to human governance, rather than as a branch of law or a collection of laws. It is more about ways of being and doing than the right thing to do.

Wild law expresses Earth jurisprudence. It recognises and embodies the qualities of the Earth system within which it exists. As an approach it seeks both to foster passionate and intimate connections between people and nature and to deepen our connection with the wild aspect of our own natures. It tends to focus more on relationships and on the processes by which they can be strengthened, than on end-points and 'things' like property. It protects wilderness and the freedom of communities of life to self-regulate. It aims to encourage creative diversity rather than to impose uniformity. Wild law opens spaces within which different and unconventional approaches can spring up, perhaps to flourish, perhaps to run their course and die.

Wild laws are laws that regulate humans in a manner that creates the freedom for all the members of the Earth Community to play a role in the continuing co-evolution of the planet. Where wild laws prevail, cultural and biological diversity, creativity and the freedom to play a creative role in the co-evolution of this planet will be found.

With a little practice you can start to recognise flashes of it even in our current legal and political systems. Wildness can be glimpsed in laws that reserve a certain amount of water to the river in order that it may flow healthily, and in international declarations that assert the inherent value of all living organisms and of biological diversity itself. It crops up in the recent amendment to the German constitution (paragraph 20(a)), which recognises that the state has a responsibility to protect animals as well as humans. Bills of rights that enshrine the right not to be unfairly discriminated against on the basis of ethnicity, nationality, gender, age or sexual preference also reflect elements of wild law in so far as they protect spaces within which human diversity can flourish.

Sometimes it is easier to identify what is not wild law. For example, laws that define seeds and genes as the property of someone and which prohibit farmers saving seeds to plant next season's crop, deny wildness. As discussed in Chapter Thirteen, the purpose behind these laws is incompatible with the purpose of wild law.

Another deeply disturbing account of judgements that reflect the antithesis of wild law is given in Brian Brown's lucid and moving analysis of decisions of the United States courts concerning the relationship between native Americans and the lands they hold sacred.[2] Again and again the courts sanctioned the severance of ancient spiritual connections between peoples and the lands that gave birth to their cultures. The fundamentalist allegiance of the courts to the notion of land as property and their failure to come to terms with the diversity of human spiritual beliefs seems to have blinded them to the consequences of their judgements. Judges who sanction the building of dams and roads through wilderness areas sacred to indigenous peoples while at the same time accepting that these actions would be enormously destructive to the ancient religious practices of these peoples, deny the soul and wildness of all humans. A worldview and jurisprudence that leads to judgements like those analysed by Brown, in whatever country, can only be described as deeply destructive.

Wildness is inherent in all people and organisms. It can even be understood as another name for the creative life force inherent in the universe. As such it is at the heart of existence and expressing it is fundamental to our role. Yet almost all of our laws and our social governance structures suppress and stifle expressions of wildness and promote uniformity and control. I hope that this book will give some ideas of how to find, recognise and develop wildness in law and society. I also hope that it will inspire you to imagine (if you dare) what our societies might be like if they celebrated and encouraged wildness rather than stamping it out!

PART 2

The world as we know it

The laws of the perfect human society can only be found within the total order of things, in the purpose of the Universe.

Alexander Solzhenitsyn, August 1914

Chapter 2

The illusion of independence

THE BANALITY OF BIOCIDE

Human societies are savaging Earth. Right now, the human societies that currently dominate our planet are precipitating what is being described as the sixth mass extinction. Periods of mass extinction have only occurred five times in Earth's fifteen billion year history. The last such event occurred about 65 million years ago, and appears to have been triggered by a massive asteroid—about six miles in diameter—smashing into the Yucatan Peninsula. The Earth was plunged into darkness, photosynthesis stalled, and the Cretaceous period ended with the extinction of the dinosaurs and most other organisms. As with all previous periods of mass extinction, it took several tens of millions of years for biodiversity levels to recover to levels comparable with what had existed prior to this cataclysmic event.

It is hard to believe, and indeed most people do not believe, that in a few centuries our species has been able to unravel the beautiful and complex web of life on this planet so extensively. Worse still, many of us are now bored by the increasingly frequent news of environmental destruction and impending ecological disasters. After all, it is old news that we are messing up the planet. Increasingly shocking stories or images are required to maintain our attention.

Most of us have used or heard similar rationalisations to the following. 'Yes, we know that as we speak rainforests are being felled and coral reefs bleached and we all agree these sorts of things shouldn't be allowed to happen. Sure, the growing numbers of shack dwellers around the world are having a hard time and there might not be much of the natural world left for our kids to enjoy. On the other hand, life goes on. Anyway, what can one really do in the face of the likes of the World Trade Organisation, the transnational corporations and governments that want to speed up the use of oil because it is running out? The best thing to do if you feel too despondent about it is to go and buy the latest 'green' product or to support the recycling project at the local school. And hey, who knows, with a bit of luck some new scientists might discover that it isn't so bad after all or invent a great new way of reversing global warming. Somebody, somewhere is bound to work it out eventually and solve these problems once and for all.'

A BRIEF OVERVIEW OF
SOME OF THE SYMPTOMS

The rapid deterioration of Earth is clear evidence that we humans are doing something awfully wrong and that our self-regulatory mechanisms (i.e. our governance systems) are defective. There are those who believe that the environmental degradation and destruction that we are observing is all part of a natural evolutionary process and we shouldn't worry too much because it will all sort itself out eventually. They may be right in the long run, but to me the thought that the gratuitous destruction of intricate biological communities will be repaired in the course of the next 30 million years or so, is cold comfort.

There are others who deny that there is a problem worth getting excited about. This is not the place to canvass all the reasons why I disagree with them, but in the interests of providing some factual basis for my views, I think it is worth pausing for a brief recap of six key points before we move on.

Ecological overshoot

The big picture is that human beings now take much more from Earth during a given period than Earth produces in that time. Each year the ecosystems and natural cycles and processes of Earth generate a certain amount of clean air, freshwater, and fertile soil, and together with the sunlight that falls on Earth, this sustains all life. Each year our species takes more than its fair share of these gifts and in so doing deprived other beings of what they require to flourish. Worse still, by consuming coal, oil, groundwater and other stores of "natural resources" far faster than they accumulated, we are using up "natural capital", and by releasing substances into water and the atmosphere faster than they can be metabolised by natural systems and processes we are destabilising them and impairing their functioning. This means that the human population is consuming not only what ecosystems produce each year (e.g. food, timber, and clean water) but is also consuming the ecosystems themselves. As we impair these natural relationships we diminish the Earth's capacity to maintain the conditions conducive to life and reduce the flow of future benefits, thereby diminishing the prospects of our children and those of most other species, flourishing or even surviving.

What a person, group of people or society takes from Earth during a given period is sometimes referred to as an "ecological footprint", and is expressed as the area of Earth that would be required to provide those benefits indefinitely. The United Nations Environment Programme ("UNEP") has published four Global Environmental Outlook reports between 1997 and 2007 which together chronicle the progressively worsening consequences of exploiting Earth far beyond ecologically sustainable levels. The Fourth Global

Environmental Outlook report published in 2007 ("GEO-4")[1] warns explicitly that 21.9 hectares of land is required on average to support each human being but at current population levels, only 15.7 hectares per person is available. Even this may understate the problem by assuming that the Earth's "resources" are available for humans to appropriate for their exclusive use. Optimising the health and functioning of the community of life as a whole would require even greater reductions in the ecological footprint of humanity.

The gap between the "ecological footprint" of humankind and the capacity of Earth to support human life is widening rapidly. This is driven by a number of interrelated factors such as environmental degradation which reduces the capacity of land to support human life, the ballooning human population,[2] increases in per capita consumption in response to economic growth, rising wealth and changing consumptions patterns spread by globalisation. In other words, what the dominant industrialised civilisations today characterise as "progress" amounts to accelerating towards their collapse.

Over-consumption

Humans are consuming or destroying those aspects of Earth that sustain human and other life at a rate that is orders of magnitude faster than they can be created. In addition, our rate of consumption is accelerating. As Lester Brown points out in Eco-Economy, while economists look with pride on the fact that the world economy expanded sevenfold between 1950 and 2000 and world trade is increasing more rapidly, ecologists see that these are based on the profligate use of Earth's "natural capital". As Brown notes:

> The economic policies that have yielded the extraordinary growth in the world economy are the same ones that are destroying its support systems. By any conceivable ecological yardstick, these are failed policies....
>
> Easily a third of the world's cropland is losing topsoil at a rate that is undermining its long-term productivity. Fully 50 percent of the world's rangeland is overgrazed and deteriorating into desert. The world's forests have shrunk by about half since the dawn of agriculture and are still shrinking. Two thirds of oceanic fisheries are now being fished at or beyond their capacity; overfishing is now the rule, not the exception. And over pumping of underground water is common in key food-producing regions.[3]

One quarter of the Earth's land area is now cultivated and since the 1960s water withdrawals from rivers and lakes doubled (70% of which is used for agriculture) and the flows of nitrogen and phosphorus from fertilisers into terrestrial ecosystems have doubled and tripled, respectively. The rapidly growing demand for food, fresh water, timber, fibre and fuel has caused humans to change ecosystems more rapidly and extensively in the last 50 years than at any comparable period in human history.[4]

To make matters worse, human overconsumption is increasing, not only due to population growth but also due economic growth, rising wealth and globalisation which are changing consumptions patterns so that per capita consumption in many countries is increasing. This is exacerbated by inequitable social systems that generate extreme affluence for a small minority and extreme poverty for the majority of people. Both extremes have negative consequences for the health of Earth. The affluent minority rapidly increase consumption and tend to have massive per capita impacts. At the other end of the scale a growing number of people who no longer have access to sufficient resources to provide sustainable livelihoods have no option but to over-exploit what is left, thereby prolonging their survival but reducing the survival prospects of their children.

Reducing human population levels may help reduce total consumption but it is clear that this would be insufficient to solve the problem of overconsumption. GEO-4 estimates that even though global population growth will probably slow and level off in mid-century the anticipated three- to sixfold increase in global GDP by 2050, coupled with the fact that the direct drivers of ecosystem change will either become more severe (e.g. climate change and excessive nutrient loading) or will not diminish, means that humans will continue to use ecosystems at unsustainable levels.

Deteriorating capacity to support life

We have known for a long time that human pressures on Earth's life-supporting systems are causing them to deteriorate rapidly, and in some cases irreversibly (at least during time periods that make any sense to humans). However in recent years, more and more studies are revealing the extent to which this is occurring and the serious implication for human well-being. One of the most authoritative was the Millennium Ecosystem Assessment ("MA") which was conducted between 2001 and 2005 by more than 1,360 experts worldwide. The MA was a state-of-the-art scientific appraisal of the condition and trends in the world's ecosystems and the services they provide to humanity (such as clean water, food, forest products, flood control, and natural resources) and the options to restore, conserve or enhance the sustainable use of ecosystems. It was also the first comprehensive audit of the status of what it referred to as "Earth's natural capital".

The MA concluded that approximately 60% (15 out of 24) of the ecosystem services that it examined are being degraded or used unsustainably, including: fresh water, capture fisheries, air and water purification, and the regulation of regional and local climate, natural hazards, and pests. Since human life is sustained by these "ecosystem services", what the MA is telling us is that that Earth's capacity to give life to human beings has already been very significantly compromised and that human activities are continuing to worsen the situation. Furthermore, as the MA points out:

> "The full costs of the loss and degradation of these ecosystem services are difficult to measure, but the available evidence demonstrates that they are substantial and growing. Many ecosystem services have been degraded as a consequence of actions taken to increase the supply of other services, such as food. These trade-offs often shift the costs of degradation from one group of people to another or defer costs to future generations." [5]

Today global warming and climate change is the most well-known symptom of how human activities are reducing the capacity of Earth to support humans and many other forms of life that have flourished during the current Cenozoic era. Although the Intergovernmental Panel on Climate Change (IPCC) has now concluded that the scientific evidence that human actions are impacting the atmosphere and contributing to global climate change is now "irrefutable" this fact was hotly contested at the time of publication of the first edition of this book and the third Global Environmental Outlook report ("GEO-3") in 2002. Now, as GEO-4 observes,

> "The challenge now is not whether climate change is happening or whether it should be addressed. The challenge now is to bring over 190 nations together in common cause. The prize is not just a reduction in emissions of greenhouse gasses, it is a comprehensive re-engagement with core objectives and principles of sustainable development. ... Climate change, while firmly an environmental issue is also an environmental threat that impacts on every facet of government and public life – from finance and planning to agriculture, health, employment and transport."

As Earth's systems begin to change in ways that create negative impacts on human societies, the international community is belatedly beginning to recognise that our belief that we could exploit ecosystems with impunity was misplaced. Instead of a one-way flow of benefits from Nature to humans, a "feedback loop" connects the behaviour of humans and the ecosystems with which they interact. The further realisation that climate change is not the problem but is only one of many symptoms of underlying systemic dysfunctions in the dominant forms of human civilisation, is now becoming apparent to more and more people. However relatively few governments seem ready to acknowledge that the symptoms cannot be cured without addressing the underlying causes which in turn will require re-examining what we believe to be the role of ours species on this planet and how to regulate our behaviour accordingly.

Mass extinctions
We are ripping apart the web of life of which we form part, and destroying our evolutionary partners, at a frightening speed. Human activities are disrupting food chains, nutrient and hydrological cycles, and the climate system on which

ecological communities depend. The rapidly increasing rate of extinction is a grim indicator of the scale of the damage being done. The extinction of species is part of the evolutionary process but the fossil record indicates that on average less than one mammal species became extinct every thousand years. Yet within a few hundred years human societies have increased this "background" rate of extinction by as much as one thousand times.

The MA explains in measured, scientifically-correct statements that human beings are having a devastating impact on virtually all ecosystems. It points out that if one applies the IUCN–World Conservation Union criteria for threats of extinction, currently 12% of bird species, 23% of mammals, 25% of conifers, at least 32% of amphibians, and 52% of cycads (evergreen palm-like plants) are threatened with extinction.[6] In the last few decades of the 20th Century alone human activities destroyed at least 35% of Earth's mangrove areas (vital breeding grounds for many marine fish), 20% of the world's coral reefs and degraded a further 20% of coral reefs.[7]

The most important factors driving the loss of biodiversity and impairing the functioning of ecosystems are habitat change (such as land use changes, physical modification of rivers and loss of coral reefs), climate change, invasive alien species, overexploitation, and pollution. These drivers are projected to remain constant or to increase in the near future. One of the key messages of the MA is that:

> "Changes in biodiversity due to human activities were more rapid in the past 50 years than at any time in human history, and the drivers of change that cause biodiversity loss and lead to changes in ecosystem services are either steady, show no evidence of declining over time, or are increasing in intensity. Under the four plausible future scenarios developed by the MA, these rates of change in biodiversity are projected to continue, or to accelerate." [8]

The measures that the global community and national governments have taken to reduce the rate at which extinctions are accelerating (let alone reducing the extinction rate to the background rate) have been woefully inadequate. At the 2002 World Summit on Sustainable Development in Johannesburg the international community pledged to reduce the rate of biodiversity loss by 2010. However in January 2010 when the Secretary General of the United Nations launched the International Year of Biodiversity he admitting that even this modest target has not been met.

The MA also cautions that successfully slowing the rate of biodiversity loss will require much stronger measures and the setting of long-term goals because the inertia inherent in human governance systems means that there is usually a significant time-lag between deciding to act and the implementation of the decision. Even after action has been taken it may be decades or centuries before any positive impact on biodiversity and ecosystems becoming apparent.

Indeed the MA estimate that by about 2050 the current extinction rate is likely to have increased tenfold![9] The soaring extinction rates are a terrifying measure of both the extent of the irreversible harm we are doing and of our inability to co-habit harmoniously within the community of life on Earth.

Decreasing human well-being

Despite our much vaunted technological advances, and the rapid growth of the human population, the human species isn't doing too well. Millions starve to death or die of entirely preventable diseases, while others in the more affluent countries eat themselves to death. The most affluent one-fifth of the world's population accounts for almost 90 percent of total personal consumption while 1.2 billion people live on less than US$ 1 per day.[10] Meanwhile some of our best scientists work on developing genetic modification and cloning technologies that will enable us to produce "spare parts" to prolong the lives of those who can afford such technologies.

Even in wealthy countries, widespread fulfilment seems stubbornly elusive. Many humans no longer live within intimate and functioning communities, or even families, and have lost any deep connection with a particular place of origin. The emotional and spiritual damage caused by a loss of community and of a sense of belonging, is evident everywhere.

Unfortunately many governments and other institutions that govern human behaviour fail to appreciate the link between human well-being and the health of the ecosystems within which people live. The health of many people around the world is affected by human-induced changes to the environment and almost one-quarter of all diseases are caused by environmental exposure. For example the World Health Organisation estimates that more than two million people die prematurely each year due to air pollution.[11] The proportion of people living in cities is growing steadily and in 1996 passed the 50% mark which can only exacerbate this problem.

To make matters worse, the harmful consequence of the reduced functioning of ecosystems are being borne disproportionately by poorer and marginalised people because they depend more directly on ecosystems to sustain them. This means that although the degradation of ecosystems is often justified on the basis that it will benefit people, for example by increasing food production, globally the degradation of ecosystems is contributing to growing inequities and disparities across groups of people, and is sometimes the principal factor causing poverty and social conflict. Indeed, the MA concluded that:

> "The degradation of ecosystem services is already a significant barrier to achieving the Millennium Development Goals agreed to by the international community in September 2000 and the harmful consequences of this degradation could grow significantly worse in the next 50 years." [12]

Inadequate Responses

Saying that the measures taken to date by the governments of the world to address "environmental issues" are inadequate is a gross understatement. Since the first international conference on the environment in 1972, the health of the community of life on Earth has not only continued to deteriorate, it is worsening more rapidly each year. Although many countries have taken measures to ensure that greater weight is given to environmental factors in decision-making and climate change is now regarded as a significant issue by most governments, few seem to appreciate the nature and extent of the responses that will be required in order for human civilisations to become ecologically sustainable and viable in the long-term.

The fact that humankind has "overshot" the capacity of Earth to sustain us has a number of important consequences. Firstly, a massive reduction in the total amount of human consumption (i.e. of the ecological footprint of our species) is inevitable. The question is no longer whether or not we should reduce human consumption, but how this will occur. Ecology and human history teaches us that unless we succeed in rapidly reducing our consumption levels, the necessary reductions are likely to occur by means of a massive collapse in human population levels. This could occur in many ways but it is probable that the changes which are occurring in ecosystems will result in a range of impacts such as floods, droughts, fires, and crop-failure, which in turn contribute to hunger, thirst, disease, social conflict and war.

Secondly, it is no longer sufficient to reduce the speed at which humans are causing environmental deterioration or to halt it. The consequence of overshooting ecological limits is that to get back within the range of what is ecologically sustainable, we must both reduce what we take from the planet and repair much of the damage that we have done to ecological systems so that their capacity to support life can begin to increase once more. For example, for as long as the total amount of greenhouses gasses emitted each year (whether caused by human activities or other causes) does not exceed the rate at which ecosystems can remove them from the atmosphere in that year, ecological sustainability can be achieved by controlling the rate of emissions caused by humans to ensure that total emissions per annum do not exceed the absorption capacity per annum. However once that limit is past (which scientists tell us happened many years ago) greenhouse gasses begin to accumulate in the atmosphere at an accelerating rate because the resultant climate change reduces the rate at which some ecosystems can absorb these gases while causing others to release more greenhouse gases (e.g. the release of methane from the tundra and submarine area of the Arctic as land and sea temperatures increase). From this point onward the situation can only be stabilised if humans succeed in intervening to ensure that the rate at which greenhouse gasses are removed from the atmosphere exceeds the total rates of emission. This will require both reducing human emissions in absolute terms and restoring the health of ecosystems so that their capacity to absorb carbon is enhanced.

Thirdly, acting swiftly and decisively becomes critical because delay alone can nullify the benefits of taking action. Once the ecological footprint of a civilisation exceeds the carrying capacity of its environment the tide turns against that civilisation and both the options and time available to it begin to run out at an increasingly speed. This means that as time passes the number of ways of responding adequately to the challenge will decrease and the amount of effort required will increase. The risk that whatever we do will be too little too late rises the longer we wait. This is particularly true in situation in which change does not occur in a smooth or "linear" manner and is interrupted by so-called "tipping-points" at which a small incremental change in impact will cause an ecosystem to move to move abruptly and rapidly to an entirely new state. Even more troubling is the fact that the likelihood of these abrupt changes occurring is increasing. One of the key findings of the 2005 Millennium Ecosystem Assessment report read:

> "Nonlinear (accelerating or abrupt) changes have been previously identified by a number of individual studies of ecosystems. The MA is the first assessment to conclude that ecosystem changes are increasing the likelihood of nonlinear changes in ecosystems and the first to note the important consequences of this finding for human well-being. Examples of such changes include disease emergence, abrupt alterations in water quality, the creation of "dead zones" in coastal waters, the collapse of fisheries, and shifts in regional climate." [13]

The details of what we are doing to Earth and how harmful our impacts are, are complex and some of the facts are controversial. However, it is obvious that we humans are behaving in a manner that is rapidly destroying our habitat. In the process we are killing millions of species that co-evolved with us and are threatening the health of the whole Earth Community. Of course this behaviour is also self-destructive because the interconnectedness of the web of life means that as the health of our home deteriorates, so does our own. As James Lovelock, creator of Gaia Theory has remarked, it's as if the human brain decided that as it was the most important organ in the body, it would mine the liver."

This raises the questions: why are we doing it, and why don't we adjust our governance systems to prevent this type of behaviour?

OUR GOVERNANCE SYSTEMS ARE BASED ON FALSE PREMISES

The human societies that presently dominate the world govern on the basis of a false understanding of the universe. The core falsehood is that we humans are separate from our environment and that we can flourish even as the health of Earth deteriorates. In fact, we humans have convinced ourselves that human health and well-being depend on exploiting Earth (preferably as fast as technology permits and the market demands) rather than on preserving the global ecosystem. The governance structures, legal philosophies (jurisprudence), and laws established by many societies reflect and entrench the illusion of separation and independence. This encourages and legitimises environmentally and socially destructive behaviour and hinders the development of more appropriate forms of social organisation by those who do not subscribe to the dominant social myths.

I believe that the dominant governance systems cannot provide the means of stopping and reversing our self-destructive behaviour. A new vision and understanding of how to govern ourselves is essential. This needs to be part of a wider social shift to a new worldview or cosmology, and is unlikely to be achieved without a shift in consciousness in many individuals. Fortunately there is evidence that this is happening. However, in this book I have focused on a single but important aspect: how to re-think our understanding of law and governance so that we can use it to govern humans in a way that will benefit the whole Earth Community, and thereby ourselves.

DEVELOPING THE MYTHOLOGY OF INDEPENDENCE

Many writers have explored the reasons why so many human societies should have 'forgotten' that we are part of a natural world and that ultimately our well-being is derived from the health of our habitat, that is, from Earth. In European history the rise of the myth of separation from nature appears to be strongly associated with a change, at the end of the Middle Ages, in people's image of nature from that of a nurturing mother to that of a machine.

The development of the myth that we are separate from nature owes much to such luminaries of Western European culture as Galileo Galilei (1564–1642), Francis Bacon (1561–1626), René Descartes (1596–1650), and Isaac Newton (1642–1727).

Galileo, the Italian mathematician, astronomer and physicist, argued strongly that science should be restricted to considering phenomena that could be measured and quantified. In *The Assayer* he stated that the book of nature is written in mathematics, and rejected approaches that focussed on the qualities of nature. In his time Galileo was a courageous free-thinker who rejected the orthodox world-view of his times in favour of a worldview that accorded with his empirical observations, particularly by telescope. He also suffered for his convictions, being forced by the Catholic Church to recant his support for Copernicus's theory that Earth revolved around the Sun and not vice versa (famously muttering after his recantation, "but it does move"), and being placed under house arrest for the last nine years of his life. However, like all of us, he was a human being embedded in his times. It is hardly surprising that in an age of religious dogma he tried to keep open an area within which free thought could flourish, by arguing that science and theology were entirely separate since science was not concerned with the unquantifiable dimensions of reality.

Francis Bacon was the first in a long line of British empiricist philosophers and is credited with having developed the empirical method of science. He argued in particular for a distinction to be made between reason and revelation, and emphasised the importance of experimentation to validate or disprove theories. He was apparently a practical, utilitarian kind of man who also held what could be described as Utopian views about how human societies could be improved if they could stop worshipping unhelpful 'idols of the mind', adopt a scientific approach and use technology to 'master' nature.

Bacon had a dramatic legal and political career. He was a favourite of King James I, and became his Attorney General, later rising to the rank of Lord Chancellor and being ennobled as Viscount St Albans. However in 1621 he was charged with corruption, fined and banished from court and finally died as a consequence of an ill-advised experiment to explore the effects of cold on his body. Bacon wrote of using experiments to hunt, constrain and interrogate Nature in order to compel her to yield her secrets. Although Bacon did not regard Earth as inert matter, his writings show how the empirical modes of thought that emerged in seventeenth century Europe began to supplant earlier reverential attitudes to Earth as a bountiful mother.

René Descartes, the French philosopher and mathematician, set out to entirely reconstruct philosophy on the basis of mathematical reasoning. He is credited with having developed analytical reasoning, but arguably his most influential theory concerns the distinction between the human mind and the human body. Starting from his famous proposition, "I think, therefore I am", he constructed an argument that mind or consciousness and matter are entirely separate and incompatible substances. In his view, we humans are intangible rational minds that have somehow become lodged in a physical body, like a ghost in a machine. The understanding of mind and matter as being entirely separate (often referred to as 'Cartesian dualism') has had, and still has, a profound impact on how we see the world and understand our place in it.

Descartes . . . killed the Earth and all its living beings. For him the natural world was a mechanism. There was no possibility of entering into a communion relationship. Western humans became autistic in relation to the surrounding world.

Thomas Berry, quoted by Ralph Metzner, 'The Psychology of the Human–Nature Relationship', in *Ecopsychology* p.59

The work of Copernicus, Bacon, Galileo and Descartes was finally synthesised by Isaac Newton, thereby completing what became known as 'The Scientific Revolution'. The physical world at this point was seen as a complex machine that could be understood by reductionist analysis (i.e. by dissecting it and looking at each of the parts to understand how it worked). The fact that human consciousness was separate from this world, coupled with religious beliefs that encouraged humans to adopt a superior, arrogant and dominating attitude towards nature, led to nature being viewed as something that existed for the benefit of humans. The idea of Earth as mother was dead.

These ideas, and particularly Cartesian dualism, are still very much alive and well today. In fact, as I argue in Chapter Four, most human governance systems are still based on this worldview. Ironically, the leading physicists and mathematicians of today who are in many ways the successors of Galileo, Bacon, Descartes and Newton, have already rejected this worldview. Yet we continue to govern ourselves on the basis of a discredited 17th Century understanding of how the universe functions. No wonder we have problems.

RE-THINKING REALITY, THE UNIVERSE
AND EVERYTHING

When I was at school I was taught that a physicist called Werner Heisenberg had formulated an 'uncertainty principle', which stated that the mass and velocity of an electron could not be determined simultaneously. It was also mentioned that for some quirky and unfathomable reason of their own, sub-atomic particles sometimes behaved as if they were particles and sometimes as if they were waves. I rather unquestioningly accepted this. It was not until several years later, when as a university student I read Fritjof Capra's *The Tao of Physics*,[7] that I realised to my intense frustration that no-one had pointed out to me how immensely significant Heisenberg's uncertainty principle is for our understanding of reality and the universe. The uncertainty principle demonstrates that we are part of the universal system and that in seeking to measure or ask questions we interact with the whole in a manner that affects its functioning. It is not possible to observe the functioning of the universe from the outside. We, the observers, are part of the system and intimately connected with what we are observing.

Indeed the 'new physics' based on quantum theory, developed by scientists such as Albert Einstein, Niels Bohr, Erwin Schrödinger and Werner Heisenberg, revealed that the universe is a single integral whole composed of a dynamic network of relationships. Quantum physics exploded the view that the universe is a vast mechanism constructed of many tiny 'building blocks'. Rather than a construction, the universe is now understood as a surging, swirling dance that unifies all the dancers and is shaped by the constantly changing relationships between them.

If the universe is more like a dance, then no part of it can be understood except in relation to the whole. Indeed the nature and behaviour of a part is determined by the whole rather than the other way round. This point of view is fundamental to what is today often referred to as 'systems thinking'. This is an intellectual approach that focuses on understanding anything by looking at its context or role within a larger system, rather than by dissecting the system and analysing the component parts in isolation.

One of the implications of this approach is that Descartes' rigid distinction between mind and matter can no longer be maintained. Descartes' statement that "There is nothing included in the concept of body that belongs to mind; and nothing in that of the mind that belongs to the body", it turns out, is incorrect. The very properties of 'matter' are evoked by its interaction with mind, while 'mind' seems increasingly to be something that matter is inherently capable of. Indeed, more and more scientists now accept that matter appears to have an inherent capacity to organise itself and to evolve in infinitely creative ways. This, surely, is an attribute of consciousness.

Furthermore, there is growing evidence that the relationships of which the universe is made are capable of a peculiar degree of intimacy. Scientists have identified that some connections between subatomic particles are maintained regardless of the distance in time or space between the particles in communion and without any need for energy to move through the intervening space/time. One of the implications of this is that if two such particles were to interact and then move apart, by observing the behaviour of one it is possible to predict the behaviour of the other, wherever it is. In a quite brilliant display of dry, academic understatement, physicists describe these connections as 'non-local'.

A most striking aspect of quantum physics and systems thinking is the degree to which their conclusions find common ground with many ancient philosophies. These parallels have been explored by several writers, perhaps most notably by Fritjof Capra in *The Tao of Physics* and Gary Zukav in *The Dancing Wu Li Masters*.[8] Of course, scientific theories come and go, but it seems to me significant that so many great thinkers from different cultures, at different times and using different techniques, have arrived at similar conclusions. All paths, it seems, lead to the conclusion that everything is interconnected. This also means that while I have chosen to use the language and insights of modern physics to explain these ideas, it is equally possible to use the teachings of many spiritual and philosophical traditions to arrive at the same point.

The dominant legal systems are all based on the assumption that we human beings exist only within our skins (i.e. that which is outside our skins is not us) and that we are the only beings or subjects in the universe. (As discussed in Chapter Five, everything else is defined as an object). These seem to be reasonable working hypotheses on which to base a system of governance. Certainly, from a lawyer's perspective, as soon as we start blurring the distinctions between humans and the rest of the universe it all gets terribly messy.

The trouble is that we now know that these assumptions and philosophies are false. We also know that from the perspective of the whole Earth (or an ecological perspective, if you prefer), the results of our governance systems are spectacularly bad. To be frank, I do not know exactly what we will need to do in order to transform our governance systems in a manner that reflects our new understanding of the universe. However, it seems insane to carry on blithely governing ourselves on the basis of discredited philosophies from the 16th and 17th Centuries. A good place to start would be to regulate ourselves as if we were part of the Earth Community—which, of course, we are. We might also like to consider applying the age-old 'golden rule' of behaving towards others as we would like them to behave towards us.

WHY HAVEN'T WE REVISED OUR GOVERNANCE SYSTEMS?

Despite overwhelming evidence that we are on completely the wrong track as far as regulating ourselves is concerned, we display an immense capacity to avoid addressing the most vital issue of our times. As Thomas Berry expresses it, the "great work" that humans must now tackle is "to establish a benign or mutually enhancing human presence on the planet". It is not rolling out glob-alisation or maximising the gross domestic product of each country. It is not even about 'development' or 'poverty reduction'. Though these are worthy and important social goals, ultimately it is the way in which they are to be achieved that will determine whether or not they are beneficial in the long term.

This is not likely to be an easy task, since most of us have internalised the false beliefs and approaches on which many of our cultures are founded. We think in a dualistic way and firmly believe, for instance, that increased con-sumption is likely to increase personal happiness. Ralph Metzner, a leading theorist of ecopsychology, notes: "Several different diagnostic metaphors have been proposed to explain the ecologically disastrous split—the pathological alienation—between human consciousness and the rest of the biosphere." [9] He goes on to suggest that standard psychological categories such as addic-tion, dissociation, autism and amnesia may provide useful diagnostic metaphors to explain our determination to distance ourselves from our habi-tat and context.

The insights of ecopsychologists will be essential in understanding how best to heal this psychological pandemic that afflicts most human societies today. Vitally important work is also being done by many others to help us understand the nature of our consciousness and to explore our full potential through enhancing our physical, emotional, psychic and spiritual connections with our bodies, with other humans and with the universe itself. One only has to look at the explosion of 'mind, body, spirit' sections in bookshops, the growth of 'new age' or 'now times' spirituality and at best-seller lists to become aware that a great many people are now questioning received philosophical foundations.

Changes in how people think will not protect Earth. Environmental destruction has also occurred in countries like China, where there are many Buddhists and Taoists who believe in the sanctity of all life. Bringing about the much-needed transformation will also require a fundamentally different understanding of the nature and purpose of law, and changes to how we gov-ern our societies.

In the next chapter I discuss how the dominant cultures have built up a whole mythology around the illusion of independence, before moving on to discuss in Chapters Four and Five the impact that this has had on our gover-nance systems.

Chapter 3

The myth of the
master species

WHEN THE MISTS CLEAR

Yesterday I read in the newspaper that a prominent young South African politician had just died of "pneumonia" — a coded reference to AIDS. The irony was that he had been a prominent 'AIDS sceptic' who didn't believe that HIV caused AIDS, and a vociferous critic of those who have campaigned for the government to provide anti-retroviral drugs to those with HIV. 'Reality One, Ideology Nil,' I thought. 'So much for denial!' He died not so much of the disease but of a failure of analysis.

When I first met this man he was a young political activist dedicated to the overthrow of apartheid. ('Apartheid' is an Afrikaans word that translates literally as 'apartness'). That time he was on the winning side. The apartheid government was not voted out of power, swept away by a popular revolution, or defeated in a war. One of the reasons why the apartheid state eventually passed into history was that it could no longer sustain the mythology that was necessary for its continued existence. The myths of inherent white supremacy and the 'Christian' duty of white South Africans to defend their wonderful land against the wicked, atheistic Communists and their brainwashed allies, began to sound less and less convincing, even to government supporters. The trouble is that reality has this uncomfortable habit of intruding into even the most complete and well worked out fantasy world. It seeps in even though legions of censors, teachers and propagandists are employed to feed the myth, and armies of soldiers and police are there to stamp out dissent.

In the 1980s, as world condemnation increased, sanctions began to hurt and internal resistance grew, the white mists began to thin. The reality behind the evaporating mists shocked many white South Africans to the core. Contrary to what they had been told and many had believed, it turned out that black South Africans did value voting and self-governance very highly and were not simply being whipped up and deluded by a few agitators. What was worse, even the Dutch Reformed Church turned around and confessed that in fact they had got it all wrong. It seems that apartheid had been a heresy all along and not, as their pastors had been proclaiming for decades, a Church-sanctioned philosophy for ensuring separate but equal development and the benign supervision of all those who are not blessed with a sufficiently pale skin. The popular notion of a 'paradigm shift' doesn't do justice to the teeth-rattling, head-spinning body-check that many whites experienced as they slammed into reality. Discovering that you have spent most of your life inhabiting a mythical world shaped by grotesque falsehoods can be somewhat disconcerting—particularly when it turns out that God did not choose you to be top of the pile after all! (Some of course simply pretended that it was all just a bad dream that would eventually pass.)

As members of the ex-master race in South Africa emerged from the fog, blinking in the sunlight of the 'new' South Africa, some began to notice that it wasn't all bad. First of all there was something liberating about not having to expend all that energy on repressing fellow citizens, denying those annoyingly disquieting glimpses of a different reality, and suppressing one's own empathic feelings and self-doubts. It seems that being a member of the master race is great for pumping up the ego but rather draining for the soul. Secondly, all kinds of possibilities for connecting with other people opened up, both in South Africa and internationally.

The dominant cultures in our world are as convinced of the superiority of our species over others and of our right to rule the planet as most white South Africans once were about their right to oppress other South Africans. However, reality is once more intruding. Today the newspaper headline said: "Earth: 30 years left. In a shock report to the United Nations ahead of the World Summit, 1,100 scientists warn of the widespread collapse of human society." I wonder what the score will be in this encounter with reality. Will this be another victory for denial?

THE HOMOSPHERE

For centuries now we humans have been enthusiastically engaged in constructing a delusory 'human world' that is separate from the real universe. We have rejected the biosphere into which we were born and have erected in our minds a vast, hermetically sealed 'humans only' world. We have lived so long within this contrived 'homosphere', breathing its myths of human supremacy, that it is now more real to us than Earth. Entranced by our own creation and fascinated by the cleverness of our abstractions, we seldom notice the unpredictable, mysterious beauty of the 'natural world' beyond the glass. Even when we set out like astronauts to examine it, the bubble-visors of our technology-oriented culture distort our vision. We have become, as Thomas Berry puts it, 'autistic' in relation to Earth. Like the old joke about both artists and scientists falling in love with their models, we have traded in the warm, sensual generosity of an Earth mother for the artificial charms of a digital cyber-babe: a techno-temptress (or hyper-hunk) that promises to satisfy our every whim at the click of a mouse but is totally incapable of satisfying our deepest yearnings. The danger is that the more we lose physical and emotional connection with Earth and our co-inhabitants, the more inclined we are to believe in these glossy lies.

By now most of us in the homosphere believe that we have a vested interest in continuing to live in it. After all, it is an ideal hothouse within which our egos can grow disproportionately large, swollen with the conceits of having mastered the universe. Within it we can give expression to our adolescent petulance at what we term 'the limits to growth' and convince ourselves that we can do things better than nature. Here only human beings matter, and some matter a lot more than others. Everything is subservient to the drive to satisfy what we perceive as our most important desires. Majestic mountains, vast grassy plains rippling in the wind, deep mysterious rivers, multitudes of iridescent fish in stately shoals, are all reduced to 'natural resources'. The process of alchemy is reversed and the intricate grace of the dance of life is transmuted into so many hectares of real estate, kilometres of road, kilowatts of electricity and tons of total allowable catch. Bit by bit we feed Earth into the mill of human greed, sacrificing all in the name of the insatiable gods of 'progress' and 'development'.

Perhaps most remarkably, we have (almost) convinced ourselves, despite the overwhelming and growing evidence to the contrary, that within this constructed world of ours we can be healthier, safer, happier and more fulfilled. More recently, however, the blanketing mists of mythology have begun to lift and the reality beyond has occasionally intruded. However, most of us, like the supporters of apartheid South Africa peering out from their mental laager of circled wagons, are terrified by what we think lies outside the homosphere. What possible role is there for an ex-master in a community of former slaves?

What is clear at this point in human history is that the industrial and post-industrial human societies of today will not survive much longer in anything like their present forms. They may well last 50 years more, but given the declining rate of oil production and escalating population levels, the chances of them lasting 200 years more are remote. The real concerns that experts have about the future can even be discerned in the careful, diplomatic language of United Nations documents like GEO-3. The report concludes: "Old troubles will persist and fresh challenges will emerge as increasingly heavy demands are placed on resources that, in many cases, are already in a fragile state. The increasing pace of change and degree of interaction between regions and issues has made it difficult to look into the future with confidence."[1]

Of course human societies will adapt in the interim. The question is how, and in what direction. The mainstream argument is that things aren't really so bad and there are no problems that a bit of research and development and some innovative technology can't fix. Those who believe that technology can fix any problem are confident that our rate of innovation will ensure that we will be able to duck and dive and weave fast enough so that we are never pinned against the ropes and knocked out of existence. Evan Eisenberg, author of *The Ecology of Eden*,[2] calls people who fall into this camp 'Managers' because they believe in 'Planet Management'. Eisenberg argues that "Planet Management has become the dominant worldview amongst scientists and policy-makers. It is the silicon version of the Judeo-Christian ethic of stewardship, which sees the earth as a garden that we are to dress, keep and humanise."[3] Even the possibility raised by James Lovelock[4] that we may have to take on the eternal task of supporting life on Earth because we have destroyed the natural life-support systems, fails to dismay the most ardent technophiles. As Eisenberg says, "This prospect should scare the Managers to death. Instead, it gets their juices flowing."[5]

Most of those who disagree with the Managers regard technology as a false god and pin their hopes on our species undergoing a metamorphosis that will radically change how we understand and relate to the universe. Their focus tends to be more on how to change or manage humans rather than the external world. I am not speaking here of a unified school of thought but rather of a diversity of views, each adopting a different approach to bringing about the change. For example, some focus on personal spiritual growth, others on creating sustainable human communities and others on developing practical ways of feeding ourselves in ways that work with, and not against, nature. If people of this persuasion were to have a bumper sticker (perhaps on their bicycles) it might read 'Change your heart and mind, not the planet'.

Eisenberg has (deliberately and explicitly) stereotyped those who stand against the Managers as 'Planet Fetishers'. As he puts it, "The name acknowledges their tendency to think of nature as a perfect, harmonious, whole—perfect and harmonious, that is, when humans keep out. By their lights, humans have no right to a larger role in nature than raccoons."[6] In critiquing the views of the Fetishers and of Deep Ecologists in particular, Eisenberg argues that "If you try to impose a paleolithic worldview on a post-industrial people, you are asking for trouble".[7]

The arguments set out in this book are, by and large, opposed to the worldview of Eisenberg's Managers. In particular, I do not have the requisite faith in technology to fix everything nor the faith in those who currently pull its levers to use it wisely. However, I am writing this on a laptop and respect the human creativity that made it possible. I do believe that advanced technology is a desirable part of future human societies, but it must be appropriate. In other words it must be designed to be made, used and recycled in a manner that is compatible with the purpose that Berry calls 'the Great Work'.

Many of the arguments advanced here can also be fairly characterised as being part of what Eisenberg calls the worldview of the Fetishers. However, in my view this is not a Fetisher book in Eisenberg's terms. This book is about developing a new vision of self-regulation for post-industrial human societies in the 21st century that is capable of practical implementation. It is concerned with learning from the aeons of Earth's experience and the millennia of human experience, not with trying to go back in time. While much of the book is devoted to discussing ideas rather than specific actions or changes, this is based on the belief that theories have great practical value, particularly in guiding action. By this I do not mean that abstraction should be valued above experience. My point is that for our species to make a concerted and coherent change in how we regulate ourselves, we need a coherent understanding of why we should do so, what the overall purpose behind our governance systems is, and how we should do it. I think that the dominant human societies and the international 'community' do not have such an understanding at present.

Understanding why we need to change our outlook on life and what we ought to change it to, is a big task. For many people in post-industrial societies this would involve changing their entire understanding of the universe and society, in short, their cosmology. This book is concerned with a more limited, but important aspect of that wider change. How can we change the way we govern ourselves so that we begin to deconstruct the homosphere and reintegrate into a wider Earth Community? How would we have to change our legal and political structures in order to move away from the 'apartness' from nature that characterises our present societies towards a post-apartheid Earth society?

Chapter 4

Why law and jurisprudence matter

In the previous chapter I suggested that the misunderstanding or denial on the part of contemporary human societies of the reality that we are part of the web of life and not the masters (or managers) of Earth is potentially fatal for many living creatures, including people. This dominant worldview is embodied in our governance systems. They are designed on the basis of this worldview and seek to regulate humans so that they act in accordance with this understanding of reality. In the next chapter I discuss some examples of this. However, I would first like to explore the role of law and legal philosophies. In particular, it is important to understand the role of law and the idea of law in the construction and perpetuation of what I referred to as the 'homosphere' in Chapter Three. It is also worth questioning whether or not rethinking the jurisprudence and laws that form the backbone of our governance systems really is a priority when right now Earth needs to be defended on so many fronts.

LAW'S ROLE

We are all aware that law is one of the principal tools that societies use to regulate human behaviour. Accordingly, if human beings are behaving in undesirable ways it suggests that the laws and how they are implemented are probably inadequate and should be reformed. That is why, as the evidence that we are ruining the environment began to accumulate faster than waste in our landfills, many societies turned their attention to developing 'environmental laws'. Indeed, many international organisations, governments, non-governmental organisations and environmental lawyers spend a lot of time and energy trying to improve laws that regulate human impacts on the environment. (Others, of course, try to remove those environmental regulations that do exist lest they irritate the corporations gorging at the 'resources' trough.)

While the regulatory function of law is easy to see, we often overlook the fact that law plays an equally important role in constituting and forming society itself. A society can be regarded as the collective creation of those human individuals that constitute it. A society will come into being when a number of individuals first conceive of themselves as having a group identity and then begin to act in accordance with those beliefs and to structure and order the relations within the group. This is a continuous and ongoing process involving the generation and development of theories, values and systems. This characteristic of societies is similar to the distinctive way in which living organisms define, structure, organise and reproduce themselves. (This quality of living organisms is referred to as 'autopoiesis', which literally means 'self-making', and is discussed in more detail in Chapters Six and Seven.)

This role of law in 'making' a society, and its relationship with the world-view of that society, is perhaps most clearly seen in those moments in history when new societies constitute themselves. The 1776 American Declaration of Independence, when the thirteen United States of America declared their independence from the British king and Great Britain, is a good example of this.

The preamble of the Declaration of Independence clearly shows that this young society shared a certain cosmology or worldview (e.g. that God had created a universe that was subject to the laws of Nature) and was based on certain shared values (e.g. equality and individual liberty). The theories and ideas that the new American society of 1776 had about itself (e.g. that all men are equal), its desires (e.g. that everyone should be able to pursue happiness), and the values that it espoused (e.g. liberty), were then incorporated into the constitution of the United States of America and its legal and political system. For example, the value placed on individual liberty directly affected the structure of the political system. In the United States political power is allocated in accordance with the doctrine of separation of powers, which requires that legislative, executive and judicial functions be vested in separate state institutions to make it more difficult for the state to abuse its powers at the expense of individual freedoms.

WHEN in the Course of human Events, it becomes necessary for one People to dissolve the Political Bands which have connected them with another, and to assume among the Powers of the Earth, the separate and equal Station to which the Laws of Nature and of Nature's God entitle them, a decent Respect to the Opinions of Mankind requires that they should declare the causes which impel them to the Separation. We hold these Truths to be self-evident, that all Men are created equal, that they are endowed by their Creator with certain unalienable Rights, that among these are Life, Liberty and the Pursuit of Happiness.

Extract from the Declaration of Independence of the thirteen United States of America on 4 July 1776

Law structures society primarily by defining the relationships between the individuals within the society, and the relationships between the individuals, groups of individuals and the society as a whole, and other individuals, groups and societies. These legally defined relationships order the society and determine, for example, how power is exercised within a society. Legal rules are also used to direct and control the actions of individuals within the

The legal constitution of society carries society's structure from its past into its future. Law is the self-directed becoming of society, the order of the self-ordering of society. Legal relations embody relations of social power among the members of the society to enable natural energy— human energy and the energy of the physical world — to be applied for the purposes of the society.

Philip Allot, *Eunomia*, p.297

society, for example by prohibiting certain conduct and punishing those who do not obey.

A society, then, consciously uses law in a number of different ways. Law is used by a society as a means of creating and defining itself in accordance with its worldview (i.e. to make or constitute itself). A society also uses law to order and structure itself by defining internal relationships, and to regulate the behaviour of its component parts (i.e. the individuals and groups within it). This latter function can also be understood as operating a bit like the feedback systems found in living organisms. For example, criminal justice systems are supposed to detect instances in which the rules of the society have not been obeyed (crimes) and then give those involved negative feedback (usually fines or imprisonment) in order to discourage them from repeating this behaviour.

Most importantly for our purposes, legal systems also perform a conservative function, because once a relationship has been defined in law or an act prohibited, this will not change until the law itself is changed by means of a specified formal procedure.

Typically, minor rules are dealt with in regulations or other legal instruments that can relatively easily be changed. Rules or principles that the society regards as most fundamental are often deliberately entrenched in constitutions or Bills of Rights in a way that makes them very difficult to change. Turning ideals into law usually makes them more powerful and durable, but also retards change. For example, more than two hundred years after the American Declaration of Independence, the worldview of those who drafted it and the American Constitution continues to shape how the members of the most powerful nation in the world relate to one another and to the rest of the world. As we know, this has both advantages and disadvantages.

THE IDEA OF LAW

Constitutions, laws and the judgements that interpret them also express and reflect our idea of what law is and ought to be, and what societies believe in and aspire to. This is the tricky bit, because it is far less visible. If one imagines the legal and political system as a painting hanging on a wall, then our idea of law and society would be like the frame of the painting. Usually when we look at the painting we don't see the frame or the wall on which it hangs. Yet they are vital. The frame marks the boundary of our vision and understanding of

Every man takes the limits of his own field of vision for the limits of the world.

Arthur Schopenhauer
(19th Century philosopher)

society. When we look at the painting or society we don't think about, let alone question, whether the painting should be bigger or smaller, or whether it should be hanging on that wall or painted on it. When we look at our governance systems, the limits of our vision and the questions that we consider are defined by the frame that is already there. We may see ways of improving the painting itself, but usually we don't even see what lies outside it.

Let me give you an example. The idea that animals should have legal rights has enjoyed little success in the courts of the United States, despite the dogged efforts of many campaigners and some dedicated lawyers. One of the reasons for this, it seems to me, is not that the American judiciary is particularly insensitive to animals, but rather that when the society that is the United States was constituted and the picture that is its legal and political system painted, animals were outside the frame. Consequently, recognising that animals should be treated in a similar way to humans goes against the grain of the whole legal system. In fact for many people it is unthinkable—unthinkable because it is right out of the frame and will remain so unless the notion of American society is 'reframed'.

However, consider for a moment what the case might be if the founding fathers of the United States of America had come to a different conclusion. If the Declaration of Independence had instead stated that it was self-evident that all creatures are created equal and are endowed by their Creator with certain unalienable rights, including the rights to life and the liberty to pursue the role that they had evolved to perform. The Constitution would have guaranteed rights for animals and the current notion that the law should treat them as objects would be 'unthinkable'.

There is then an intimate relationship between a society's view of itself and its law. As the legal philosopher and academic Philip Allot points out:

> Society cannot be better than its idea of itself. Law cannot be better than society's idea of itself. Given the central role of law in the self-ordering of society, society cannot be better than its idea of law.[1]

This means that in order for any fundamental change in how a society perceives itself to be translated into an actual change in how it functions, it is necessary first to change that society's idea of law. By this I mean not only changing the content of the laws themselves, but rather how the society conceives of law and its role. In other words, the fundamental reorientation of our societies that Berry's 'Great Work' demands cannot be achieved unless we simultaneously entirely reconceptualise the jurisprudence of the dominant cultures.

The jurisprudence of our dominant cultures provides the theoretical foundation for a self-ordering system within the glasshouse of the homosphere that we have constructed. It is conceived of as the legal theory for human society (or a particular human society) that is separate from the rest of the universe. This jurisprudence is based on a number of premises that we know to be false, such as the belief that our well-being is not derived directly from the well-being of the Earth Community as a whole, and the belief that the Earth is an infinite resource for our use. It is also bolstered by a dangerous arrogance that assumes, for example, that technology will provide a solution to any problems that we create in the course of destroying natural systems. However, what makes these human self-delusions so dangerous is the fact that because of the extraordinary degree to which humans have altered the natural functioning of the Earth, they affect the survival and well-being of the whole Earth Community.

SHIFTING OUT OF THE OLD GOVERNANCE PARADIGM

In the 1960s Thomas Kuhn, in writing about the development of scientific ideas, suggested that a scientific 'paradigm' (from the Greek word for 'pattern') is created in the minds of a community of scientists. This paradigm then defines how they see and understand the world. He defined a paradigm as "a constellation of achievements — concepts, values, techniques, etc — shared by a scientific community and used by that community to define legitimate problems and solutions".[2] It is clear that communities of people involved in governance also operate within certain paradigms or 'frames of reference', which effectively restricts the extent of what they see, and what they regard as acceptable in terms of methods and approaches. The dominant paradigm in governance is, I believe, still largely a mechanistic, Cartesian, human-centred worldview. In short, the philosophy of the homosphere.

Thomas Kuhn postulated that a change from one paradigm to another does not happen gradually but in a discontinuous, revolutionary break that he called a 'paradigm shift'. A good example was the 'Copernican Revolution', which involved abandoning the notion that the sun moved around Earth (which had been regarded as proof that God had made us the centre of the universe) and accepting that the reverse was true. It was not possible to move gradually from one view to the other, as they were mutually incompatible.

I imagine that going through a paradigm shift might be likened to one of those futuristic space programmes on television when the captain grimly gives the order for the craft to be brought up to 'warp speed'. The engines rev up, everything starts shuddering, space rushes toward them at frightening speed, and everyone hangs on tight looking rather anxious. Just as it seems as if the whole ship will fall apart, they pop out somewhere else in the universe. In fact, the experiences of those physicists and others who were at the cutting edge of making the paradigm shift in physics in the early 1900s were probably more traumatic. One of the foremost writers on the philosophical implications of modern science, Dr Fritjof Capra, describes the intensely personal dimension of this experience as follows:

> The exploration of the atomic and subatomic world brought them in contact with a strange and unexpected reality. In their struggle to grasp this new reality, scientists became painfully aware that their basic concepts, their language, and their whole way of thinking were inadequate to describe atomic phenomena. Their problems were not merely intellectual but amounted to an intense emotional and, one could say, even existential crisis. It took them a long time to overcome this crisis, but in the end they were rewarded with deep insights into the nature of matter and its relation to the human mind.[3]

At present, I think that it is fair to say that few of the people who make most of the decisions that affect the relationship between humans and other aspects of the Earth Community have made the shift from a mechanistic worldview to a holistic or ecological worldview. These decisions are made or guided mainly by politicians, lawyers, bureaucrats and the managers of private corporations, each of whom operates within existing legal and political structures that entrench the old mechanistic paradigm. This makes it difficult to change. It is also clear from the feedback that we are getting that we do not have unlimited time to make this transition. The intricate and exquisite fabric of life is rapidly unravelling and slipping through our fingers. Earth desperately needs a completely new paradigm for social governance. However, we need not only to understand, but also to behave in new ways. Consequently we also need practical new ways of constituting societies and regulating human behaviour so that we are for, and not against, Earth.

I think our ideas of law and governance, our laws and our legal and political structures have such a decisive impact on our relations with the Earth Community that a very special responsibility now rests on people involved in social governance. We need to confront and seek a way through whatever intellectual, emotional or existential crises may be facing us. Like the crew of the spaceship approaching warp speed, we should also be prepared for some anxious moments. We are unlikely to break through to the verdant vistas of the Ecozoic period without experiencing some of the personal confusion, frustration, and despair felt by pioneers of quantum physics such as Niels Bohr and Werner Heisenberg, as they came up against the limitations of their own worldview.

It is most important to distinguish between, firstly, changing how we personally understand the world; secondly, shifting the governance paradigm of a human society or even of the dominant human societies in general; thirdly, developing an Earth jurisprudence; and fourthly, adopting the wild law approach and implementing wilder laws. How I think is constantly changing and in this book I have tried to give some examples of moments and writings that I think affected *how* I understand the world. This is something that is constantly evolving within me and is not necessarily visible or immediately apparent to others.

Shifting the paradigm of the homosphere to an Earth-centred worldview will take the efforts of many people in many fields, but I think that there are many encouraging signs that this is well underway. One of the images of social change that I like best is the image of a flock of birds wheeling in the sky. The flock has no single leader yet will suddenly turn as one. Apparently how it happens is that individual birds begin to signal their wish to turn by momentarily altering course and then quickly rolling back to the original course. This communicates their intention and more start doing the same until a critical mass is achieved and so many alter course that the rest follow simultaneously. This book is me flicking my wings and hoping others might follow.

As with all paradigm shifts, if the shift to a new Earth-centred paradigm occurs, it is likely to happen within a relatively short space of time. The nature of the shift will also require abandoning the old notions in favour of the new understanding. It will not be achieved by synthesising the old with the new since they are mutually incompatible. The shift is therefore, by definition, a radical one.

One of the effects of such a paradigm shift is likely to be a fundamental change in the purpose or goal of our governance systems. However, this does not mean that governance structures or laws themselves will also change in a single evolutionary leap. There the process is likely to be more gradual and evolutionary and indeed, as discussed in Chapter One, there are already signs of wildness discernible in our governance structures.

Chapter 5
The conceit of law

LAWS OF OPPRESSION

I was probably fortunate to have studied law in apartheid South Africa. It meant that right from the beginning I was very aware that states use law as a method of social control, that laws reflect a particular view of the world held by those with political power, and that there is not necessarily a healthy relationship between law, justice and morality. It also meant that I was never in awe of the 'majesty of the law' or believed that having a complex yet rationally consistent set of rules was an end in itself. The fact that I was involved in organising student marches and other anti-government activities that were illegal at the time, also gave me a healthy disrespect for many of the involved debates that some legal theorists immersed themselves in. Issues such as whether or not there is a moral obligation to obey the law simply because it is the law, or whether or not a morally repugnant law is law, seemed simple in those days. Whatever the niceties of the various academic points of view, when confronted with really repugnant laws that are nevertheless enforced with whips, imprisonment and worse, the doubts evaporate. I, and many others, found that at these times we took guidance from our consciences and hearts and not from logic or theory. Valuable though logic is in discerning truth, sometimes the heart or intuition is a better guide in the turbulence of experience.

The proof of the pudding, as they say, is in the eating. In my view, the deteriorating condition of Earth is the proof that the human self-governance pudding has gone bad. Our systems for regulating human behaviour are not protecting Earth, our home, from destruction, because that it not their purpose. The problem of inadequate self-regulation cannot be solved at the level of legislative reform. The problem is not simply that our laws need refining to be more effective. The fact is that, by and large, these laws do give accurate expression to the defective worldview that underlies them. Our legal and political establishments perpetuate, protect and legitimise the continued degradation of Earth by design, not by accident.

In this chapter I will discuss some examples that I think illustrate this point, as well as referring briefly to some of the jurisprudence that lies behind the legal systems of the cultures that currently dominate world society.

SYMPTOMS

There are few areas in which the arrogant and obsessively anthropocentric worldview of the dominant societies is more apparent than in the law. The law reserves all the rights and privileges to use and enjoy Earth to humans and their agents (and usually only selected categories of those, at that). It has also reduced other aspects of Earth and the other creatures that live on it, to the status of objects for the use of humans. The grandiose constitutions of the mighty nations form the arching vaults of the homosphere, and describe it and its aspirations. The law prescribes how we relate to other humans, to other cohabitants of this planet and to Earth itself. It punishes and takes revenge on those who do not conform. It legitimises the eternal extermination of species and the most profound disrespect and abuse of the Earth that sustains us.

If all this sounds like hyperbole, consider the following, which is true of the legal systems of almost all the cultures that currently dominate human society.

OTHER ASPECTS OF EARTH ARE DEFINED AS OBJECTS WITHOUT RIGHTS

A fundamental difference between our culture and Eskimo culture, which can be felt even today in certain situations, is that we have irrevocably separated ourselves from the world that animals occupy. We have turned all animals and elements of the natural world into objects. We manipulate them to serve the complicated ends of our destiny. Eskimos do not grasp this separation easily and have difficulty imagining themselves entirely removed from the world of animals. For many of them, to make this separation is analogous to cutting oneself off from light or water. It is hard to imagine how to do it . . . A most confusing aspect of Western culture for Eskimos to grasp is our depersonalisation of relationship with the human and animal members of our communities.

Barry Lopez, *Arctic Dreams*

Animals, plants and almost every other aspect of the planet are, legally-speaking, objects that are either the property of a human or artificial 'juristic person' such as a company, or could at any moment become owned, for example by being captured or killed. For as long as the law sees living creatures as 'things' and not 'beings', it will be blind to the possibility that they might be the subjects (i.e. the holders) of rights. It is simply legally inconceivable for an object to hold rights. In other words, the jurisprudence of most of the world does not recognise, as Thomas Berry expresses it, that "the universe is a communion of subjects, not a collection of objects".[1]

Another consequence of recognising only humans as beings, is that any sacred or spiritual dimension of any other form of life, or of Earth itself, is denied, and in the eyes of the law, does not exist.

The only rights recognised by law are those that are enforceable in a court of law, and these may only be held by human beings or by 'juristic persons' like companies. This means that from the perspective of our legal systems, the billions of other species on the planet are outlaws, and are treated as such. They are not part of the community or society that the legal systems concern themselves with, and have no inherent right to existence or to have a habitat in which to live. This may sound like an exaggeration when most countries have laws that protect designated species and habitats, for example in national parks. However, this type of legislation does not confer rights on non-humans, it merely restricts some aspects of human behaviour, usually to ensure that other humans can continue to enjoy wild areas and creatures.

Even if a legal system were to recognise that other species are beings, we must still overcome the difficulties of how any 'rights' that they may have will be protected and asserted. This is difficult but essential. A right that cannot be enforced is not a right at all. (The question of rights is discussed in more detail in Chapter Eight.)

FICTIONAL CREATURES HAVE TOO MANY RIGHTS AND FEW RESPONSIBILITIES

In our 21st-century world, fictional, incorporeal beings are given enormous, largely unfettered powers to dominate and exploit virtually every aspect of Earth. These corporations and other juristic persons have no emotions, consciences, values, ethics or ability to commune with the other members of the Earth Community. Indeed, companies have inherently rapacious appetites because the laws that create them and their own constitutions require them to compete aggressively for control over the Earth's bounty and to consume it as fast as possible, heedless of the long-term consequences for Earth itself or its inhabitants.

In the 1970s there were about 7,000 corporations operating internationally, but by 2008 this had increased to about 82,000 transnational corporations with 810,000 foreign affiliates.[2] Corporations account for 51 of the largest 100 economic units in the world (the others are countries)[3] but although the top 200 corporations account for more than 25 per cent of the world's economic activities they employ less than one per cent of the world's workforce. The sheer size, financial resources and influence of corporations in the world today has given them an almost mythological status in our minds, like the giants of ancient times. In fact they have only been around for a few hundred years, and their continued existence depends on whether or not our legal systems continue to recognise them.

We tend to assume that corporations have always existed in more or less the form that we know them today. In fact, corporations were first constituted under English law as 'not-for-profit entities' established to advance the interests of the society as a whole. They included churches, schools, universities and at a later stage, municipalities. Initially what they could do was strictly controlled, but as Daniel Bennett[4] has described, in the United Kingdom (as in many other countries), public control of corporations has now been eroded to such an extent that it is almost non-existent.

In England the Crown began to grant Royal Charters of incorporation to trade associations during the late 1500s, and in 1600 granted a Royal Charter to the East India Company giving it a monopoly on trade in 'the Indies'. The East India Company eventually created shares in itself and began to trade in this stock and to make a profit for its members, despite the fact that it was not authorised to do so by its constitution and consequently was acting unlawfully. Other corporations followed suit, and in time new commercial corporations were created by both Royal Charter and Acts of Parliament. All this came to an end when the so-called 'South Sea Bubble' burst. The South Sea Company, formed in 1711, had been given a monopoly on trade to Spanish-controlled South American ports. When it became clear that it would never be given access to these ports the founders fled the country and a stock market crash followed. The government responded by enacting the 1720 'Bubble Act', which provided that all commercial undertakings "tending to the common grievance, prejudice and inconvenience of His Majesty's subjects" would be illegal and void. The Act also prescribed that shares could only be legally sold to persons genuinely involved in running the corporation or partnership, and speculative trading in shares was banned. Until the repeal of the Bubble Act in 1825 most trade was carried on by way of partnerships, although the Parliament did pass special Acts to create corporations for limited periods for specific purposes such as building canals or waterworks.

As Bennett points out, ever since 1825 corporations have been granted more and more extensive powers under English law, while the legal powers of the courts and governments to control them has declined. Originally, corporate powers were circumscribed and limited by the Crown or government that drafted and approved the corporation's constitution. However in 1844 the Joint Stock Companies Act empowered companies to define their own purposes, and in 1855 an Act was passed that limited the liability of shareholders for the debts of the company to the amount that they had paid for their shares.[5]

After the 1844 Act, the courts attempted to exercise some control over what corporations did by ruling that if a corporation tried to act in a manner or for a purpose that was not authorised by its constitution, it was purporting to exercise a power that it did not have. Consequently a court could declare the act to be unlawful and of no effect (i.e. in legal terms the act was ultra vires). However, companies continued to flout any restrictions on the ambit of their activities, and the effectiveness of the ultra vires doctrine was undermined by a series of cases that limited who was entitled to invoke the doctrine. Eventually in 1966 the Court of Appeals accepted that the Board of Directors could decide on the limits of the company's powers if authorised to do so by its constitution.[6] The Companies Act 1989 finally removed even this paltry qualification by allowing a company to define its objects in a manner that covered all commercial activities and prevented corporate acts being challenged on the basis that they were inconsistent with its objects.[7]

Real people are, of course, involved in these corporations. However the law allows the people who invest in, and run, these artificial 'legal persons' to structure them in such a way that they avoid criminal, financial, social and moral responsibility for the actions which the corporations (at least theoretically) do on their behalf. The courts recognise the rights of participants in corporations to hide behind the 'corporate veil', and are seldom prepared to look through the fiction that a company is a person, in order to hold those who pull the strings liable for acts done in the name of the corporation. Responsibility has also been diluted by the fact that most shareholders in listed companies are themselves companies in whom people have invested. In most cases individual investors neither know nor care whether the groups of companies in which they invest are being environmentally and socially responsible. An absence of personal responsibility for acts done in the name of the corporation is also common among those actually involved in running companies. Most directors and managers act on the assumption that both the law and 'business ethics' demand that their highest priority is to maximise the short-term financial reward to shareholders. Consequently we now have a situation where the vast majority of humans involved in corporations, whether as investors, managers, employees or customers, do not feel any personal responsibility for destructive acts committed in the name of the corporation.

It is high time that we took a long hard look at corporations and asked ourselves whether this form of social organisation is still in the interests of people and Earth. Is the level of social and environmental destruction that they cause worth the benefits that they supposedly deliver, particularly when the benefits accrue only to a small minority? If not, then we must do something about it, despite the enormous lobbying power of the corporations. Human beings used law to create corporations and we can use law to modify or abolish them. For example, I have little doubt that corporations would substantially reduce the harm that they cause to the environment if there were an effective legal mechanism for ensuring that if a business caused ecological harm, both the individuals concerned and the corporation would be required to rectify the damage, regardless of the cost.

EXTERMINATING LIFE ON EARTH IS LEGAL

We rightly outlaw genocide as a crime against humanity. As such it can be prosecuted as a crime anywhere in the world, even if it was legal under the laws of the country in which it occurred. But what about exterminating other species or living systems? With few exceptions, the most dangerous and harmful acts of human beings, those that kill or threaten to exterminate other forms of life or even the life-support systems of Earth, are not even recognised as crimes. I do not know of any countries that prohibit what might be called 'biocide' or 'ecocide'. In fact, the most powerful human society on Earth at this time continues to demand the right to continue to destroy the climate system on which life depends, unfettered by even the most paltry restrictions.

Furthermore, many of our governance systems promote behaviour that threatens life. Incentives are provided to encourage the development and use of technologies that facilitate the faster exploitation of Earth, and even those that alter the genetic coding of humans and other forms of life. Huge amounts of public funds are spent on the development of weapons of mass destruction that if used, would result in massive, and probably irreparable, environmental damage.

JUSTICE SYSTEMS TEND TO WEAKEN, NOT REPAIR, RELATIONS

In most modern states, what are euphemistically described as our 'systems of justice' are in fact specifically designed as formalised methods by which the state exacts revenge on behalf of the victims of crime so that they do not resort to vigilantism and undermine social stability. In most cases these systems merely exacerbate the very alienation of the individuals concerned from the community that led to the crime in the first place, and are sometimes an expensive way of making criminals worse.

However many customary law systems, which place a high value on the health of communities, view crimes and social conflict as symptoms of a deterioration in the social bonds that create a community (which may include the dead, animals and deities). Accordingly they focus primarily on restoring the quality of damaged relationships rather than on meting out punishment. Typically this 'restorative justice' is achieved by a process of mediation and discussion involving all concerned and wrongdoers are required to make amends to any injured parties (which may include deities) and to reaffirm the social bonds.

In recent years the Peace and Reconciliation Commission that investigated apartheid crimes in South Africa under the leadership of Nobel Laureate Archbishop Desmond Tutu, adopted a restorative justice approach.

This approach is also beginning to be used in several countries in dealing with youthful offenders.

The inadequacies of the retributive form of justice are even more apparent when one is dealing with human behaviour that is destructive of the wider Earth Community. Although fining corporations and individuals who harm the environment may have a deterrent effect, it does not repair any damaged relationships within the ecological community concerned.

OUR LAWS DENY THAT THEY EXIST WITHIN A WIDER CONTEXT

The sources of law are entirely human. Although some legal systems claim to be divinely inspired, all are based on human texts for practical purposes. There is no recognition, even at the international law level, of any need for human laws to take account of the wider context of 'laws' of the universe or of nature. So it is that even the sophisticated governance structures of the European Union allocate greater fishing quotas than the fish stocks can bear, year after year. They have many scientists who advise them against doing so, but at the heart of it they do not accept (or do not care) that human governance systems are subservient to the unyielding rules of nature. No directive from Brussels can overrule the principle that continued over-exploitation will reduce the fish population until it reaches levels that are so low that commercial fishing is not viable. The penalty for transgressing nature's laws cannot be plea-bargained away, and no lobbyist can get them repealed.

We have not only forgotten how to live in accordance with the rhythms of the planet, we have also forgotten that doing so was once the chief purpose of human regulatory systems. Probably all human communities once regulated themselves with the purpose of ensuring that their members lived in accordance with the requirements of the wider ecological community. This was seen as necessary for the health of the human society. Unfortunately the customary laws and practices of those indigenous peoples who still prioritise maintaining a mutually enhancing relationship with their habitat, have had virtually no influence at all on the governance systems of the dominant cultures.

THE DEMISE OF 'NATURAL LAW'

When I was at law school I studied jurisprudence—the philosophy of law. We covered a range of theories and discussed ideas like 'justice' and 'rights'. We even touched on the issue of 'natural law'. This was treated as an interesting but outmoded notion that there existed a universal and unchangeable 'higher' form of law, discoverable by reason, which could be used as a yardstick for

True law is right reason in agreement with Nature; it is of universal application, unchanging and everlasting; it summons to duty by its commands, and averts from wrong-doing by its prohibitions. And it does not lay its commands or prohibitions on good men in vain, though neither have any effect on the wicked. It is a sin to try to alter this law, nor is it allowable to attempt to repeal any part of it, and it is impossible to abolish it entirely. We cannot be freed from its obligations by Senate or People, and we need not look outside ourselves for an expounder or interpreter of it. And there will not be different laws at Rome and at Athens, or different laws now and in the future, but one eternal and unchangeable law will be valid for all nations and for all times, and there will be one master and one ruler, that is, God, over us all, for He is the author of this law, its promulgator, and its enforcing judge.

Cicero, *De Republica* iii, xxii, 33
(quoted by Harris (1997) p.8)

determining whether or not actual human-made laws were morally binding. In other words, natural lawyers believed that good laws were based on an inherent sense shared by all humans (or at least 'civilised' humans) that some things were right and others wrong. The classical form of the concept was expounded by the Roman Stoic philosopher Cicero in the first century BC, and it was subsequently developed within a Christian context by the Dominican jurist St Thomas Aquinas (1225–1274) and later in a more secular context by the great Roman-Dutch jurist Grotius (1583–1645) and by Puffendorf (1632–1694).

In European legal thought, the idea that legal philosophies and the laws themselves ought to be shaped by principles of natural law was widely accepted for several centuries, but gradually lost currency during the 18th Century and was largely discredited in the 19th Century. However, a few vestiges of this thinking can still be found in many European legal systems and those based on them. For example, in many countries in the field of administrative law, decisions by individuals or bodies performing public functions are required to conform to certain basic standards such as hearing both sides of the story before making a decision. Requirements such as these are sometimes referred to as aspects of 'natural justice'.

This waning of natural law philosophies was brought about primarily by two schools of thought. The first, 'noncognitivism', is usually associated with the work of the Scottish philosopher David Hume (1711–1776). In his *Treatise of Human Nature*, first published in 1739, he pointed out that no matter how much we know about the functioning of the world or of human nature (i.e. what 'is'), we cannot logically deduce what is morally right or wrong (i.e. what 'ought' to be done). In other words, a moral conclusion (i.e. relating to values) cannot be derived from two factual statements, as moral philosophers of the time, including proponents of natural law, tended to do. For example, if one starts with the major premise 'All mammals have sex in order to procreate', and the minor premise 'Humans are mammals', one can logically arrive at the conclusion 'Humans have sex to procreate'. However, these premises do not support the conclusion 'Humans *ought* only to have sex to procreate'.

What Hume showed was that the observation on life, society and human nature, which many philosophers and jurists relied on to establish the content of natural law, did not provide a logical basis for the conclusions that they drew as to what law ought to say, particularly in the future. Many jurists assumed that Hume's observations destroyed the basis for natural law. However, this is not the case. As Harris points out, if this syllogistic, deductive reasoning is the only way of proving something then we cannot logically establish that the sun will rise tomorrow because it has risen in the past. Furthermore, if we start with statements that contain value judgements (i.e. 'ought' statements) then we can logically deduce others.[8]

The second school of thought that attacked the idea of natural law is usually referred to as 'legal positivism'. Adherents of this school of thought argue that law has no inherent moral content (i.e. the question of what law 'ought' to say is meaningless) and what is law can be empirically determined, typically by reference to legislation, judgements and custom.

At a more pragmatic level, one of the reasons why the natural law approach lost currency is that there is a strong tendency for various interest groups in society to claim that their beliefs are 'natural' and therefore inherently superior to competing beliefs, which they pillory as 'unnatural'. Certainly, if one looks over the centuries at what different societies have treated as crimes and what has not been prohibited, it is easy to understand why positivist legal philosophers conclude that a 'crime' is whatever those in control of the political machinery of the state choose to define as such. Today, relatively few jurists would even support the notion advanced by many legal philosophers in the past that there are certain acts that are inherently evil or wrong (*mala in se*) and are consequently universally recognised as crimes. Even homicide is a very relative concept when one takes into account the circumstances in which it is legally defensible and therefore not murder. For example, the premeditated killing by a wife of her violently abusive husband is murder, while the deliberate killing of thousands of millions in wars or as a consequence of foreign policy decisions is not, and may even be regarded as laudable.

Furthermore, the deliberate killing of a living thing will only be regarded as murder (i.e. a crime) if the deceased is a subject recognised by law. Legally speaking, all owned things are objects, not subjects. So, for example, killing a slave was not murder under Roman law because a slave was an object and there was therefore no crime involved. However, if one killed a slave belonging to someone else the owner was entitled to compensation for the loss of his or her property. Similarly today, legally speaking, it is not possible to murder an animal or a forest no matter what the magnitude of the slaughter is or what degree of brutality, depravity, or cruelty is involved. At worst one might fall foul of animal cruelty laws (which are probably mainly intended to protect human sensibilities) or be convicted of failing to comply with regulatory procedures such as undertaking an environmental impact assessment.

In more recent times the idea of natural law has been supported by eminent jurists such as H. L. A. Hart (1907–1992), who argued for the recognition of a minimum content of natural law. It has even enjoyed a limited revival, particularly through the reinterpretation of the idea by writers such as John Finnis, the author of *Natural Law and Natural Rights* (1980). However, these new interpretations of natural law are still firmly anthropocentric. For example, Finnis argues that 'justice' consists of fostering the 'common good' by putting in place the conditions necessary to enable the members of a community to achieve basic values and other reasonable objectives. However, the 'community' is the human community, and he then goes on to justify private ownership on the basis that it promotes a good of 'personal autonomy in community' and is based on the observation that resources are more productively exploited by private rather than public enterprises. Clearly if we shift our point of reference from what we consider to be good for the individual in (Western) societies to what is good for Earth, the conclusions are likely to be very different.

From an Earth jurisprudence perspective, the inherently anthropocentric flavour of current concepts of natural law makes the debates that have raged around these ideas seem rather artificial. Nevertheless, the history of natural law as an idea is instructive for at least two reasons. Firstly, it demonstrates that ideas that cannot easily be defended on the basis of empirical fact or strict logic are likely to be attacked vigorously by those with vested interests in existing power structures. Secondly, it provides a warning of the need to guard against making facile or ideologically-loaded generalisations about how humans ought to behave based on observations of specific circumstances. Perhaps it also reveals the limitations of relying virtually exclusively on formal logic and the scientific method in the search for wisdom.

THE LAWS OF NATURE

One of the subjects that we did not discuss in our jurisprudence classes were the laws of nature. The laws of nature, as we currently conceive of them, self-evidently have no place in the lawyer's world. They figure in the popular imagination as grossly inaccurate cartoon caricatures. We are all familiar with terms such as 'the law of the jungle', 'kill or be killed', and 'survival of the fittest' (misconceived as the person or animal that is the strongest or the most cunning at a particular time). In general these are inaccurate projections of human perceptions onto the natural world.

More seriously, we might think of the laws of nature as aspects of the physical world that govern the lives of animals and plants but that self-evidently have little relevance to modern human beings. In other words, insofar as we even use the term 'laws of nature' seriously, we do not conceive of them as 'real laws' but rather as principles that describe the functioning of the universe and have little relevance to the hermetically sealed human world.

Our secular legal philosophies then almost universally deny that our jurisprudence need take account of any rules, norms or considerations that lie outside human society. Laws are generated entirely within our glass 'homosphere'. Our laws are understood literally, as laws unto themselves. All that matters are the legal convictions of the human community at the relevant time and the content of the written law. At first glance this may not appear wholly unreasonable. After all, human laws have been written by humans and are only intended to apply to humans—what use would even the most intelligent dolphin have for a set of Halsbury's *Laws of England*? All social animals have their rules and punish transgressors—witness a pride of lions eating at a kill, or the complex social structure of chimpanzees. Are our laws not more complex versions of the same? The problem is not that we have developed human laws or human rights; it is rather that we are no longer aware that our legal systems exist within the Earth system and consequently do not see the need for any connection or continuity between our legal systems and the Earth system.

What makes this particular delusion so pernicious is the fact that the evolutionary process has vested such prodigious abilities in the human species that we now have an enormous capacity to do harm as well as to give glorious expression to universal qualities such as creativity and consciousness. If a group of chimpanzees were to persist in aberrant social practices that destroyed their habitat, it probably wouldn't have a very significant effect on other species, and the self-destructive nature of these practices would tend to result in the extinction of those animals in the long-term. Our greater ability to control aspects of our environment, however, appears to mean that before our species meets its evolutionary fate, we may be able to devastate the life-supporting systems of the Earth. It has been estimated that if the current rate of human impact on the Earth's systems continues throughout this century, by the year 2100 (i.e. during the lives of our grandchildren and some of our children) a third of the species alive today may be extinct.[9]

HEALING LAW

It would be obvious to any members of the Earth Community other than humans that the governance systems of the dominant human societies are dangerously dysfunctional. It is less obvious to many humans that our governance systems are also failing us. As long as our societies continue to fail to identify and stop human practices that threaten the health of the whole, these practices will continue to multiply. Sooner or later we will either suffer catastrophic consequences (along with the rest of the Earth Community) or make very substantial changes to how we regulate ourselves. The question is, will our societies be able to undergo the requisite metamorphosis fast enough? From the perspective of many of the great forests, ancient coral reefs and many other exquisitely intricate communities of life the answer to this question is 'no'. They will be gone forever, long before there is any significant change in human behaviour. For our species and many others, the answer to the question may well be decided during the lifetimes of the next two or three human generations.

Recognising the symptoms of the malaise that are described in this chapter is the first step to healing. The second is diagnosing the deeper nature of the illness and acknowledging that we need to do more than merely treating the symptoms. Healing however, requires an understanding of what health looks like, and practices to restore that condition. In Part Three (Chapters Six to Nine) I discuss how we might discern a healthy role for humans once more, and what the characteristics of governance systems that support this role might be. In Part Four (Chapters Ten to Fourteen) I discuss what we could do to begin transforming curerent governance systems into 'Earth governance' systems. Part Five (Chapter Fifteen) reviews the arguments for urgently transforming human societies and governance systems, and surveys the way forward, while the Postscript records the progress made to date.

PART 3

Earth governance

The ecological ego matures toward a sense of ethical responsibility with the planet that is vividly experienced as our ethical responsibility to other people. It seeks to weave that responsibility into the fabric of social relations and political decisions.

Theodore Roszak

Chapter 6

Respecting the Great Law

THE MOUNTAINS

The Table Mountain range outside my window is calm, as ever. Long wispy white clouds are floating serenely across its rugged grey face. A few minutes ago the slowly seething manes of the clouds were radiant, shot through with slanting shafts of glory as the sun sank below the sea beyond the mountains. Now, as the clear evening cools, the clouds look bluer and heavier as they drift down towards the forested slopes. Suddenly the mountain is gone, blanketed by the softly shifting mists.

I can't see the mountain any more, and as the dusk gathers even the forest and mist fade from sight. I know it is there though, and if I seek it I will find it. I will know it by the quickening of my heartbeat as I climb its slopes. Its steepness will swell my muscles and its beauty will call to my soul. It has a physical reality that demands respect, as the unprepared or unwary wanderer on the summit may discover to their peril in the sudden mists.

However, if I try to engage it with my rational mind alone, it is more elusive. Where does it begin and end? What is the mountain and what is the range? What is it made of, and are the clouds, forests and streams part of it? What is it to me, and me to it? Is it an object of reverence? A muse to inspire me? Or is it merely a pleasingly shaped pile of sandstone and granite? In my confusion I flee to the comforting abstraction of the dictionary definition ('a large natural elevation of earth's surface') and the closely serried contour lines of the ordinance map. All the while the mountain remains as it is, solid and still, yet playing its part in co-creating the microclimate around me, the meaning in my head and the gladness in my heart.

DIFFERENTIATING BETWEEN THE GREAT JURISPRUDENCE AND OTHER EARTH JURISPRUDENCE

I am not part of the mountain, nor is the mountain part of me. We are distinct from one another and yet we are both part of the same Earth, and the same subatomic particles and energy flow through us. The characteristic of being both part of a whole while remaining distinct within it, also applies to how we understand Earth jurisprudence, for it too has different aspects. On

Man takes his law from the Earth; the
Earth takes its law from Heaven;
Heaven takes its law from the Tao.
The law of the Tao is its being what
it is.

Tao The King (Tao Te Ching), ch.25

the one hand there are the 'laws' or principles that govern how the universe functions. These are timeless and unified in the sense that they all have the same source. This 'Great Jurisprudence' is manifest in the universe itself. For example, the phenomenon of gravity is expressed in the alignment of the planets, the growth of plants, and the cycle of night and day. All are manifestations of the existence of this 'law'.

On the one hand, 'Earth jurisprudence' refers to legal philosophies developed by humans that are to a large extent derived from, and consistent with, this 'Great Jurisprudence'. For the sake of clarity in this book I use the term 'Earth jurisprudence' in this narrower sense. However, it is important to appreciate that any true Earth jurisprudence must be embedded within, and be an extension of the 'Great Jurisprudence'. Both are therefore better understood as different aspects of the same pattern than as separate things.

THE NATURE OF THE GREAT JURISPRUDENCE

The Great Jurisprudence is like the mountains. It is what it is, and our descriptions of it are abstract approximations. It is neither right nor wrong, and it is inherent in all things by virtue of the fact that they are part of the universal whole. In this sense it is better understood as a quality of the universe rather than as a rule or principle that governs it. It is not applied, as a rule or principle might be, in order to arrive at a particular outcome. Instead its existence and how it operates can be observed in the phenomena of the natural world. It can also be understood as the design parameters within which those of us engaged in developing Earth jurisprudence for the human species, must operate.

If we are to be guided by the Great Jurisprudence in developing a viable Earth jurisprudence for our species, we need to start by trying to discern the nature and content of that Great Jurisprudence. The natural world (i.e. the universe functioning as it should) provides the best guide we have to the essential nature of the universe. In order to rediscover Earth jurisprudence and develop forms appropriate to our times, it is essential to start by looking at the fundamental laws and principles of the universe, since these provide the ultimate framework within which any human legal framework must exist. For most practical purposes this means understanding the functioning of the natural world on Earth. In attempting to reintegrate ourselves into the wider Earth Community it is helpful to remember that the earth beneath our feet and beneath the roots, paws, fins and tentacles of those with whom we have co-evolved, is the common ground that unites us. It provides our common home, the stuff of which we are made and the sustenance that supports us.

HUMAN NATURE AND
THE GREAT JURISPRUDENCE

The empirical knowledge gathered by the scientific community, particularly in recent decades, provides valuable insights into the functioning of the universe. However, I believe that rational analysis is not the only method of accessing valid and useful information and insights. The Great Jurisprudence is 'written into' every aspect of the universe. Everything about our species, from the size of our brain, the shape of each tooth, and our sense of beauty and colour has been shaped by our interaction with the universe and the plants, animals and microbes with which we have danced in the intimacy of co-evolution. Had anything been different—gravity perhaps—we would have been different. Therefore in a sense the Great Jurisprudence is also written in the bones, muscles, sinews and thought patterns of our own bodies.

Since we humans are part of that universe, it seems to me logical that we also have the capacity to understand the principles of the Great Jurisprudence by empathic engagement with nature and by introspection. In other words, unlike the classic understanding of 'natural law' discussed in Chapter Four, there are other routes to discovering the Great Jurisprudence besides using 'reason' (at least in the narrow sense of the term). In developing Earth jurisprudence, it is also important to take account of the nature of human beings and its connection with the wider universe. Earth jurisprudence is to the Great Jurisprudence what human nature is to nature.

CHARACTERISTICS OF
THE GREAT JURISPRUDENCE

What then are some of the primary characteristics of the Great Jurisprudence? In *The Universe Story*, Brian Swimme and Thomas Berry refer to a 'Cosmogenetic Principle', which postulates that the evolution of all parts and dimensions of the universe will be characterised by three qualities or themes: *differentiation, autopoiesis* (meaning literally 'self-making') and *communion*.[1] They point out that these features of the universe have been derived by examining the universe, rather than being deduced from a theory. Consequently we can expect our understanding of them to deepen over time as our knowledge and understanding increases.

These terms are not capable of simple definition, but for our purposes we can understand 'differentiation' as referring to an inherent tendency towards diversity, variation and complexity; 'autopoiesis' as an inherent ability to self-organise and to be self-aware, and 'communion' as referring to the interconnectivity of all aspects of the universe. The universe orders itself by way of differentiating itself into different aspects or parts, autopoiesis structures those different parts, and communion organises them in relation to one another.

There is also the distinct possibility that Earth, as a system, is evolving, in spurts, to more and more complex levels of organisation. At each new level, new properties appear to emerge, with the result that the new system is greater than the sum of its parts and cannot be understood as a mere combination of the lower level systems.

Jan Smuts (1870–1950), another frequent walker on the mountains of the Table Mountain range, wrote that:

> Both matter and life consists of unit structures whose ordered grouping produces natural wholes which we call bodies or organisms. This character of 'wholeness' meets us everywhere and points to something fundamental in our universe. Holism . . . is the term here coined for this fundamental factor.[2]

Smuts argued that inorganic matter produced life, which in turn produced mind. Each superior level is greater than the sum of the lower levels, and cannot be reduced to its constituent parts.

Support for a vision of the Earth as an evolving system that is being co-created by the interaction between living organisms, and between living organisms and the non-living environment, has been strengthened by a number of hypotheses and discoveries. These include the 'Gaia Theory' of former NASA scientist James Lovelock. He makes out a convincing case for regarding Earth as an effective self-regulating system, rather like other organisms that we are familiar with.[3] Certainly more and more evidence is emerging that indicates that for millions of years Earth has regulated and stabilised the chemical composition of the atmosphere and the temperature of its surface at levels that are optimal for life. For example, around 21 per cent of the atmosphere is made up of oxygen, which is highly reactive, while methane is found at a fairly constant level of 1.7 parts per million. In sunlight, oxygen and methane react to produce carbon dioxide and water. Maintaining methane at this level requires living organisms to produce about 500 million tons of methane a year. If life on Earth were to cease, all its elements would continue to react with one another until no more reactions were possible and the planet would become a hot, inhospitable place without oxygen or water.[4]

The theories of David Bohm (former Professor of Theoretical Physics at Birkbeck College, University of London) may also support the idea that the Earth is 'unfolding' like a bud toward its full potential. Bohm argues that aspects of a whole system are enfolded into each part of the whole in the same way as fragments of a holographic picture retain the image of the whole picture. He points out that the whole system of order that is 'folded into' into each part and not visible to us, can unfold in a natural way and become explicit, in the same way that a television can reveal the visual image that was implicate in the radio signal it received.[5]

Others, like the Catholic priest Teilhard de Chardin and Peter Russell, author of *The Awakening Earth* (1982),[6] see Earth as an organism that is evolving towards being a super-organism. Having made leaps from energy levels to matter, and from matter to life, Earth is now poised to make a leap to a form of ordered global consciousness.

These ideas may seem far-fetched. I certainly remember laughing derisively when, as a would-be hard-headed young shipping attorney, I heard about Lovelock's hypothesis that Earth could be regarded as an organism. Later, when I read his careful scientific arguments, I regretted my prejudice. Sufficient supporting evidence has now been discovered for the hypothesis to be accepted as a scientific theory. For example, scientists like Lynn Margulis have shown that micro-organisms such as marine algae help stabilize the composition of Earth's atmosphere. She has also argued that the evolutionary process has been driven not so much by the divergence of one species from another, but more by independent entities combining in symbiotic relationships in order to form complex entities ('symbiogenesis'). In other words, co-operation and mutual reliance has been more important in evolution than competition.[7]

Life did not take over the globe by combat but by networking. Beneath our superficial differences we are all walking communities of bacteria . . . The world shimmers, a pointillist landscape made of tiny living beings.

Margulis and Sagan, *Microcosmos*, p.15 and p.191

At this stage, however, I think that it is reasonably safe to say that in developing Earth jurisprudence for our times we would be wise to bear in mind that natural systems exhibit what Edward Goldsmith[8] calls 'whole-maintaining' characteristics. In other words, each aspect of a properly functioning system acts in a manner that contributes to the health and integrity of the whole. If this were not the case, then the whole system would begin to deteriorate with adverse consequences for all the component parts. Self-regulation is an essential part of any living organism or community of organisms. Any organism or community that is unable to regulate itself in a manner that ensures that its component parts or members function in a way that benefits the whole, will ultimately disintegrate. It also means that a viable self-regulating system must have feedback mechanisms that allow it to identify and correct any functions within it that undermine the whole.

Of course, a cynic might argue that if Earth is a properly functioning natural system we need not worry because in time balance or 'homeostasis' will be restored as our poor 'management' of the planet either results in our own extinction or drastically reduces our numbers. Personally, I don't find this a very comforting thought and prefer to think that we might just be clever enough to evolve sufficiently sophisticated and appropriate self-regulatory mechanisms in time to avert this long-term correction. However, even if we do, the question is how much more life will Earth lose forever in the interim.

TAKING GUIDANCE FROM
THE GREAT JURISPRUDENCE

In order to understand the implications of the Great Jurisprudence for human legal systems and jurisprudence, it is necessary to consciously shift one's reference point away from a purely human-centred one. Doing this is analogous to the shift of mental perspective that was required in order to appreciate the validity of Copernicus's discovery that Earth revolved around the sun and not vice versa. At the time many people, including the authorities, so feared what they understood to be the negative consequences of accepting that Earth, and ultimately human beings, were not the centre of the universe around which everything else revolved, that they tried to force Copernicus to recant. In doing so they failed to realise that this would have no effect on reality, and if he were correct (as he turned out to be) it only proved that having Earth move around the sun wasn't the disaster they thought. In fact, the only real damage was to certain self-aggrandising conceits cherished by the Church and peoples of the time. In the same way, accepting that human jurisprudence must be subsidiary to the Great Jurisprudence may appear threatening but, in fact, has always been true.

What then are the implications of the primary characteristics of the universe (i.e. the Great Jurisprudence) for the development of Earth jurisprudence?

Firstly, if we recognise the validity and relevance of the Great Jurisprudence to human jurisprudence, then the ultimate source of jurisprudence and of law shifts out of the homosphere and beyond human control. In other words, as Thomas Berry puts it, "the universe is the primary lawgiver".[9] With it goes the political power to be the supreme arbiter of right and wrong and of legitimacy. This may at first seem threatening, particularly to existing political and legal establishments trying to maintain power. However, it is important to be aware that this is the price of re-admission to the Earth Community, which offers the prospect of far greater fulfilment than is possible within the homosphere.

Secondly, if one accepts that the ultimate source of 'rights' is the universe and not human society, it follows that human jurisprudence is embedded within, and bounded by, the larger and more significant Great Jurisprudence. In other words, we must be conscious of the limits of what our legal theories and laws seek to regulate.

Thirdly, human laws and governance systems must be designed to promote human behaviour that contributes to the health and integrity not only of that human society, but also of the wider ecological communities, and of Earth itself. Any self-regulating community or ecosystem is part of a larger system, which itself is part of a larger system, and so on. Accordingly, in the process of evaluating and designing governance systems according to 'whole-maintaining' criteria, we are also ordering and structuring integrated communities. In this sense, applying the whole-maintaining principle means restoring integrity.

Fourthly, we must re-evaluate our desire to impose uniformity, and celebrate a diversity of self-regulatory systems—an Earth democracy if you will. What we know about the quality of differentiation suggests that stability and creative evolution lies in the direction of diversity rather than uniformity. It is interesting to note that most legal systems expend a great deal of energy on attempting to impose uniformity — in both approach and substance. Globalisation is also founded on the promotion of uniformity and the reduction of cultural and regional differences. To some extent our desire for uniformity is rooted in our firm belief in the need to manage everything, including the environment (i.e. everything around us). The managerial mind must of necessity reduce the complexity of the real world to abstract approximations that allow decisions to be made in bulk. Managers in the World Bank, for example, cannot possibly spend sufficient time on all the projects under their purview to understand the nuances of each one. What they need is categories and classifications so that they can generalise and facilitate decision-making in bulk.

If Earth jurisprudence is to be consistent with the quality of differentiation (as it must), it must reject a management approach based on human superiority and seek to create an environment within which diverse approaches can flourish. Once we recognise the essential unity of all things and honour this truth by acting in a whole-maintaining manner, we no longer need to fear that permitting diversity or 'deviance' will cause our social systems to fall apart. In fact we need to reduce our emphasis on legal controls in some areas in order to allow greater freedom of expression for the innate creative and self-ordering (autopoetic) forces in our communities and in ourselves.

One of the central questions is, of course, how we discern what is 'whole-maintaining' and what is not. This is where communion is vitally important. Communion can be understood as the web of relationships or the dance between different aspects of the universal whole. In this sense it is the 'stuff' of which the universe is made. This interconnectivity always exists because of the essential unity of the universe but its quality varies. A relationship characterised by strong and mutually beneficial interconnectivity can be described as intimate. If it is to be a lasting relationship, it must also exhibit features such as exchange and reciprocity that benefit all involved.

This is true as much of human lovers as a predator-prey relationship. This suggests that those most intimately involved in a particular relationship or community are best placed to 'negotiate' mutually beneficial terms. If the relationship is mutually beneficial a dynamic balance will arise, the relationship will last and it will contribute to the maintenance of the whole. Since in most cases we will be concerned with relations with beings other than humans who do not speak our languages, we must first learn (or re-learn) how to be sensitive to the needs of the other members of the Earth Community in order to increase intimacy. However, first we must know who we are.

Chapter 7

Remembering who we are

WHERE HAVE WE COME FROM?

In the part of Africa I come from, when greeting someone in Zulu, as soon as you have established their name you ask *"Uphumaphi?"*, "Where are you from?" For many African peoples, establishing where a person's roots lie and where his or her people live, is fundamental to understanding who that person is. In Zulu and Xhosa cultures, when a child is born the umbilical cord is buried in the earth of the cattle *kraal* (enclosure), which is both the spiritual and economic heart of the community. Understood in the context of this practice, the traditional greeting has a deeper significance. It is not only an enquiry about the homeland of your community but also about where you took root on Earth. For this reason, a man or woman who may have left the rolling green hills and warm smoky mornings of rural Zululand as a child to grow up in a city, will still answer the traditional enquiry by naming the place where he or she belongs.

Human beings originated in Africa roughly seven million years ago. Several different species of earlier hominids have been found in the Great Rift Valley in East Africa, Southern Africa, and recently in West Africa. However, our earliest human-like ancestor is usually taken to be *Australopithecus africanus* (remains of which have been found in the deep limestone caverns at Sterkfontein near Johannesburg). *Australopithecus* is thought to have evolved into *Homo habilis*, then *Homo erectus* and finally, about half a million years ago, into *Homo sapiens*. As far as we know, these species were confined to Africa for about the first five or six million years. About 50,000 years ago human history took off with what Jared Diamond has referred to as our 'Great Leap Forward',[1] and abundant artefacts have been found at the sites of what are now referred to as Cro-Magnons. Our ancestors appear to have begun to spread out of Africa around a million years ago, with the more advanced Cro-Magnons entering Europe around 40,000 years ago and displacing the Neanderthals who were already there.

All these people were hunter-gatherers, and it is only within the last 11,000 years or so that people began to produce food by domesticating wild animals and cultivating wild plants as crops. For thousands of years agriculture

*When a Karen child is born, the
father of the newborn takes the
placenta and umbilical cord and
walks deep into the forest, where he
selects a large tree and offers to it the
afterbirth by placing it in the crook of
a branch. The tree, which exemplifies
both life and longevity, becomes a
lifetime reminder to the Karen child
that his or her own health and well-
being are related to the health and
well-being of that tree . . . When the
child is old enough to walk and
understand, the father will guide his
daughter or son to the forest to see her
or his 'life tree' and to know that she
or he must nurture and care for this
ancient being.*

Seri Thongmak and David L. Hulse,
The Winds of Change: Karen People in
Harmony with World Heritage, about
the Karen people of the Myanmar
and Thailand highlands

and hunter-gathering coexisted as alternative survival strategies. Some groups chose not to adopt agriculture at all, others converted completely, others supplemented their hunting and gathering, and some even adopted farming for a period before abandoning it again for long periods.[2] Over time and for a variety of reasons, the balance tipped in favour of agriculture. Population densities were growing as technologies for collecting, processing and storing wild food improved. This in turn led to a demand for more food. Provided that a community had appropriate crops and the technologies to grow, store and process them, agriculture yielded more edible calories per hectare than hunting and gathering. As the agriculturalists remained in one place, the intervals between births were shortened and the population density grew, thereby further increasing the demand for food. This dynamic was so strong that these early farmers had to spend more time securing food and were less well-nourished than their hunter-gatherer ancestors, because the population increased faster than the food supply. This relationship between population and food supply created an ongoing pressure to expand. The denser populations of food producers were almost invariably able to displace those hunter-gatherers who did not convert to food production, a trend that has continued until the present.

It is clear that for the vast majority of human history our species has lived in small tribal groups in an intimate relationship with nature, either as hunter-gatherers or food producers, or as a combination of the two. The question as to whether or not our tribal ancestors lived 'in harmony with nature' (which I take to mean without causing significant long-term degradation to the environment in which they lived) is a much-contested one. There is certainly (contested) evidence that early hunter-gatherers might have caused the extinction of large animals (so-called 'megafauna') in Australia, New Guinea, and North America, because they appear to have disappeared at around the same time that humans arrived. Certainly there is little hard evidence that all contemporary and ancient hunter-gatherer societies were ecologically benign.

The relationship between agricultural production (particularly large-scale farming) and ecological damage is much stronger. Indeed there is considerable evidence that several ancient food-producing civilisations declined because they degraded their environments. The Mesopotamians of the Fertile Crescent denuded the hills of trees and irrigated their lands until the water table of brackish groundwater rose high enough to affect the roots of the crops. For a while they were able to sustain food production by changing from wheat to the more salt-tolerant barley. However, archaeologists tell us that in Southern Mesopotamia the ratio of wheat to barley declined steadily from about 3500 BC until by 1700 BC no wheat was being grown. Eisenberg suggests that the increasing salinity of the soil (which would have manifested itself first in the lower lying lands), may have been a factor in the steady shift of political power "up river from Sumer to Akkad and Babylon (with a southward detour to Ur), from Babylon to Nineveh."[3] Today much of the land in the area is saline, and yields of both barley and wheat are less than in ancient times. However, it is also true that some societies, like the Indians of South America, have been able to maintain their agricultural practices and have 'farmed' the rainforest for millennia without destroying the environment.

Unsurprisingly, the key issue in determining whether or not a human society degrades its environment is probably not whether its people hunt and gather, or farm, but how they do it. The link between agriculture and population growth, however, means that large-scale agriculture based on the exclusive cultivation of a few crops tends to create a pressure for humans to continually convert wild lands into farms. In more recent times, 'modern' agricultural practices have further weakened most humans' contact with wildness. Many rural areas have become depopulated as the growth of large-scale 'agri-business', with its heavy reliance on expensive inputs such as tractors, pesticides, fertilisers and hybrid or genetically engineered seeds, and close links with major food retailers, has displaced small farmers and agricultural labourers. This has fuelled the exponential growth of city and slum populations.

The relevance of this quick and rather superficial tour of human history over the last seven million years or so is that our ideas about what happened in the past have a great impact on our ideas of who we are today and who we (and our societies) might become. Some people believe that we are on the right track because, thanks to technology and science, at least some of us can sit comfortably on a flush toilet instead of squatting in filthy garments around a fire wondering if something big and fierce will eat us before we die of disease. Others believe that we have fallen from the Garden of Eden which our ecologically wise ancestors once inhabited, and are now horribly corrupt and soulless shadows of humans, condemned to lounge obesely before our television sets or to scratch for survival amidst the filth and violence of squatter camps. A third point of view is that humans are inherently destructive creatures and the only reason that most ancient human cultures did not destroy their habitats as we do is because there were not enough of them or they did

not have sufficient technological capacity to do so. Each camp tends to draw
on human history as evidence of the correctness of their point of view.

My own view is that some contemporary 'Greens' who extol the virtues
of indigenous societies over the destructive practices of modern industrial or
post-industrial societies, probably do sometimes overstate the 'greenness' of
indigenous cultures. The temptation to portray some of these peoples as
inherently wise 'noble savages' whom we have displaced from Eden, can be
very strong. On the other hand, there are many commentators who heap
scorn   on   the   idea   that   there   is   anything   useful   that   a
modern society can learn from these 'primitive' cultures. However, it is clear
that many of them are far less informed about indigenous peoples than those
whose views they ridicule, and their own cultural prejudices are often only
too apparent from their writings.

INSPIRATION FROM INDIGENOUS PEOPLES

I am neither an anthropologist nor an ecologist, and do not have the exper-
tise to draw definitive conclusions about which human cultures have acted
in an ecologically sound manner and which have not. However, my own limited experience and understanding of African customary law and of indigenous cultures in Africa, South America and elsewhere, has been enough to
convince me that there is much we could learn. I certainly believe that the
dominant cultures of the 21st century could learn important principles and
techniques from the systems of governance of these indigenous peoples that
would be useful in developing more Earth-centred governance structures for
our times. At a time like the present, when we are facing a governance crisis
of terrifying proportions, we need all the inspiration we can get. Much of the
wisdom of these communities is already lost and the remnants that are still
available to us are in many cases fast disappearing, due to the persistent and
overwhelming advance of the dominant cultures. It is therefore fundamentally important that we seek to protect these societies and to learn from
them. Not to do so would be extremely arrogant, foolish, and criminally irre-
sponsible.

Even for those sceptical of the value of indigenous knowledge about
human governance, I think that there are at least three good reasons for taking a closer look at indigenous cultures. Firstly, it appears that certain cultures
did manage to evolve laws and other means of regulating human conduct that
enabled them to live successfully over very long periods of time as part of a
wider community of living and non-living beings. In other words, they
appear, by and large, to have succeeded in avoiding degrading their environments as we have. To me this suggests that they probably know things that we
don't and which would be helpful for us to know.

*Although the wisdom of the
indigenous peoples is rooted in
primeval origin, it is both an
accumulative and an active cultural
experience. It is not the findings of an
individual specialist searching through
libraries but wisdom learned from our
direct contact with the land. Nature's
raw elements are truly the source of
enlightenment. The discovery of one's
infinite links to the universe gives us a
sense of being, of rootedness and
contentment.*

Mutang Urud, Kelabit tribesman,
Borneo

Secondly, as the World Summit on Sustainable Development demonstrated, there is a terrible dearth of plausible new ideas about how to govern ourselves in a manner that will improve our relationship with the rest of the Earth Community. The fundamental issue that we are dealing with here, our relationship with Earth, is as old as humanity itself. We would be foolish indeed not to consult the fantastic library of different techniques of human governance that have succeeded over thousands of years.

Thirdly, after being in the stifling, virtual monoculture of governance thinking within the homosphere for so long, it is immensely inspiring and invigorating to be exposed to cosmologies and worldviews that lie outside it. These governance systems are from another paradigm. They can help us to 're-frame' our thinking and broaden our horizons about what is possible. Let me give you a personal example. One of the great stumbling blocks for people from Western European cultures when considering how to develop a governance system that takes into account the interests of other species, is the fact that we cannot talk to them. This means that we cannot discover what they want and this seems to thrust us back into the role of managing their lives for them. It also, of course, poses apparently insuperable problems when it comes to briefing lawyers to represent for example 'nature' or the whales in court, in order to protect their rights. I had no answer to this problem. However, one evening during our meetings at the Airlie Centre, Martin von Hildebrand, an anthropologist who works very closely with Amazonian Indian communities in Colombia, gave us a fascinating overview of the cosmology of one of the groups that he knew well.

One of the aspects that he mentioned was that one of the responsibilities of the shamans of each community is to ensure that 'vital energy' continues flowing and that an appropriate dynamic balance is maintained between the energy within the human community and that within the animals that they hunt. The shamans communicate during trances with the guardian spirits of the game animals in order to regularly 'negotiate' what humans may take, or to restore balance if too much has been taken. I am not suggesting that we should model ourselves on these societies and convert our judges into shamans (although there may well be merit in pursuing that idea further). My point is simply that I did not even consider attempting to communicate with other species until I knew that the cosmology of these

Peoples that have lived in the same place for a long time without ruining it are not 'natural'. They are smart and they are lucky. And because they have lived in the same place for a long time, they have been able to fine-tune their dealings with nature. No primitive people that is still around today can really be primitive. All have thousands of years of trial and error under their belts. In many cases, they have had the same basic technology for centuries, which has allowed them to work out the kinks—the places where technology rubbed the wrong way against nature, or against people, or against itself. From this point of view, it is we who are primitive.

Eisenberg, *The Ecology of Eden*, p.317

peoples contains within it an understanding of how to do so. I was so conditioned by my own cosmology to believe that such things were not possible that I didn't notice the cultural framework limiting my field of vision. Now that I know that other cultures have found a way to deal with this issue it seems possible that we too could devise methods, appropriate to our cultures and times, to fulfil the same purpose.

In Chapter Two of this book I argued that the defective worldview or cosmology of the societies that dominate this 21st-century world was at the root our problems. What we need, I argued, is to go through a 'paradigm shift' to a new understanding of ourselves as part of, and not detached from, Earth. We also need to develop governance systems imbued with this new understanding, that are effective in preventing people acting in a manner that harms Earth, and thereby ourselves. Inherent in this argument is the belief that there is a close connection between the cosmology of a society and its system of governance. If this is the case, is it really possible to learn anything useful from a governance system that is based on an entirely different cosmology?

TUKANO COSMOLOGY

In considering these issues, I think it is useful to look at an example. Gerardo Reichel-Dolmatoff argues convincingly that the cosmology of the Tukano Indians of the Colombian Amazon plays a very important part in shaping everything that they do to increase the probability of their survival as a group or as individuals (what he calls their 'adaptive behaviour'). In his article he seeks to demonstrate that:

> Aboriginal cosmologies and myth structures, together with ritual behaviour derived from them, represent in all respects a set of ecological principles, and these formulate a system of social and economic rules that have highly adaptive value in the continuous endeavour to maintain a viable equilibrium between the resources of the environment and the demands of the society.[4]

The Tukano cosmology is particularly interesting in this context because, unlike the cosmology of today's dominant societies, each individual sees him or herself as part of a universal network of interrelationships. Preserving the ecological balance is of overarching importance, and each individual understands that this requires each person to behave in a co-operative manner in relation to all components of the environment. In their understanding the world has a limited amount of energy that flows continuously between humans, society, animals and nature. Humans may use the energy of animals and plants (e.g. by eating them) but they use only what is needed and a great deal of attention is given to ensuring that the flow of energy does not become blocked or imbalanced.

This cosmology has significant implications for how the Indians behave. To begin with they have little interest in trying to develop technologies that will enable them to increase what they take from the forest beyond what is actually needed. On the contrary, their interest is in finding out more about their environment and what it requires *from them*. Reichel-Dolmatoff explains that "this knowledge, the Indians believe, is essential for survival because man must bring himself into conformity with nature if he wants to exist as part of nature's unity, and must fit his demands to nature's availabilities." One of the reasons that they observe animal behaviour so closely is because animals present a model of what is possible in terms of successful adaptive behaviour. In other words, the Indians might be inspired by the jaguar's masterful adaptation to its environment to adapt their own behaviour in order to move more gracefully within the dance of Earth. In the same way, their intimacy with the natural world can provide us with an inspirational model of what is possible.

The Tukano have a wide range of practices that have the effect of preventing environmental degradation, although they may be explained in other ways. Population levels are controlled primarily by the use of oral contraceptives made from plants and sexual abstinence, supported by social disapproval of large families. Harvesting levels are kept at sustainable levels by a wide range of techniques, including enforcing ritual food restrictions and requiring elaborate ritual preparations for hunting and fishing. In their understanding, game animals are protected by a spirit referred to as the 'Master of the Animals', and a hunter must comply with rigorous requirements in order for the Master to give permission to kill an animal. These include abstaining from sex, observing food restrictions and undergoing purification rites. When game is scarce, the shaman must go into a narcotically-induced trance in order to make contact with the Master of the Animals. The shaman will then negotiate for game to be made available in return for promising that he will send the souls of any people who die to the Master's storehouse in order to replenish the energy lost by the killing of animals.

The shaman plays a very active role in controlling harvesting, including determining how many animals may be killed at particular times and which

fish are to be thrown back. Since diseases or injuries are understood to result
when a person upsets the ecological balance (e.g. by over-hunting or wasting
some scarce resource), the shamans tend to focus on treating the affected part
of the ecosystem in order to cure social malfunctions. This usually requires re-
establishing rules to avoid over-use of the environment or undesirable population increases.

The Tukano believe that the universe is steadily deteriorating (rather like
the physicist's understanding of entropy) and consequently regularly engage
in ceremonies during which all the aspects of the universe are ritually recre-
ated. As Reichel-Dolmatoff explains:

> In the course of these ceremonial occasions, when the universe and all its com-
> ponents are being renewed, one goal becomes of central importance: the reaffir-
> mation of links with past and future generations, together with the expression of
> concern about the future well-being of society. The emphasis of the ritual is upon
> unifying the social group, upon continuity, upon the close bonds of identity that
> unite society with the past and make it the foundation of the future. It seems that
> this sense of union provides deeply motivating values and strong incentives for
> ecological responsibility. The lengthy genealogical recitals and the ritual dia-
> logues have a powerful cohesive function, and in many of these rituals animal
> and plant spirits are thought to participate, expressing by their presence their
> inter-relatedness and interdependency. It must be pointed out here that the rit-
> ual re-creation of the universe is generally accompanied by the collective use of
> narcotics of plant origin. During these drug-induced trance states, . . . the par-
> ticipants establish contact with the mythical past, in fact, they see themselves
> return to the time of divine Creation and thus take part in it.[5]

The contrast between the pathetically inadequate methods used by most governments or the international community to convey the importance of 'intergenerational equity' with the physical, spiritual and emotional depth of the
Tukano's methods is striking. Our diplomats and ministers responsible for
environmental issues cough timidly in the corridors of power about sustainability, and annotate international documents with references to the importance of not prejudicing the ability of future generations to meet their needs.
It is difficult to speak with authority without drawing on a shared mythological past or genesis story that provides a sense of history and collective purpose for our peoples. The Tukano culture, on the other hand, speaks to its
people with the power of thousands of years of history, the authority of the
mythological creators and in the language of experience. The results of each
approach are self-evident.

LEARNING FROM INDIGENOUS PEOPLES

The Tukano have an intricate and sophisticated cosmology that is intertwined with the rivers, hills and forests in which they live. Although the cosmology of each tribe or group of tribes is unique, there are also recurrent themes that are strikingly similar throughout the world. Like the Tukano, many tribal cultures:

• have a very real sense of belonging, and of being part of a larger context or community that embraces the living, the dead and the unborn, as well as non-human beings;

• have developed sophisticated means of communing with non-human beings including other species and the dead;

• respect laws or principles that they believe are immutable and do not have a human source;

• believe that human beings have an important role to play in ensuring the proper functioning of the natural world of which they are part (for example, the Aboriginal peoples of Australia believed that it was their responsibility to sing the world into existence and to maintain it as it was on the first day);

Tribal laws are never invented laws, they're always received laws. They're never the work of committees of living individuals, they're always the work of social evolution. They're shaped the way a bird's beak is shaped, or a mole's claw—by what works. They never reflect a tribe's concern for what's 'right' or 'good' or 'fair', they simply work—for that particular tribe.

Daniel Quinn, *The Story of B*, p.314

• are very conscious of the need to adapt their social practices to accord with the natural world rather than focussing on changing the natural world to suit them;

• place great emphasis on respecting other aspects of the environment (particularly animals that they hunt for food) and avoiding waste or excess;

• seek to maintain some sort of dynamic balance within the universe, by emphasising the importance of reciprocity, and that every taking requires a giving;

• have rituals and restrictive practices designed to restore any perceived imbalances or conflicts between human and non-human societies; and

• devote a great deal of attention to ensuring that their mythological history, worldview and laws are internalised by each member of the community.

An adequate discussion of what we may learn from these cultures is beyond the scope of this book and is a potentially inexhaustible area of study. It is also

Innuit emphasise that the core of the relationship between humans and animals is human recognition that an equity exists with animals as participating members of a shared environment . . . Through a life that unifies the land, the animals and the community past and present, the Inuk hunter acquires, reconstructs, and lives out a world-image which provides security both in his own identity and direction for his behaviour. He does not hunt only to eat, but also to structure his community and ultimately to build a cognitive model of the world by which he is defined and directed. To be inummarik (the process of becoming a genuine person), is to be actively engaged in lifelong cycles of interaction with, and cognitive interpretation of, the human and the non-human environment.

Stairs, Arlene and Wenzel, George, 'I am I and the Environment: Innuit Hunting, Community, and Identity', *The Journal of Indigenous Studies*, Winter 1992, 3:1, pp.4 & 6

difficult to imagine convincing many people in post-industrial 21st-century states to adopt a cosmology similar to that of the Tukano. (Although I confess to a certain attraction to the idea of facilitating a global paradigm shift by involving world leaders at the next G8 meeting in a ritualised, drug-induced trance!) Nevertheless, I think that the many examples of workable systems offered by indigenous tribal communities are instructive. Even if the governance mechanisms that they use are inappropriate for highly technological 21st-century societies, we still need to develop alternative mechanisms to achieve the same ends.

Remembering where we have come from and who we are is a necessary part of recovering our lost role in the Earth Community and of creating a vision of who we may become. The remaining tribal communities that still maintain strong bonds with the natural world can show us much about our human past and what we have left. Going back even further to the birth of Earth and beyond, reminds us that we are all part of a greater unfolding reality and that separation is an illusion. Only by seeing our present situation within the great sweeping arc of our planet's life story and the ongoing co-evolution of our kind, will we gain the perspective we need to choose wisely in the present.

Chapter 8
The question of rights

TAKING RIGHTS SERIOUSLY

The difficulties inherent in moving from the current philosophy of governance to Earth jurisprudence surface as soon as one mentions 'rights' for animals or the environment—particularly if there are lawyers present. The average lawyer responds with either scorn or humour — probably because the unconscious assumption is that since such propositions lie outside the conceptual framework of law as we know it, they are self-evidently absurd. Professor Christopher Stone, who in 1971 wrote the seminal article 'Should Trees Have Standing? — Towards Legal Rights for Natural Objects' (referred to in this chapter as *Trees*), records how legal critics resorted to humour instead of engaging seriously with his suggestion that the American legal system should allow lawsuits to be brought on behalf of aspects of nature, like trees, as if they were people.[1] Many in fact responded in verse to Stone's article (which was cited with approval by Justice Douglas in *Sierra Club v Morton*).[2]

THE QUESTION OF RIGHTS

Even the courts got in on the act. When the owner of a tree sued a negligent driver for damage to the tree, the Oakland, Michigan, County Appeals Court upheld the dismissal of the claim with the following judgement:

> We thought that we would never see
> A suit to compensate a tree.
> A suit whose claim is prest
> Upon a mangled tree's behest.
> A tree whose battered trunk was prest
> Against a Chevy's crumpled chest.
> A tree that may forever bear
> A lasting need for tender care.
> Flora lovers though we three
> We must uphold the court's decree.[3]

Stone himself rather self-deprecatingly admits that he started seriously researching the possibility of trees having rights only in an attempt to restore his credibility with his students. He recalls that in trying to maintain the interests of his property law students during the dying minutes of a lecture, he had wondered aloud:

"What would a radically different law-driven consciousness look like? . . . One in which Nature had rights, . . . Yes, rivers, lakes, . . ." (warming to the idea) "trees . . . animals."[4]

This "vague if heartfelt conclusion tossed off in the heat of lecture" created uproar among his students. Stone, to his credit, then set out to show that his idea was not incoherent by writing an article that might influence the outcome of a real case (*Sierra Club v Morton*).

Stone's original *Trees* article, as well as his subsequent writings, canvassed many of the practical difficulties that need to be surmounted if we are to use our courts to enforce rights held by other members of the Earth Community in the same way that people enforce their rights. (In fact, for most lawyers, if a court will not recognise a right then it does not exist.) However, rather than examining the complexities of trying to bring other members of the Earth Community into our courts and treating them as honorary humans, I wish to focus on the nature of these 'rights' themselves.

SHOULD BEINGS OTHER THAN HUMANS HAVE RIGHTS?

Thomas Berry's views on the issue of rights from an Earth-centred perspective are clearly and succinctly set out in *The Origin, Differentiation and Role of Rights*, which is reproduced on page 103. His justification for recognising that other members of the Earth Community have rights is elegant, and to my mind, convincing. In essence, he argues that the rights of all beings are derived from the most fundamental source of all, the universe. Since the universe is, in his words "a communion of subjects and not a collection of objects", it follows that all the component members of the universe are subjects capable of holding rights, and have as much right to hold rights as humans. One of the beauties of this approach is that it avoids the difficulties that have bedevilled those who have tried to argue that only certain 'sentient' or 'higher' forms of life should have rights.

Lawyers normally use the term 'right' to mean an interest that is legally protected in the sense that it can be enforced in a court of law. However the term is a slippery one, even for lawyers. In fact the American jurist Wesley Newcomb Hohfeld famously pointed out that 'right' is routinely used by lawyers and judges to refer to at least four different legal concepts: rights which give rise to a duty on the part of someone else, privileges, powers, and immunities.[5] If one interprets the term in the strict legal sense it means that terms like 'insect rights' are meaningless because no court would recognise or enforce any right claimed on behalf of an insect. It would, however, be only too happy to allow artificial legal persons created by legal fictions to hold extensive rights. In short, the notion of recognising the rights of any other aspects of the Earth Community is literally unthinkable. (Christopher Stone was obviously acutely aware of this, and his *Trees* article begins with a section entitled 'Thinking the unthinkable'.)

However, Berry uses 'rights' in a wider sense than lawyers normally do. As he explained at the Airlie meetings in April 2001 when questioned on his use of the term in *The Origin, Differentiation and Role of Right*s,

> When we use the term 'rights' we mean the freedom of humans to fulfil their duties, responsibilities and essential nature and by analogy, the principle that other natural entities are entitled to fulfil their role within the Earth Community.

If we accept Berry's propositions that the Earth is a communion of subjects, and that rights originate where the universe originates and not from human jurisprudence, it means that we cannot claim that humans have human rights without conceding that other members of the Earth Community also have rights. In other words, the rights of the members of the Community are indivisible—there cannot be rights for some without there being rights for all. If this is so, the discussion about the legal rights of 'non-human' members of the Community is about whether or not the legal system chooses to recognise these inherent rights. In other words, if the term 'rights' as used in our legal systems is incapable of being applied to other members of the Community it is simply an indication that the legal system is insufficiently developed to reflect the reality of their existence. (From an Earth-centred perspective, the myopia of a philosophy that cannot recognise the 'right' of a river to flow, of a species to remain free of genetic pollution or even of Earth to maintain its climate, beggars belief.)

If we use existing legal systems and human jurisprudence as our starting point for discussing this issue of rights, it is easy to become entangled in complex legal arguments. Resolving these questions is difficult because they are caused by the anthropocentric worldview itself and are not capable of resolution within the existing jurisprudential or legal frameworks. Thomas Berry avoids these difficulties by going back to the origin, the deepest of first principles, the root of all roots.

SHOULD WE BE SPEAKING OF RIGHTS?

Several people have questioned whether it is appropriate to use the term 'rights' at all if one does not mean 'rights' in the way that a court of law would understand the term. It is a valid question. In my attempt to escape the conceptual prison of contemporary jurisprudence, I have noticed repeatedly how language shackles us to the world we know. It is as if one were gazing beyond the homosphere one day and glimpsed a colour that did not exist within the homosphere. How would one describe it? If you called it a colour others would point out that it was not to be found on the palette of colours and so couldn't be a colour. If you made up an entirely new name for it you would be obscuring the important fact that it was a type of colour.

This difficulty arises with the use of the term 'rights' when describing relationships that involve non-human members of the Earth Community. While we insist that humans and juristic persons have rights in relation to, say, rivers and land, then we must also recognise that as subjects, rivers and land must have rights in relation to humans. If we do not, we will be maintaining a fundamental inequality that will obstruct our attempts to describe the reality of the situation in legal terms. On the other hand, even if the law were to acknowledge that, say, a river had the capacity to hold rights, extending the language of rights and duties to relations with non-human subjects is potentially confusing. Terms such as 'rights' and 'duties' are infused with our experience of existing legal systems and burdened with the connotations of conflicts. The very language that we use is coloured by the worldview of the homosphere.

Debating the use of 'rights' in the legal sense is not just a matter of using terminology accurately. If a 'right' cannot be conceived of and described in the language of law, our governance systems will not recognise it or give adequate weight to it when making decisions.

In the absence of an appropriate alternative term to describe the 'rights' of all the members of the Earth Community, including humans, I too have used the term in relation to other members of the Earth Community. I also occasionally use the term 'Earth right' in order to emphasise the distinction between a fundamental right of a member of the Earth Community derived from the universe, and other rights created by our legal systems. The fact that the use of the word 'rights' may sound jarring or inappropriate at times is a valuable reminder of the inappropriate limitations of our legal thinking and terminology.

RELATIONSHIPS AND RIGHTS

Rights exist within the context of relationships. As discussed above, the American jurist Wesley Hohfeld believed that law could be analysed in terms of legal relationships in which any right held by one person could be correlated with a duty owed by another, every power could be correlated with a liability, and so on. Not everyone agrees with this analysis. However, since we are discussing how people should govern themselves so as to avoid further degradation of Earth, discussing rights without considering the context of the relationships within which they are being asserted, is meaningless. So let us start with relationships as the context for rights.

A relationship between subjects can have many different aspects and can be described in many ways, depending on the context or purpose. For example, my relationship with my son could be described in terms of its quality ('we are close'), in biological terms ('he is my offspring') or in legal terms. From a legal perspective, the nature of our relationship is determined both by the inherent nature of each of us (insofar as it affects the relationship) and by our roles in relation to one another. In this case the fundamental nature of the relationship is determined by the fact that the law recognises our biological relationship but the legal relationship is also affected by our respective roles vis-à-vis one another, which may change over time. While my son is young I have a legal obligation to maintain and support him, but one day if I am old and penniless, this situation may be reversed and he may have a legal duty to support me. Therefore the legal rights and duties of each subject only exist within the context of a particular relationship and are closely related to the inherent qualities of each participant.

From a governance perspective, the most important way of analysing and describing a relationship is in legal terms. This is because the institutions of the governance system use a legal analysis to decide whether or not to become involved in the relationship. The state is not concerned if I cease to have a close relationship with my son, but if I do not fulfil my legal obligation to maintain him while he is a dependent child, he is entitled to call upon the power of the state to compel me to do so. In other words, the language of the law is used to define how people ought to act in relation to one another, and the consequences if anyone does not respect the terms of the legal relationship.

The situation is different where one is dealing with beings that the law does not recognise as subjects capable of participating in legally recognised relationships. For example, a person may beat his or her dog with impunity unless there is a provision in the law that prohibits them from doing so. If the law does not prohibit dog-beating, neighbours will have no legal right to interfere to prevent it. In fact a person would be entitled to call upon the police to prevent neighbours from entering his or her garden and interfering with the beating of the dog. Of course many countries have laws that prohibit cruelty to animals, in which case if a person beats a dog, some social institution could intervene and ultimately that person might be fined or imprisoned. However, it is important to appreciate that in this scenario the dog has no legal right not to be beaten. The law does not describe the relationship between a person and a dog, since the dog is not a legal subject. The legal analysis deals only with the extent of the powers, rights and obligations of humans and state institutions.

EARTH'S RIGHTS

If humans are not the only members of the Earth Community that have rights, and the source of those rights is not human laws, then we must ask ourselves: what rights does Earth as a whole have, and what rights do the other members of the Earth Community have? Of necessity this also means defining the rights of humans.

Within the Earth system, the well-being of the planet as a whole is paramount. None of the components of the Earth's biosphere can survive except within the Earth ecosystem. This means that the well-being of each member of the Earth Community is derived from, and cannot take precedence over, the well-being of Earth as a whole. Accordingly, the first principle of Earth jurisprudence must be to give precedence to the survival, health and prospering of the whole Community over the interests of any individual or human society. Giving effect to this principle is actually also the best way of securing the long-term interests of humans. It is only our failure to appreciate that we are part of the Earth Community that has led us to believe and act as if the reverse were true.

In looking for a way to express this in conventional legal terms, we could choose as an analogy the relationship between the state and its citizens in most legal systems today. The state, and the constitution that establishes it, are regarded as the source of all the rights of the citizen (with the possible exception of human rights). The state demands allegiance from its citizens and defines any citizen who attempts to destroy it as a traitor, who is then liable to the most extreme forms of punishment available. I am not suggesting that Earth jurisprudence follow this model. However, it does to some extent convey that if we are to express the relationship between humans and Earth in legal language, the primary nature and fundamental importance of this relationship must be emphasised. It is not a relationship between equals but between the whole and a part. Accordingly, while the needs of the part must be respected, attempting to balance them against the rights of the whole is inappropriate. The rights of the whole cannot be compromised.

The 'allegiance' that we humans owe Earth is therefore more analogous to that which a cell owes the body. The 'duty' of the cell is to fulfil the functions for which it evolved and to continue acting in a manner that contributes to the health of the body. If it ceases to do so it dies or becomes a cancer. Similarly, our obligation to Earth is to play our proper role in the functioning of the Earth system and to act in a way that maintains the integrity or 'wholeness' of Earth. If we cease doing so, we betray the Earth Community which sustains us, and ultimately, our species.

THE RIGHTS OF THE MEMBERS OF THE EARTH COMMUNITY

The Earth (and indeed the universe) can be understood as a vast network of interrelationships that is also a process because it is constantly changing. Physicists tell us that mountains, rivers, humans, lilies and dragonflies are different aspects of Earth, composed of the same subatomic particles re-arranging themselves in specific ways for a period. However, our senses tell us that the world around is not the same as us: on the contrary, it contains a kaleidoscope of different entities, each with its own role to play. In a sense, both these apparently contradictory views are correct. It is the interaction between the many different components of the system that creates a whole that is greater than the sum of its parts. I, like others before me, have used the metaphor of a community composed of different members to convey the sense of Earth as a whole created by the relationship between the parts. How might one translate these relationships into the concepts of governance and the language of law?

Thomas Berry has proposed that: "Every component of the Earth Community has three rights: the right to be, the right to habitat, and the right to fulfil its role in the ever-renewing processes of the Earth Community." Taken together, these 'rights' describe the essence of the role of each member of the Community in relation to other members and to the Community as a whole. Recognising these rights amounts to an acknowledgement that each member of the Community is a subject who has an inalienable right to be part of the Community, and to continue expressing itself in relationships with the other members of the Community.

Whether one expressed it in legal terms or not, it is clear that the system as a whole (i.e. Earth) requires each member of the Community to maintain its identity and to enter into relationships with other members of the Community. It is these relationships that are critical, both for the health of the whole and also for each member to define itself clearly. As Xhosa people say: "A person is a person because of people" (*Umntu ngumntu ngabanye*), meaning that it is through our relationships with others that we experience our full humanity.

Translated into 'rights-speak', we could say that each member of a community has both the right to be part of that community and the 'right' to be recognised as a distinct entity within it. (If it were not recognised as being distinct, it would be part of a larger entity rather than a member of a community.) Each member must also be able to enter into relationships with other members of the community, and in this way define its role and make its contribution to the community. This 'right to be recognised as being distinct' is therefore closely linked with what might be called a 'right of self-determination'. For example, during the process of de-colonisation, emerging nations that were part of colonial empires fought for the right to be treated as distinct entities within the world community (i.e. independent states). Once this was recognised, they would have the right to regulate themselves internally and to negotiate their relationships with other states. Members of the Earth Community, whether they be species or communities, must be recognised as having similar rights.

In recent decades many indigenous communities have also fought for the recognition of their right to be allowed to live and regulate themselves within their habitat, without the imposition of outside law and cultures that define how they must relate to one another and other members of the Earth Community. It is important to note that, by and large, these communities have not been asking the dominant cultures to extend certain 'human rights' to them. Their plea is for the dominant culture (represented by the national government) to cease trying to impose its idea of an appropriate human role on their relationships with one another and with the Earth Community as a whole. If the national governments accept that such a right of self-determination exists, then by necessary implication it must limit and reduce the extent of its influence and power, and allow the indigenous communities to self-regulate to a greater extent. In the same way, the first step is for our human jurisprudence to recognise that the dominant cultures of our times have no right to prevent other components of the Earth Community from fulfilling their evolutionary role. This is more important, I believe, than attempting to determine the precise content of the Earth rights of rivers, animals and plants.

BREACHING EARTH RIGHTS

One of the most dangerous misconceptions of the dominant cultures is that because human governance systems do not penalise most infringements of the Earth rights of other members of the Community, there is no sanction. Nature has its own way of responding to a failure to observe Earth rights. Each infringement violates the Earth Community and causes a further deterioration in the relationships between humans and the rest of that Community. We humans have evolved, and are genetically coded, to be part of that Community, and share a consciousness with it. Consequently the growing detachment of the dominant human societies from the Earth Community is matched by an increasing sense of loss and emptiness. It is already apparent that by replacing what were relationships of respect and reverence with other members of the Community with exploitative relations, we have lessened not only the beauty and complexity of the whole Earth Community, but also ourselves.

The Origin, Differentiation and Role of Rights

1. Rights originate where existence originates. That which determines existence determines rights.

2. Since it has no further context of existence in the phenomenal order, the universe is self-referent in its being and self-normative in its activities. It is also the primary referent in the being and the activities of all derivative modes of being.

3. The universe is a communion of subjects, not a collection of objects. As subjects the component members of the universe are capable of having rights.

4. The natural world on the planet Earth gets its rights from the same source that humans get their rights, from the universe that brought them into being.

5. Every component of the Earth Community has three rights: The right to be, the right to habitat, and the right to fulfil its role in the ever-renewing processes of the Earth Community.

6. All rights are species-specific and limited. Rivers have river rights. Birds have bird rights. Insects have insect rights. Humans have human rights. Difference in rights is qualitative not quantitative. The rights of an insect would be of no value to a tree or a fish.

7. Human rights do not cancel out the rights of other modes of being to exist in their natural state. Human property rights are not absolute. Property rights are simply a special relationship between a particular human 'owner' and a particular piece of 'property' for the benefit of both.

8. Species exist in the form of individuals and groupings—flocks, herds, schools of fish and so forth. Rights refer to individuals and groupings, not simply in a general way to species.

9. These rights as presented here also establish the relationships that the various components of Earth have towards each other. The planet earth is a single community bound together by interdependent relationships. Every component of the Earth Community is immediately or mediately dependent on every other member of the community for the nourishment and assistance it needs for its own survival. This mutual nourishment, which includes the predator–prey relationship, is integral with the role that each component of the Earth has within the comprehensive community of existence.

10. In a special manner humans have not only a need for but a right of access to the natural world not only to supply their physical needs but also to provide the wonder needed by human intelligence, the beauty needed by human imagination, and the intimacy needed by the human emotions.

Thomas Berry, 2001[6]

HUMAN RIGHTS

Humans, of course, can hold a very wide variety of rights. However, when we use the term 'human rights' we mean a particular category of rights that we consider worthy of special protection because they relate to essential characteristics that define our humanity. Although lawyers may argue that many of these rights have their origin in, say, a Bill of Rights, most people regard the core human rights, such as the right to life, as inherent. In other words, we regard them as Earth rights. There may be arguments about the precise content of various rights. However, most people believe that all humans are entitled to have certain fundamental rights respected by others and that any attempt to deprive anyone of these rights is 'unlawful' and morally wrong. Laws that are enacted to protect human rights are understood as reflecting, clarifying, and perhaps adding to these core rights, to make it more difficult for us to be deprived of them.

The protection of human rights can also be seen as guaranteeing our freedom to play a role in life that gives full expression to our natures. Without the freedom to have a family, to express ourselves freely, to be safe from arbitrary imprisonment and so on, our ability to express our humanity fully is restricted. If the state or some other party does not allow us the freedom to exercise these liberties, then we say that they have abused our human rights. Today, people all over the world will protest against human rights abuses, regardless of where they occur. There is a sense of solidarity that flows from the perception that the violation of fundamental human rights also violates our common humanity and it is our collective responsibility to resist those who deny these rights. In fact we define some of the worst systematic violations of these rights like genocide and apartheid as 'crimes against humanity'. These are regarded as so serious that some of the usual legal rules can be overridden. For example, a person may be tried for having committed a crime against humanity anywhere, whereas the usual rule is that someone accused of a crime must be tried in the country in which the crime was committed and according to the law of that county.

If we now imagine that we are talking about rivers instead of people, we would conclude that a fundamental river right (i.e. the riverine equivalent of a human right) would be the right to flow. If a water body couldn't flow it wouldn't be a river, and so the capacity to flow (given sufficient water) is essential to the existence of a river. Therefore, from the perspective of the river, building so many dams across it and extracting so much water from it that it ceased to flow into the sea, would be an abuse of its Earth rights.

LIMITING HUMAN RIGHTS IN THEORY

In order for human jurisprudence to be integrated into and consistent with the Great Jurisprudence, it must firstly not contradict the principles of the Great Jurisprudence, and secondly it must recognise that the ambit of human jurisprudence is circumscribed. By this I mean that the human jurisprudence must itself recognise that there are certain issues that are beyond its province to regulate and to the extent that it purports to do so, it is acting beyond its realm and those actions are invalid.

Put another way, it is clear that in order for humans (or any other species) to play a 'whole-maintaining' role within the Earth Community, we must recognise that human rights must be limited by the 'rights' of other members of the Community. This means that Earth jurisprudence, in order to give effect to the 'right of self-determination' discussed above, must recognise its limitations, and that its focus ought to be on human governance. The task ahead of us is not about developing and expanding human jurisprudence so that it can serve as a jurisprudence for all members of the Community. This would amount to humans trying to philosophise and regulate for all members of the Community: in short, a kind of 'neo-colonialism'. Instead what we need to do is to appreciate that human jurisprudence and governance is a part of a larger system of Earth self-governance and develop a better appreciation of the need to limit its scope and to respect other governance systems.

Therefore, the starting point for humans is the principle that each member of the Earth Community should be at liberty to fulfil its role within the Earth Community. In order for this liberty to exist, humans must have no right to prevent another member of the Community from fulfilling its role. This means that we must establish governance systems that prevent humans from being able to dam a river to the extent that it can no longer fulfil its role in an ecosystem, or from destroying the habitat on which a species depends for its survival. However, it does not mean that we must ensure that, for example, a species continues to play a role or even to exist. Extinctions also occur without human intervention. It is another matter, though, if we create the conditions that are likely to result in extinction, since we would then clearly have restricted or extinguished the freedom of the species in question to play its role.

BALANCING AND LIMITING
HUMAN RIGHTS IN PRACTICE

Part of the challenge posed by Earth jurisprudence is to develop governance methods that prevent humans infringing the fundamental Earth rights of other members of the Earth Community. How can we ensure that our species does not infringe the right of another member of the Earth Community to fulfil, as Berry puts it, "its role in the ever-renewing processes of the Earth Community"?

Let us look, for example, at the zebra. The recognition by human Earth jurisprudence of the 'right' of all zebras to fulfil their natural role would offer the zebra no protection against the lions. First, because human Earth jurisprudence is of no concern to lions, secondly even if it were, it doesn't apply to them, and thirdly because part of the natural role of zebras is to provide nourishment for lions. This means that even though a lion eating a zebra means the end of that zebra's life, it continues to fulfil the role of zebrakind (and so contributes to the continued existence of the species) even as it passes through the gut of the lion.

On the other hand, does Earth jurisprudence entitle a human hunter to shoot a zebra? I think that the answer to that is: 'It depends'. It will depend on the circumstances and different communities will have different versions of Earth jurisprudence. For the Bushman/San hunter killing for food, the answer might be 'yes'. (Although from the perspective of their Earth jurisprudence, it could be 'no' if he had not complied with the appropriate rituals, for example.) If the hunter is someone out to make some extra cash by shooting pregnant zebra mares in the hope that every so often the foetus will be at just the right stage of development to yield a fluffy, brown-striped pelt, the answer is probably 'no'. In the first case the killing will reinforce the intimacy of the relationships within the local Earth Community. In the latter the killing would be the wasteful, disrespectful, and harmful act of a person who regards wild animals as commodities. Nevertheless, between these extremes there would be more difficult cases to decide. We will need to develop far more sophisticated mechanisms for making these decisions in accordance with the dictates of the Great Jurisprudence—as the Tukano have done (see Chapter Seven).

The rights and wrongs of zebra killing don't arise too often in most countries, so let us consider the example of river rights. Imagine that a small group of humans settle near a river and begin to use its water for domestic purposes and to water their cattle and crops. In Earth jurisprudence terms, the use by the humans of the river water is a good thing since it strengthens the relationship between people and the river. The water that the people scoop from the river doesn't affect its flow and the aquatic ecosystem benefits from the increased nutrients from the humans and cattle.

Let us assume that over time the population of the small human settlement on the banks of the river grows and a city develops. There are now extensive farmlands nearby and the farmers are pumping out large volumes of water for irrigation, which reduces the flow of the river. Soon the municipality wishes to dam the river so that there will be sufficient water to meet the growing demand for water among city dwellers. At this point the relationship between the river and the people begins to become strained. As we all know from our own relationships, a bit of give and take is fine, and even taking without giving can be tolerated for a period. However, in the long run, balance is essential. When one of the parties begins to take so much that it begins to affect the essential character of the other, the relationship becomes dysfunctional and abusive.

In terms of Earth jurisprudence, once the fundamental Earth right of the river to flow is threatened, the legal system must prohibit the human activities that threaten it. A law that reflects this understanding should therefore prohibit any such activity. However, let us say that the river's ability to flow was not at risk. On the contrary, it flooded every so often and washed away the shacks that landless people had built along its banks. (They had settled here because this was the only area in the city where they could find open land with an accessible water supply.) People died. Should the river be canalised? Would that be an infringement of the rights of the river? Surely it would be justified to protect human rights, since the river's Earth right to flow is maintained?

The answer depends on what we consider the essential nature of the river to be. Fortunately rivers communicate rather a lot about their essential natures. We know that they need to flow, tend to rush over rocks in a highly oxygenated, high-energy flurry in their upper reaches, and have a distinct inclination to meander languidly in their lower reaches. They create microclimate and riverine ecosystems along their banks and they flood from time to time, compensating for what they destroy with rich silt and demarcating a flood plain as their territory. In other words, a flooding river is almost certainly acting in accordance with its nature. This means that the river should be given precedence (at least within its customary floodplain) and the people should be accommodated elsewhere. Canalising rivers to stop them flooding is analogous to shooting aardvarks to stop them digging holes under jackal-proof fences. As long as aardvarks are aardvarks they will dig, and as long as rivers are rivers they will flood. It is part of their essential nature and is part of the contribution that they make to the ecosystem. This is the very wildness that wild law must preserve.

Earth jurisprudence demands that we do not respond by exterminating the aardvarks, or controlling the rivers until they cease to be rivers and virtually become sewers boxed in concrete. It requires that we develop and implement wild laws that are able to recognise and celebrate the unique qualities of rivers and aardvarks. This may mean finding suitable land for landless people, preventing the construction of dwellings within the floodplain, or restoring wetlands to help prevent floods. I have little doubt that once canalisation is no longer an option, human ingenuity will find better ways of co-habiting with the rest of the Earth family.

RIGHTS FROM THE PERSPECTIVE
OF EARTH JURISPRUDENCE

Earth jurisprudence therefore approaches the question of rights by starting with Earth and the origin of Earth. This is the common ground that unites all the members of the Earth Community and that defines that Community. From this starting point we conclude that to be a being is to have certain inalienable 'rights'. These Earth rights can be understood as: defining what it is that makes that member of the Community distinct; and describing the freedoms that the member must be allowed in order to fulfil its role within the Community and the ongoing Earth story. These rights are expressed in relationships with other members of the Community. These interactions limit and balance the different rights at a particular level in the Community in a way that strengthens the next level of the Community. So, at the level of the individual, the right of the predator to feed may end the life of the prey, until the day when the lack of prey ends the predator's life. However, the maintenance of this dynamic balance contributes to the stability and good functioning of the ecosystem of which they are both part. In a healthy ecosystem, whether the fox or the rabbit dies on a particular day, the 'right' of the ecosystem (of which they are part) to play its part in the Earth story, is maintained.

Governance systems based on Earth jurisprudence must include not only a conceptual framework that recognises that nonhuman members of the Earth Community can hold 'rights', but must also devise a language to describe those rights, and legal mechanisms for giving full recognition to them. In doing this we must approach the task with the proper degree of humility and perspective. The issue is not, as is so often conceived, deciding whether or not we humans should deign to grant rights to other species or to the environment. (They already have them, but they are invisible to our legal system because it cannot conceive of them.) The challenge is rather to re-conceptualise and develop the philosophical basis on which we organise and regulate our species so that it accords more closely with the reality of an interconnected universe of subjects.

EARTH RIGHTS TRUMP OTHER RIGHTS

We must also recognise that not all rights must be given the same status or weight. We already recognise that certain fundamental rights, like the right to life, should not be weighed up against say the right to enter into contracts and to have them enforced in court. Yet we do not apply the same approach to all Earth rights. For example, in the international arena the trade rules of the WTO are weighed against many Earth rights that are, to a limited extent, protected by international environmental agreements, and even the rights of human communities. Usually the trade rules are given precedence. In order to give effect to Earth jurisprudence, it will also be necessary to abolish, or significantly adapt, some of the rights that are supported by conventional jurisprudence. For example, once we see the universe as a communion of subjects instead of a collection of objects, it becomes immediately apparent that defining land and living creatures as property to be owned and used for humans, is unhelpful and destructive of the Earth Community. Property rights of this nature reflect a worldview in which it is right and proper for human subjects unilaterally to dominate all other aspects of the Earth Community as objects. In fact, by defining the rest of the Earth Community as objects, the dominant legal philosophies not only legitimise and facilitate our exploitative relations with the Earth Community; they also prevent the emergence of two-way relationships between subjects that both have legally recognised 'rights'.

The conceptual and legal transformation of a natural reciprocal relationship into a unidirectional exploitative relationship also creates imbalance. The virtually unfettered rights of the property owner to do as he or she likes with land or living creatures represents a dangerously unbalanced force. The destructive consequences of this imbalance are plain to see and are discussed more fully in Chapter Fourteen.

If one is able for a moment to step outside the homosphere, the truth of Berry's observations regarding the inherent nature and origin of the rights of all aspects of Earth is clear and easily understandable. It is only the strongly anthropocentric hue of most of the legal discussions of this issue that has obscured this. The idea of a universe of right-holding subjects may well sound very radical to someone steeped in the legal traditions of the homosphere. However, it is only our autism in relation to nature and our cultural amnesia vis-à-vis tens of thousands of years of our tribal histories that make this seem so outlandish. From the perspective of an indigenous tribal person, the idea that people might invent a fictitious being such as a corporation, ascribe enormous powers to it, and then dedicate much of their lives to enabling it to devastate their natural habitat, may seem far more perverse.

Chapter 9

Elements of
Earth governance

EARTH JURISPRUDENCE

In Chapters Six, Seven and Eight I discussed different aspects of Earth governance. I began with the need to acknowledge the context of the Great Jurisprudence (Chapter Six), went on to draw attention to the importance of drawing on the knowledge of human communities who practise forms of Earth governance (Chapter Seven), and then discussed how it required us to understand rights in a new way (Chapter Eight). In this chapter I try to put these different aspects together in order to give an overview of some of the main characteristics of Earth jurisprudence and Earth governance.

Earth jurisprudence should reflect a particular human community's understanding of how to regulate itself as part of the Earth Community, and should manifest the qualities of the Great Jurisprudence of which it forms a part. In other words, a healthy human Earth jurisprudence should be a species-specific elaboration of the Great Jurisprudence. It could be expressed in many forms. It may appear in the pages of a book or the provisions of a law. However, it could also be found in a single seed. The seed of a traditional crop contains within its genes the results of hundreds, if not thousands, of years of human selection, guided by close observation of what grows best in that particular place. This is conscious co-evolution in practice. The intimate co-operative relationship between many generations of farmers and their local environment produces seeds that encapsulate the needs of both: nutritious enough to justify the farmers' efforts, resilient enough to cope with the variability of the micro-climate, and specifically adapted to the availability of soil nutrients, water and light in the place where it evolved.

The seed does not, however, contain the whole story. Essential to its continued propagation by humans is a context of traditional knowledge and practices about how to plant, cultivate, harvest, store and cook the seed. Associated with these are specific skills and technologies, and cultural practices such as rituals to celebrate and honour the process. Frequently the exchange of seeds will itself be used as a means of strengthening social bonds, and in many communities seeds for planting are deliberately exchanged in a manner that strengthens these bonds, whereas grain for food is often sold as a commodity. Where there is an intimate relationship between people and Earth, the nature and diversity of the people's culture is inseparable from the nature and diversity of the plants, animals and soils.

However, developing these Earth-centred practices takes time and a commitment, like that of the Tukano, to consciously and continually participate in a process of adapting human practices to Earth rather than vice versa. By this I do not mean that humans should not leave their mark on Earth. That is inevitable. In fact, even the Tukano and other Amazonian Indian groups have deliberately and significantly modified the Amazon rainforests that appear so pristine to outsiders. The difference is in the purpose or intention. There is all the difference in the world between developing seed varieties in a manner that will benefit a human community by producing more food within the constraints of a particular social and ecological system, and genetically engineering seeds that can be mass-produced and owned for the purpose of increasing profits and the price of shares on a stock exchange. Genetically engineered seeds have been manipulated by humans not to fit in with and contribute to a specific environment, but rather to co-exist with a patented herbicide, also developed to increase profit. These are products not of long-term intimate relationships, the timeless communion between members of an Earth Community, but of hurried, forced unions in the glassy sterility of a corporate lab. In this world the accumulated wisdom of evolutionary experience and the integrity of life forms count for nothing, and the share options of the CEO for everything.

If the human cultures that currently dominate the planet were to change their worldview so that we once more understood that the role of humans is primarily to fit in with, and contribute to, the larger Earth system and process, the purpose of governance would change. It would no longer be important to try to make national and world Gross Domestic Product grow year after year, or to increase international trade for the sake of it. Our governance efforts would focus rather on re-constituting our society's image of itself and on increasing the sophistication of our regulatory systems to ensure that the net impact of humans strengthened rather than weakened the web of life. The main role of Earth jurisprudence in a human governance system is to provide a philosophical basis to guide the development and implementation of that governance system (which may include ethics, laws, institutions, policies and practices and the like). In relation to laws, it can be seen as functioning like the spirit of the law (to borrow from Montesquieu), a spirit that I believe will restore wildness to the heart of law. In this chapter, I identify some of the features that I think would characterise Earth jurisprudence for a particular human society.

THE SOURCE AND LEGITIMACY
OF LAWS AND RIGHTS

Fundamental to Earth jurisprudence is the recognition that it exists within a wider context that shapes it and determines how it functions. (Put in terms of systems thinking, this means that we must recognise that it is the wider context of the system that shapes how any component of it functions, rather than vice versa.)

In the context of legal philosophy, this insight has profound implications for two issues of central concern to lawyers—the source and the legitimacy of laws. Among other functions, laws regulate the exercise of power in society. This makes it crucial to have theories that explain why it is that certain people or institutions may make laws, and how the exercise of the powers conferred by those laws can be controlled. For example, many states will point to a moment in history when the 'founding fathers' of the society (and they usually were almost exclusively men) collaborated in the formulation of a constitution. A constitution typically records that a legislative body, by following defined procedures, can create any laws that are not in conflict with the constitution itself. The laws made in this way then confer powers on various state officials and others, but they may only exercise these powers strictly in accordance with the legislation that conferred them. In Western legal systems, official acts that go beyond the boundaries set by the empowering legislation are described as ultra vires (beyond their powers) and are invalid. In this way the society establishes a system for determining whether or not a law is legitimate and whether or not the exercise of a public power (usually used to limit a private liberty) is valid.

However, if human jurisprudence (even Earth jurisprudence) is derived from the higher order of the Great Jurisprudence, it is, by definition, limited and subordinate. First, its ambit is determined and circumscribed by the Great Jurisprudence. For example, if the rights of other species arise directly from the Great Jurisprudence, it must follow that they cannot be validly circumscribed or abrogated by human jurisprudence. Secondly, human jurisprudence and the constitutions and laws that give expression to it, must be subordinate in that they must conform to the Great Jurisprudence. To the extent that they do not, they must be regarded as illegitimate and so powers exercised under them could be regarded as analogous to acts that are treated as ultra vires in national legal systems.

Legal theorists have long argued over the issue of the extent to which certain rules in a legal system should be treated as invalid, or as not really being laws, because they are in conflict with a higher system of law (usually natural law). I do not propose to revisit these arguments here in relation to the Great Jurisprudence or Earth jurisprudence. My attitude is simply that if we accept conceptually that our governance systems ought to be consistent with, firstly, the Great Jurisprudence, and secondly with any Earth jurisprudence that our society may develop, then we will need to develop legal and other mechanisms to achieve this.

DISTINGUISHING RIGHT FROM WRONG — THE QUESTION OF ETHICS

The jurisprudence, laws and particularly the criminal justice systems of the dominant cultures rely heavily on being able to distinguish between right and wrong. The dividing line is often a fine one, but the consequences of being on the 'wrong' side of the line may be severe. Moral and ethical beliefs influence what a society considers to be acceptable and what is not. In practice, exactly where the line lies is determined by a range of factors including the precise wording of legislation or contracts, the 'facts' that can be proved, the court's opinion of the state of mind of the relevant person, and the degree to which that person acted 'reasonably'.

Even in the field of environmental law, whether or not a person is sanctioned for harming another aspect of Earth is likely to be determined by interpreting texts that set standards for human conduct. Thus the rights of the human, or more typically of the corporate entity, are determined independently of the context of the Earth Community that defines the particular set of relationships that have been impaired. For example, a company may be fined for discharging effluent into a river if it contains a higher concentration of a particular pollutant than the law permits to be discharged into rivers. Our governance systems are, on the whole, not sophisticated enough to consider the situation from an ecological perspective and to enquire into the effects of the discharge on the functioning of the river and ecosystem (which might include humans). Stone suggests that it would be helpful if instead of drawing boundaries between what is permissible and what is not in relation to what he calls "Non-persons" on the basis of numerical standards, "we can transport into the legal rules that govern our relations with Non-persons, norms that try to capture essences. In regard to a river, rather than using a standard expressed in parts per million, or some opacity index, we would examine the issue in terms of whether the river's 'riverhood' was being endangered." [1] It might, with some justification, be argued that approaches such as this will be impractical and the difficulties in enforcing such standards might allow more polluters to escape the consequences of their actions. That may well be so within the parameters of our current governance structures. However, the practicalities do not change the point that we ought to change the philosophical basis for our approach to these issues. Once we accept this, human ingenuity, being what it is, will rapidly discover new ways of improv-

ing implementation. For example, as Stone mentions, American environmental law already contains remedies that come close to what would be
required to implement this approach. The Marine Mammals Protection Act
provides that the courts may intervene to protect endangered marine mammals such as porpoises, if a human activity like fishing threatens the 'optimum
sustainable population' within a particular habitat. The courts have interpreted this to mean that once this point is reached, the 'balancing of interests
between the commercial fishing fleet and the porpoises is irrelevant; the por-
poise must prevail'.[2]

Even if a human act that harms some non-human aspect of the Earth
Community is adjudged to be wrongful, our governance systems typically
respond by imposing a fine or requiring the payment of compensation to
other humans. This does not address the fundamental issue of how to restore
healthy, wholemaintaining relationships in that particular context. Nowadays
many countries have environmental laws that require polluters to pay so-
called 'clean-up' costs. These provisions could go some way toward strengthening the relationships with an ecological community by reversing some of
the physical damage. Unfortunately in practice such provisions are usually
designed to allow public authorities to recover expenses that they have
incurred rather than to restore a healthy relationship between the polluters
and, say, the river in a manner that reduces the likelihood of a recurrence of
the incident.

Earth jurisprudence is concerned with maintaining and strengthening
relations between all members of the Earth Community, and not just between
human beings. In this context, thinking in terms of a strict division between
right and wrong is generally unhelpful, particularly when the distinction is
based on inflexible standards determined solely by humans. (In any event
many standards are not even in the long-term interests of human society, but
are determined by powerful interest groups within human society on the basis
of what they perceive to be in their short-term interests.) If our concern is to
maintain the integrity or wholeness of the Earth Community, it is more useful to evaluate the extent to which an action increases or decreases the
integrity and health of the whole system and the quality or intimacy of the
relationships between the component parts.

This approach is similar to Aldo Leopold's famous land ethic, which states
that "a thing is right when it tends to preserve the integrity, stability, and
beauty of the biotic community. It is wrong when it tends otherwise."[3]

In a similar but more personal vein, Thomas Berry describes how as an
11-year-old boy, he crossed a creek near his home and suddenly encountered
the beauty of a meadow of white lilies in the afternoon sun. This scene
became a very important touchstone in his life. As he explains, the experience
was normative in that from then on he judged whether something was 'good'

An ethic, ecologically, is a limitation on freedom of action in the struggle for existence. An ethic, philosophically, is a differentiation of social from anti-social conduct. These are two defini-tions of one thing. The thing has its origin in the tendency of interdepen-dent individuals or groups to evolve modes of co-operation. The ecologist calls these symbioses . . . All ethics so far evolved rest upon a single premise: that the individual is a member of a community of interdependent parts. His instincts prompt him to compete for his place in that community, but his ethics prompt him also to co-operate (perhaps in order that there may be a place to compete for).

Aldo Leopold, *A Sand County Almanac*, 1948

or 'bad' by reference to the field of lilies. As he put it, "Whatever preserves and enhances this meadow in the natural cycles of its trans-formation is good; whatever opposes this meadow or negates it is not good. My life orientation is that simple."[4]

In his 1987 book *Earth and Other Ethics* Christopher Stone makes what he refers to as "the case for moral pluralism".[5] He rejects the conventional approach of trying to devise a unified body of principles that can be applied to determine the 'right answer' in every situ-ation. He argues that we need a diversity of moral frameworks, with different principles and approaches. This does not mean that any ethical or moral framework is appropriate, but only that we should recognise and respect the importance of diversity here too.

I think that once we recognise that the uni-verse, like a dance, exists by virtue of the co-operative relationships between all involved, it must follow that our governance systems should focus on fostering and nur-turing intimate relationships between the members of the Earth Community. A focus on relationships also suggests that we should determine what is good or bad by looking at whether or not it tends to strengthen or weaken the bonds that constitute the Earth Community. Put another way, something that contributes to the integrity, beauty and ongoing 'unfolding' of the whole ought to be preferred over something that detracts from it. How one deter-mines whether or not this is the case can vary, provided that it is consistent with the Great Jurisprudence. The Great Jurisprudence itself not only recog-nises, but insists upon, diversity.

BALANCE, RECIPROCITY AND JUSTICE

Earth jurisprudence must take account of the central importance of balance in the natural world. Not the stasis of equal weights in each pan of the scales of justice, but the ever-changing flux, the 'creative disequilibrium' of the uni-verse: always moving, always changing, but never moving in one direction for long without swirling back to seek equilibrium or re-establish the pattern again. As the symbol of Yin and Yang graphically demonstrates, as Yin waxes, so Yang must wane, until the reverse occurs, but all the while the cycles of response and counter-response maintain the whole.

Allied to the question of balance is the principle of reciprocity—for every taking there must be a giving. As every good farmer knows, if we take from the soil we must replenish and nourish it or it will become barren. In indigenous tribal cultures this principle is recognised and honoured by means of many rituals, particularly in relation to hunting and harvesting. Hunters all over the world have small rituals to thank the dead or dying animal for its sacrifice of life so that the hunter's family might live, and to acknowledge that one day it will be the hunter's turn to surrender the nutrients and energy in his or her body back to the Earth system. Practices such as these not only keep these principles present in the minds of people, they are also expressions of the respect and humility necessary to function as an integral member of the Earth Community. Where the universe is understood as the cyclical ebb and flow of energy or spirit, trying to accumulate anything beyond a certain point is synonymous with seeking imbalance.

Our current jurisprudence does give some recognition to the idea that a balance between the rights of human beings is important (the term 'justice' is usually understood as incorporating this notion). Many jurists and political scientists would also recognise that in governance systems it is important to link rights and responsibilities. The greater the rights or privileges, the greater the responsibilities that ought to go with them. We also know from experience that without the counterbalance of responsibilities, an unfettered power will inevitably destroy that over which it is exercised. Furthermore, as Cicero recognised, the unlimited power of one will destroy the liberty of all. Yet we seem blind to the reality that the privileges of being born a creature with such wondrous talents and great powers in relation to other species and Earth, cannot exist without correspondingly great responsibilities. Put another way, the role of humans in the Community encompasses both extraordinary powers and responsibilities and the principle of reciprocity suggests that our vast taking from the Earth in the past will in future require a huge giving.

EARTH GOVERNANCE

The world's democratic states boast of being 'governments of the people for the people'. The response of many citizens to such a statement may well be to snort derisively and to point out that this often means 'governments of the élite, for the corporations and at the expense of most'. However, if one takes a step back and contemplates the role of governments from an Earth-centred perspective, it is immediately obvious that our notion of human governance does not even pay lip service to the wider Earth Community. Even a government that is truly 'by the people for the people' is likely to be destructive unless it consciously orientates itself towards and prioritises the well-being of Earth from which human well-being is derived.

Earth governance is therefore government of people, by the people, that is for Earth. It requires us to expand our understanding of governance and democracy to embrace the whole Earth Community and not just humans. This point of view is reflected in the Earth democracy movement in India about which Dr Vandana Shiva has written:

> Earth democracy re-contextualises humans as one member of the Earth family (*Vasudhaiva Kutumbkam*), and diverse cultures in a mosaic of cultural diversity which enriches our lives.[6]

Earth governance is based on the recognition that in the long-term, humans will not thrive unless we regulate ourselves in a manner that is consciously oriented towards, and prioritises, the well-being of the Earth system from which human well-being is derived. By governing for Earth in the sense of prioritising the health of the whole system, we are also governing for people because our well-being is derived from that system. In fact the long-term, holistic approach that Earth governance requires will be far more beneficial to humanity than the current systems of governance based on the pursuit of short-term political goals and political advantage. However, it is important to understand that Earth governance does not imply attempting to manage every aspect of Earth.

In order to achieve the objectives of Earth governance, our human governance systems must incorporate methods of guiding human behaviour to ensure that in exercising our freedoms we neither destroy the well-being of other Earth citizens nor prevent them from fulfilling their evolutionary roles.

Earth jurisprudence provides the philosophical and theoretical basis for such governance systems and will foster wild law. Earth jurisprudence will vary from society to society, but each variation is likely to share common elements. As outlined above, it is likely that these common elements will include:

- a recognition that the source of the fundamental 'Earth rights' of all members of the Earth Community is the universe, rather than human governance systems;

- a means of recognising the roles of non-human members of the Earth Community and of restraining humans from unjustifiably preventing them fulfilling those roles;

- a concern for reciprocity and the maintenance of a dynamic equilibrium between all the members of the Earth Community determined by what is best for the system as a whole (Earth justice); and

- an approach to condoning or disapproving human conduct on the basis of whether or not the conduct strengthens or weakens the bonds that constitute the Earth Community.

PART 4

The journey into wildness

All life came out of the ocean; each one of us comes out of the waters of the womb; the ebb and flow of the tides is as alive as the ebb and flow of our breathing. When you are in rhythm with your nature, nothing destructive can touch you. Providence is at one with you; it minds you and brings you to your new horizons. To be spiritual is to be in rhythm.

John O'Donohue, *Anam Cara*

Chapter 10
Seeking Earth Jurisprudence

In Part Three I have tried to convey a sense of the forms that Earth governance might take. In the next five chapters (Chapters Ten to Fourteen) I will explore how we might move towards Earth governance.

My own experience of discovering Earth jurisprudence has been like wandering through the wilderness after a long absence. Scary, exhilarating, unsettling and deeply satisfying. I recommend it to all who despair about our present governance systems and dysfunctional relations with Earth. Like wilderness, Earth jurisprudence and wild law can be food for the soul.

STEPPING OUT OF THE CAR

After spending a decade in Europe, I returned with my family to my native South Africa in 1999. In April 2001 I met Robert Greenway at the discussions with Thomas Berry at the Airlie Center in Virginia. Robert, who has been exploring the psychological aspects of the wilderness experience since the 1960s, asked me when I had last been in the wilderness. With surprise I realised that it was many years since I had had more than a superficial encounter with the bush, and immediately resolved to renew my connection. Another of the participants in the Airlie Center meeting was Bruce Dell, Director of the Wilderness Leadership School in Durban, South Africa, and a man who has spent most of his life in the bush. We flew back from the United States together and I decided to go on a trail with him as soon as I could.

In September 2001 I went on a five-day wilderness trail in the Umfolozi game reserve. The trail was led by Bruce, assisted by Mandla Buthelezi, a local man whose people are from that part of Zululand. We drove into the reserve, then leaving our watches in our vehicles, donned our packs and struck out into the bush behind Bruce and Mandla. Before we had gone more than a few hundred metres a small bird flew up from behind a large bush ahead of us in the game trail, crying in alarm. It was an oxpecker, a friend to large game and a tell-tale sign to experienced rangers. Bruce and Mandla signalled urgently and we froze. Simultaneously a great horned head swung up a few metres in front of us in response to the oxpecker's warning. Fortunately the rhino that had been dozing, head down, behind the bush had its rump to us and we were downwind. Thanks to our guides' alertness and understanding of the signs of the bush, we were able to move quietly and safely around the group of rhinos and, a few minutes later, to avoid an old buffalo bull concealed in the scrub.

Shortly afterwards we saw lion spoor and began to feel puny and vulnerable in what seemed like a very dangerous place. We had left the safety of the vehicles, and despite the rangers' rifles, were very conscious that we had surrendered the power of our technology and were no longer in control of the situation.

Over the course of the next few days our perceptions shifted. As we gradually let go of the need to know exactly where we were, what the clock time was, and where we were going next, our fear began to be replaced with a sense of belonging. We all experienced in different ways a deep, unexpected, and perhaps partially unrealistic yearning to be part of this world. It became very clear that it was the guides' intimacy with the bush and their knowledge, rather than their rifles, that kept us safe. We also realised with shock that in many ways this place was safer than where we had come from. Here we could drink the water from puddles because there were no humans to pollute it or contaminate it with disease. Here, despite the presence of wild lions, hyenas, hippos and crocodiles, we could sleep safely in the open, near a fire to warn other creatures of our presence. Doing the same in many city areas would be risking serious assault or worse.

Now, at the beginning of the 21st century, we desperately need a new vision of how to govern ourselves. The rapid deterioration of our beautiful planet and the mounting evidence that we are in the early stages of the sixth major period of extinction tells us that something is dreadfully wrong with how humans are behaving. The only living models of truly sustainable human governance available to us are those of the few remnant indigenous communities who live in harmony with nature but with very limited technology. To suggest that we can emulate these societies in an age of space travel, global communications and nanotechnology, seems implausible.

So far, the response of the governors (governments, international organisations and powerful private companies) has been to look for security in more technology and more 'control' over nature. This approach is a bit like staying in the car in the wilderness. It certainly feels safe, but the possibilities of interacting with the environment are limited and in the long term there is no sustenance to be had. Sooner or later the petrol will run out and you will have to venture out for food or die in the 'safety' of the vehicle. This is not too difficult to understand while we are enclosed in a technological bubble surrounded by wilderness. Today, however, most of the wilderness has already been destroyed by the world of the car. The more we surround the wilderness with roads and cities, the less easy it is to see why we still need to get out of the car. Sitting in a car seems normal in an asphalt parking lot, and if all the trees are already gone, there seems little point in getting out.

One of the reasons why getting out of the car and walking away from it into wildness is scary, is because it defies conventional wisdom. This tells us that 'wild' is dangerous, that what we need is a properly controlled, sanitised, all-eventualities-insured-against world. In fact, the conventional 'wisdom' of our societies encapsulates the prejudices and fallacies on which they are based, and is one of the main obstacles. Seeking a new form of governance requires us to become aware of, to question, and ultimately to discard, much of what our societies assume to be true. Trying to think in a way that not only transcends our socially constructed compartmentalisation of knowledge, but also to a large extent, our cultures themselves, is difficult.

SEE THE HEALED STATE

Usually, when we think about the future we tend to extrapolate from the past and present. This is not helpful if we want to change entirely our approach to governance. One of the methods that I find helps me to avoid extrapolating from the past is to start by leaping ahead and imagining what it would be like if I had already achieved what I am seeking to achieve. For example, I might try to imagine a human society living as productive and valuable members of a community of living beings. Then I try to imagine what laws and other governance mechanisms such a human community might have. Having imagined what Robert Greenway refers to as 'the healed state', it is far easier when looking at contemporary societies to see what is likely to take us closer to or further away from the desired future healthy state.

This approach also has its limitations. My culture, upbringing and training predisposes me towards abstractions and theories. I find it a constant challenge to restrain myself from soaring too far from Earth in pursuit of them. As Carl Anthony of the Earth Island Institute has observed, "Abstraction means distance from immediate experience, from annoyingly concrete particulars, the substitution of a remote symbol for a given sensuous reality. But that's what ecology is all about: the real complexity."[1] I suspect that thinking about governance in an 'ecological' way requires not only grounding theory in practice, but also engaging on an emotional and physical level. I need to feel soil sifting softly and sinuously through my fingers and to admire its fine richness, if I am going to begin to understand land. Discerning Earth jurisprudence clearly will require us to engage more than our imagination and logic. We must also use both fingertips and heart to feel the meaning of it fully.

ECOLOGICAL THINKING

I hope that this more complex, ecological way of sensing and understanding will eventually become second nature to me, but at the moment I find that I constantly need to watch my own thought processes. In this regard I have found it helpful to keep in mind a few simple lessons that life has taught me so far. Firstly, it is important to free my mind by identifying and getting to grips with my prejudices, and by remembering the importance of humility. Secondly, I always try to go back to first principles and to keep digging down for simple truths. Thirdly, I constantly remind myself that I need to learn how to learn, and to be open to new approaches. Finally, I find that it is enormously valuable to listen to, and be guided by, those who are already skilful and knowledgeable about the terrain that I wish to traverse.

GET TO GRIPS WITH PREJUDICES

I first became conscious that many of my beliefs were not my own when I was a 17-year-old Rotary Youth Exchange scholar at a school in New Zealand. It happened when one of the boys at school showed me a photograph of the sister of his Nigerian pen friend. Having overcome his earlier disappointment that I did not know his pen pal despite the fact that we were both from Africa, he had raved about the pen friend's gorgeous sister and offered to bring a photograph of her to school. It was only at the moment that I saw her smiling face in the photograph that I realised that because my friend had said that she was beautiful and sexually attractive, I had assumed that she was white. At that moment, the manifest absurdity of my assumption struck me with full force. The chances of a Nigerian girl being white must be incredibly small, yet the worldview of the white South African society in which I was raised had blinded me to the possibility that any young woman who was not white could be sexually attractive.

I was shocked and horrified at my assumptions. How could I hold such absurd ideas without even realising it? How had I uncritically and unconsciously absorbed many of my ways of thinking from the apartheid society in which I grew up? I did not even support the legal prohibition on so-called 'mixed' marriages! I then thought back to when I had walked down the street in South Africa as a pimply schoolboy, subconsciously scanning the passing crowd for attractive women. I realised with renewed shock that I had been subconsciously screening out most women on the basis of their colour. Needless to say, it was I who until then had been impoverished by that unconscious prejudice. Now I wonder how many other beautiful beings I am screening out of consideration. I can only guess at the extent to which I and other humans are impoverished on a daily basis by our prejudices concerning the nature of the relationships that we can have with other beings.

My first encounter with Thomas Berry's work also exposed some of my own prejudices to me. On the one hand, the beauty and simple logic of his writings resonated with me clearly, both at an intellectual and an emotional level. On the other hand, when I began to consider the implications of what he was saying, my instinct was to draw back and recoil from what once again seemed to be conclusions that were too radical, too green. I had previously regarded an animal rights approach to environmental law as well-intentioned but ultimately unhelpful and potentially counter-productive to scientific conservation methods. (Bringing back old circus lions to die in Africa might make animal lovers feel good, I thought, but it might also introduce diseases that could decimate wild prides.) I was also aware of the difficulties associated with trying to accommodate rights for animals within Western legal systems. The idea that not only the rights of animals but also those of trees, mountains and rivers should be recognised in our courts seemed clearly impractical, despite the arguments of scholars like Christopher Stone.

Then I remembered how I felt when I first went to University. I was intellectually and emotionally drawn to the points of view of the students who belonged to the so-called 'left'. (In fact in the 1980s in South African virtually all political views except those to the right of the apartheid government, were considered to be 'left wing'.) However, I continued to argue against what I saw as the more radical consequences of these arguments for almost six months. I lost one argument after another, until I finally accepted that the arguments that I had been resisting were simply better. However, the reason that it took me so long to abandon my previous positions was that as a schoolboy I had unknowingly absorbed the belief that it was somehow wrong or bad to be 'radical' or 'left wing'. My self-image as someone who was 'reasonable' as opposed to 'radical', 'sensible and balanced' as opposed to 'left wing', actually obstructed my understanding. In order for me to make the intellectual and emotional shift to actively working for the demise of apartheid and of white privilege in South Africa, I first had to recognise and then let go of these warped prejudices and to adjust my self-image. Letting go of human supremacy and privilege demands a similar self-adjustment.

Many people, particularly lawyers, who come across these ideas experience similar turmoil as they are drawn to the clarity, and what I believe to be the essential truth, of an Earth-centred approach. For people who like to think of themselves as sensible and well-respected members of a modern human society, even reading a book like this may induce a sense of furtive shame. (Perhaps cover it in brown paper if you are thinking about reading it in a law firm, government office or other bastion of 'good sense'.) Certainly the temptation to retreat in the face of the magnitude of the challenge and to slip into intellectual compromises and platitudes for fear of being dismissed as daft, is very great and understandable. It also needs to be over-come in order to go beyond the fear and move into a larger and more promis-ing future.

Discovering and developing Earth jurisprudence also requires a certain degree of humility. We need to be humble in order to discern roles for humans that will enhance the whole. In other words, each of us needs to learn to be a team player.

START AT THE BEGINNING WITH THE WHOLE

If we are to re-conceptualise completely our understanding of law and human governance, it is important that we go back to first principles and start at the beginning. Regardless of our religious beliefs, the ultimate source of all that we know is the universe. What, if anything, existed before the universe is unfathomable, and our ideas about this are grounded in faith. I think there-fore that the origin of the universe is the most useful starting point. This then is the 'whole' of which we are part.

Remembering that Earth is not only our habitat, but that we are, in a very real way, part of it, is crucial. We have forgotten that we are not only on Earth but also of Earth and that our existence and fulfilment is derived from Earth. As Thomas Berry puts it:

> The human is less a being on the earth or in the universe than a dimension of the earth and indeed of the universe itself. The shaping of our human mode of being depends on the support and guidance of this comprehensive order of things. We are an immediate concern of every other being in the universe. Ultimately our guidance on any significant issue must emerge from this comprehensive source. (*The Dream of the Earth*, p.195)

Understanding on an intellectual level that we are part of a single system is relatively easy. After all, even our Western physicists confirm that the same atoms and sub-atomic particles may be part of the soil on Monday, a plant on Tuesday and us on Wednesday. It can be more difficult to 'get it' or know the truth of this essential oneness at a deeper, non-intellectual level, particularly if one is not in close contact with the natural world.

I was very privileged to grow up on a smallholding in the hills outside a medium-sized South African town called Pietermaritzburg. Our home was surrounded on three sides by a combination of plantations and indigenous bush that was home to bushbuck, monkeys, porcupines and a host of other animals, plants and birds. Walking in those hills and playing in the streams as a child gave me a sense of connection and empathy with the natural world. However, it was only in my twenties that I consciously understood that I was part of this whole. I remember clearly when it happened. I was walking, meditating at the Buddhist retreat centre at Ixopo, when I suddenly knew with great clarity that I was part of a single whole, like a cell in a body. I can't explain it and I certainly don't always act in accordance with this realisation. Nevertheless, since that moment I have 'known in my bones' that this is so. From this perspective, if I were to pollute a river it would be self-destructive, like slashing my own arm. Therefore the question of whether or not I should pollute a stream when I can avoid doing so, does not arise. The decision to avoid polluting the stream is not based on a desire to comply with the law, or even on moral principles; it is simply that to pollute would be nonsensical.

DIG DOWN TO THE ROOTS

A retired professor friend of mine in London was fond of reminding me, "Go back to first principles!" I have found this to be good advice in most situations, but particularly when facing complex situations with very limited knowledge. At that time, I was regularly engaged as an 'international legal expert' and sent to developing countries in order to give advice on governance systems or to help draft new legislation. This required getting to grips with the relevant elements of the governance system (including the laws) of a country within a few weeks at most. That sort of time period is clearly inadequate. The main problem was usually that I didn't know what I didn't know. In other words, no matter how much I discovered, it was always possible that there were more crucial laws or facts out there that I didn't know about. However, I found that if I thought carefully about what the country was trying to achieve and tried to reduce it to first principles, I usually asked the right questions. It also meant that my recommendations were likely to be helpful and correct, in principle, even if I was unaware of some important fact.

I think that this advice also applies in the search for Earth jurisprudence, a search that confronts us both with the ultimate mysteriousness of the universe and the limits of our understanding. This is why I have devoted so much of this book to discussing theories about the nature of the universe and of reality, which may seem irrelevant to many people involved in law and governance. These theories may, of course, be wrong, or my understanding of them incorrect. I have no doubt that in any event they will change over time. Nevertheless, I think that it is fundamentally important that our approach should be to go back to what we know of the nature of Earth and the universe and then seek to reconcile our systems of governance with these principles.

My friend's advice also reminded me of the importance of taking a radical approach in the sense of going to the root (*radix*) of a problem in order to solve it, rather than attempting to treat the symptoms. This was something I had learnt as a student activist, but it still amazes me how threatening this idea can be to those who are comfortably ensconced in stable societies. Perhaps it is because, unlike reformers, radicals do not rule out the possibility of uprooting the whole system should the problem prove to be systemic.

LEARNING HOW TO LEARN

Despite our delusions of separation and the mythical realm of human mastery that we inhabit, we humans are still of Earth. This means that we still have the inherent capacity to understand the Great Jurisprudence that manifests itself in how the universe works, although we may need to do some work to enhance our ability to do so. Fortunately there are still wild places and indigenous cultures from which we can learn. First, though, we must learn how to learn.

Accepting the premises of Earth jurisprudence has fundamental implications for the study of jurisprudence, law and governance. Currently we learn about jurisprudence and law in law libraries and lecture theatres from which nature is meticulously excluded. From an Earth-centred perspective, this means that we are devising our legal philosophies and laws without reference to the 'primary texts' (i.e. nature) and seeking answers in libraries that do not contain those answers. Many lawyers and law schools will find (or at least ought to find) this proposition deeply disturbing. Is it really possible that the approaches adopted by the Yales, Oxfords and Sorbonnes of this world could be wrong? For many, I suspect, it will be easier to reject the ideas of Earth jurisprudence entirely than to contemplate such a blasphemous proposition seriously.

The language of the universe is primarily experiential. It speaks to us in the language of hot and cold, beauty and fear, patterns of events, symbols and associations. However we must engage with it to 'hear' this language. Book learning and scientific rationality can only take us so far. We also need direct experiences of nature, intuition and emotions. Therefore in order to become ecologically literate once more and to regain an awareness of the principles which govern life on Earth, we must strive to reconnect and engage empathically with wildness and nature, and if possible, with the wilderness.

Next, we must observe and listen carefully—'listen' in the sense of fully experiencing the richness of life and the universe around. In order to reconceptualise the role of our species and how we govern ourselves, we must set aside our prejudices, theories and limiting views of what is possible.

This is particularly important for those of us who have been brought up in Western-oriented cultures. The beliefs and worldview of the dominant cultures have suffused our consciousness to such an extent that it is very difficult even to imagine our societies functioning in a manner that is integrated with nature. We have few direct personal experiences to draw upon. Many hundreds or thousands of years have elapsed since our communities had mutually enhancing relationships with the other members of the Earth family. In most cases the oral traditions that taught us how this is done were severed long ago.

Consequently, perspectives of the role of humans within the biosphere that were widely accepted for perhaps 99 per cent of human history, sound bizarre and dangerously radical to the urbanised humans of the 21st century.

Therefore, learning how to learn requires firstly that we should cleanse the doors of perception, to paraphrase William Blake.[2] We must strive to let in the direct experience of life, and when we interpret what we experience we must be alert to the potentially distorting effect of the culturally tinted lenses through which we see the world. Doing this will not necessarily be easy—it may require some dedication and close attention, before we are able to hear the song of the universe clearly. The guidance of those few wise people who are well practised in doing so will be invaluable in this regard.

Although as humans we will inevitably think like humans, we must also try to see the world from other perspectives to arrive at a more empathic understanding of Earth. If we are to transcend the mental fetters of species and culture and engage fully with the wider Community we must strive, not only as Aldo Leopold suggests, to think like a mountain, but also to breathe like a tree and allow our minds to move like water. By this I mean we need to feel and consciously experience the supportive symbiosis of our relationship with the other members of the Earth family, the give and take of carbon dioxide and oxygen, the constant exchange of nutrients and energy. We must also, metaphorically, allow our own consciousness to trickle deep, deep into the soil until it connects with Earth's vast and ancient subterranean waters. Until we allow ourselves this freedom to experiment with new ways of knowing we will never believe that the capacity to share a degree of consciousness is more than a romantic metaphor.

We need to remember too that knowledge of the universe is not only to be gained by careful observation of the world around us. The inherent properties of the universe also reside in every cell of our bodies: its life-force animates us with every breath and pulse, and our minds are interconnected with consciousness outside our bodies. For this reason, listening to and understanding the universe must also mean listening carefully to the intuition or wisdom inherent in each of us.

Our societies rightly respect action taken on the basis of empirically verifiable data. However, scientific rationality has become so pervasive that we often (irrationally) refuse to accept that knowledge and wisdom may also be accessed in other ways. Consequently, a degree of self-confidence is required to assert ideas based on knowledge gained from deeply personal experiences that cannot be scientifically verified and that do not accord with generally held beliefs. However, it is important to accept that if we are not going to rely exclusively on 'scientific' means of developing and evaluating our ideas, we still need ways of ensuring that we are not simply abandoning rationality and being lead astray by our egos and prejudices. There is also the danger of over-generalising from very subjective experiences.

BEWARE THE UNIVERSAL PANACEA

In particular, we must beware of succumbing to the temptation of devising the 'Great Solution' that will enable all human theories of jurisprudence to be transformed instantly into a reflection of the Great Jurisprudence. Already by scaling up the dominant human cultures to a mass level we have bred over-simplification, uniformity and shallowness at the expense of wildness, diversity and subtlety. Communities cannot be scaled up massively without the relationships that create them becoming shallower and less intimate. We need to remember that the evolution of Earth tends towards diversity, not uniformity.

Chapter 11
The rhythms of life

TIME AND TIMING

The themes of harmony and discord run through this book like a melody. Musical metaphors for life, nature and the universe seem to resonate with both the mind and ear. Music, both real and metaphorical, is also valuable in healing discord and promoting harmony. As Eisenberg points out, "Since the eye individuates and the ear unites, music has long been thought the art best able to give humans a sense of oneness with each other and the universe." [1]

Music is also about rhythm and beat and timing. Timing is related to time, but not to the linear, punctuated, cut-up-in-pieces-and-sold, deadline-determined time that we are used to in modern societies. It is about listening so that you know the right moment to whack that cymbal, about drumming to the same heartbeat until great, cyclical sound waves sweep drummer and dancer along in the unity of the dance.

Where I come from we say that rhythm is the soul of life because the whole universe revolves around rhythm; and when we get out of rhythm, that's when we get into trouble. For this reason the drum, next to the human voice, is our most important instrument. It is special.

Babatunde Olatunji, Nigerian drummer

Time and timing are also a dimension of governance that we seldom consider. We speak of our societies being at a critical point in time, meaning usually that we fear that we are approaching a major deadline — a line that when crossed will determine the deaths of so many species. This linear understanding of time has a certain reality about it and may be helpful in creating a sense of urgency among humans. However, it may be more helpful not to separate time and action in our thinking: to think in terms of events that are composed as much of when they happen as what happens, in the way that a musical beat is composed both of the action of striking the drum skin and of the moment chosen to do so. From this perspective, we must be attentive to what is going on around us in order to choose the right moment to act and when not to. Earth governance (and life) is not about trying to squeeze as much 'doing' into the gaps in an unforgiving linear framework of time compartmentalised by deadlines, schedules and targets. Earth governance is about listening carefully, allowing wisdom to arise in the fullness of time, and recognising the moment to act and the moment not to. It understands that it matters whether something is done now or later, because it will not be the same event and the effects on the cosmos may be very different. Timing (not time) is what is most important.

I am not necessarily suggesting that we abandon action plans and timetables altogether. Indeed, I have difficulty imagining how a governance system could operate without them. What I am trying to point out is that this is another area where we need a reality check so that we notice the discrepancy between how the universe works and how we behave. Wisdom cannot be crammed between the lines of a diary on the third Wednesday of the month. It needs unhurried spaces and the fullness of time to flourish. This is one of the reasons why it is so unlikely that any great insights of wisdom on the profound issues facing us will emerge from great international meetings such as the World Summit on Sustainable Development. There is no space for wisdom in the jostling mob of interest groups and governments whose increasingly frenzied doings during the year or so before the Summit seem to disappear down the spinning vortexes of preparatory committees, ministerial meetings and sundry other holes in time. Soon it will all be over and the feverishness will subside for a while. We will probably all be none the wiser but will comfort ourselves with a new collection of shiny promises of things to be done within ever tighter deadlines.

THE TYRANNY OF TIME AND MONEY

I work in a law firm where we use a special computer programme to record how much time we spend working on each file. This is to help us turn time into money. We, and probably all of our clients who stop to think about it, know that measuring the value of the service we provide by how long we spend providing it, is absurd. Yet clients and lawyers everywhere persist with the system (with minor variations). This is because we can measure how long we take to do a task and we think that time is money. This is essentially a convenient, though clearly inadequate, way of turning our particular knowledge and skill into a commodity with a price. (You can get experienced Ms X for so much per hour, or inexperienced Mr Y for half the price.)

Like many of us, I am a busy person. In our world that means that I do not have time. I have, of course, time to work and I set aside time to spend with my children, but I never seem to have enough time. I convince myself that I don't have enough time to devote much to myself or to my close relationships, to go on holiday or to write a book like this. When I do 'spend' a lot of time on these things I often feel profligate and self-indulgent. As the years pass, I can feel my life speeding by faster and faster. The culture I live in encourages me to do more and more, lest I 'waste' some of this dwindling time. In fact I feel sure that it is only a matter of time before I have no time to live at all!

None of this is true, of course. But on a bad day in the office it all seems so real I could swear that it is true, and that I can prove it to you.

It's not just me either. Sometimes I hear other people, busily hurrying about their techno-lives, talk unconvincingly of the importance of 'taking time to smell the roses'. It sounds like they are reaffirming the value of reconnecting with nature and the real world of sensory experience. However, like me, their unacknowledged starting point is the understanding that within the homosphere such activities require time to be 'taken'. It must be diverted from the primary purpose of existence. Taking a little time, we silently agree, is okay, but take too much and you are stealing time and not really contributing to society what you ought.

WILD TIME

Some years ago, I had a bit of 'free' time because I was attending a conference and got chatting to Jay Griffiths. She is a sparky, irreverent woman who delights in the creative ambiguity of words and has a gift for puncturing pomposity. Jay gave me a copy of her book *Pip Pip: A Sideways Look at Time*.[2] As I read it (in chunks over a period of time as I didn't have enough time, obviously) it began to dawn on me how central our constructed, linear version of time is to maintaining our current governance systems. In her book, she demonstrates clearly how we have abandoned the abundant, cyclical time of nature where things happen when the time is ripe rather than at half-past three Greenwich Mean Time. We now live by the linear, quantifiable time which the ancient Greeks associated with the god 'Chronos' or 'Kronos' (who, incidentally, was famous for swallowing his children alive). We have forgotten about the qualitative aspects associated with 'Kairos', the god of timing. This has been an important part of reinforcing our dissociation with the natural world. As Jay Griffiths points outs, "Nature was once the biggest public clock, its rhythms establishing 'time communities' of joint activities, a shared observation of a natural event or season, a shared sowing, a shared harvest."[3]

If I try to track the evolution of some of these ideas in my own consciousness and think back over the fraught process of committing them to paper, it is clear that almost all of it happened when I was not measuring and accounting for my time. I have seen and heard most clearly not when I have been 'spending my time productively', or working hard, but rather when I have set aside linear time: in the dreamy consciousness of the hour after wakening, amidst the sensations of a morning shower, or when the beauty of sun filtering through the forest canopy brings me into the present. Insights or new

Let us preserve religiously, secure,
protect the coincidence of our life with
the life of nature . . . My life as
essentially belongs to the present as
that of a willow tree in the spring.
Now, now its catkins expand, its
yellow bark shines, its sap flows, now
or never you must make whistles of it.

Henry Thoreau (quoted by Griffiths
1999, p.21)

perspectives swim up into consciousness when, in little bursts of rebellion against the iron progression of chronological time, divided, measured and sold, I 'take time off'.

Thinking of time in any way other than as linear, ordered, and (usually) speeding by is difficult. However, if we again go back to first principles and look both at the nature of the universe and at how indigenous communities live in nature, it is clear that Earth time is very different. The time that forms part of the Great Jurisprudence is elastic and cyclical as well as progressive. It is, as Jay Griffiths points out, live, unconstrained, 'wild time'. It doesn't run out, it is abundant and so elastic that, as children know, it is possible to "hold eternity in an hour", as the poet William Blake put it. What matters is the fullness and richness of living time, not deadlines. The right time for plucking fruit is when it is ripe; any externally imposed schedule is meaningless.

RACING TO DEATH

Talking of 'wild time' sounds very abstract and romantic to the modern ear. I for one have difficulty holding onto the truth that time is abundant. Nevertheless, governing entirely by clock-time with no sense of the importance of wild time and timing, has very real consequences. It is sometimes easier to see this by looking at Kronos's modern henchman, speed. Speed kills. We know this, but don't really believe it will happen to us. Even though we know it can kill, speed comes in such beautiful, shiny, ego-enhancing forms that it is so difficult to resist. Speed is also the alchemist that turns chronological time into money.

One of the places where speed runs up against the wild time dimension of Great Jurisprudence is in the area of genetic engineering. The organisms which are now being engineered co-evolved as part of a specific Earth Community over aeons of evolutionary time. As the seasons wheel around, the members of the Community interact repeatedly in many ways, each shaping the other. Over time the most successful relationships are maintained and others fall away. In this way both the slender beak of the nectar-eating sun bird and its habits accord with the shape and seasons of the local flowers and vice versa. At some point early humans began consciously to direct the evolution of species of crops and domestic animals by breeding only from those that displayed the traits most beneficial to humans. However, this did not have a very significant impact on these communities and can even be understood as a new form of symbiotic relationship.

Everything changed when a few countries used law to create legally enforceable property rights in genetically engineered life forms. This had several effects. First, it enabled companies that could modify an organism to privatise and monopolise the whole organism, including the accumulated experience of the Earth Community was inscribed within its cells. As Jay Griffiths eloquently puts it: "Genetic engineering, using patent laws as fence posts, steals everyone's common past so that a few multinational 'time-owners' can profit from its privatisation."[4]

Secondly, by creating a new form of property, these laws also create an irresistible new food source for the rapacious mega-corporations. Property, of course, can be converted into money. In order to make more money it is important to be fast—to be first into the market and always to have something new. The pressure is even greater when the participants are public companies expected to report rising profits every quarter, and managed by executives with stock options. Enter speed.

Companies started swallowing each other in their mad rush to 'take the lead' in the biotechnology 'race'. Governments, led by politicians focused on the short-term objectives of maintaining their parties in power, now compete to promote biotechnology 'before we get left behind'. Legislators are admonished in the press, and extensively lobbied in private, about the dangers of passing laws that might slow down the development of new genetically engineered species or restrict cloning. Delay is bad, speed is good!

In many ways this is an everyday scenario in the capitalist world. The big difference is that we are now releasing life forms into the Earth Community that are fundamentally different from those that have evolved in those communities. These new genetically engineered organisms have been consciously designed, hurriedly engineered and mass-produced to maximise profit. Typically they incorporate what their engineers believe will be technological 'quick-fixes' to human-created problems (mostly associated with large-scale monoculture). Unlike indigenous organisms they have not had to manifest an ability to enhance, rather than degrade, a particular Earth Community over long periods of time, in order to survive. Of course, some may prove to be beneficial to the Earth Community, but at present the belief that they will be beneficial over a long period of time is based primarily on faith, rather than science or logic. Certainly, if the genetically engineered living organisms that we are releasing into nature turn out to be responsible Earth citizens, it will be by luck not design. They were designed to maximise profits, rather than to contribute to the integrity of the Earth Community.

One of the things that the debate about genetic engineering demonstrates is that one of the reasons that our governance systems are so out of kilter with the Great Jurisprudence is that our timing is out. As is often pointed out, our political structures encourage, even demand, short-termism. Politicians generally do not look much further than the next election, a time-horizon of four years at most. From an Earth-centred perspective this is absurdly short. In the case of genetic engineering, we are trying to turn up the tempo of the evolutionary process to breakneck speed without having taken the time to consider the wisdom of doing so, or to explore fully what the consequences might be.

DANCING TO AN EARTH BEAT

Some say that Earth itself has a measurable 'heart beat' and that there are certain notes that we can use to renew our connection with Earth—to harmonise ourselves with Earth. The idea that music plays a part in ordering the universe and that there is a connection between our inner desire for rhythm and music and the greater cosmic symphony, is an old and persistent one. For example, in European culture, the followers of Pythagoras (the Greek philosopher, mystic and mathematician who died in the 6th century BC), believed that the regular movements of the celestial bodies produced a sublime, heavenly music inaudible to human ears. This idea of the 'music of the spheres' captured the imagination of generations of poets, and the idea of universal harmony is still powerful today.

How do you collaborate with Gaia [Earth] if you don't know exactly how she works, or what she wants? You do it, I think, by playing Earth Jazz. You improvise. You are flexible and responsive. You work on a small scale, and are ready to change direction at the drop of a hat. You encourage diversity, giving each player—human or non-human—as much room as possible to stretch out. You trade fours with the goddess: play four bars, listen to her response, respond, listen, respond. True, sometimes her response may not be clear for centuries. But then no one said this would be easy.

Eisenberg, *The Ecology of Eden*, p.294

Certainly all people make, love, and respond to, music. Everywhere you look, our species is drumming and humming, swaying and swinging, tapping and rapping, jumping and jiving, bopping and be-bopping: we are sounding boards for Earth. Singing and dancing bursts out of every happy child. Music engages the full range of our human nature. It stimulates the imagination, sweeps our emotions along with it, and gets our bodies swaying, tapping, stamping and gliding.

Evan Eisenberg, after a detailed exploration of 'humans, nature and human nature',[5] argues that the 'Planet Fetishers' want humans to play a faint part in a harmony of nature that they imagine to exist, while the 'Planet Managers' want the whole Earth to play in a symphony composed and conducted by them. He rejects both, and concludes that in relating to nature we should imagine our species to be the saxophonist in a bebop quartet playing 'Earth Jazz'.[6] I am not wholly convinced that we should see ourselves as a band leader separate from Earth (after all, we won't be able to harmonise unless we know the chords of the Great Jurisprudence which Earth wrote).

However, I think that his metaphor is still apt. In particular, it conveys the importance of listening carefully and responding with sensitivity and flexibility. It also communicates the importance of allowing the time dimension of our relationships to be structured by a beat and rhythm that arises from the ebb and flow of the interaction between the players, instead of on the basis of a predetermined time line.

Rhythm, music and time are also relevant to governance. Even though we may not be conscious of it, different governance systems operate at different rhythms and at different times. Some rattle through decision-making at the rapid, heart-racing, staccato techno-beat favoured by the corporates (and ravers on ecstasy). Other bureaucracies move towards a conclusion with the stately, self-absorption of a Viennese waltz. However, all think in linear clock-time and don't give a fig about whether or not the time is ripe for making the decision. It may be an 'opportune' moment politically, but its relationships with Earth rhythms are not considered.

Earth governance is going to require us to rethink the time dimensions of governance, particularly in relation to the making of decisions. We need to be able to act swiftly when the moment demands it. In other situations we need to develop the wisdom to recognise when we are not yet ready to make a decision, and the confidence to delay action until the time is ripe. If we want to participate fully in the dances of the Earth Community we need to listen carefully for the beat and adjust our rhythm and timing accordingly.

Chapter 12
The law of the land

SACRED LAND

Land is another name for Earth. We are of the land, given physical form by its minerals and the plants rooted in it; our minds and sense of beauty are formed in relation to its contours, colours, textures, tastes and smells; we are destined to melt once more into it on death. Many cultures and philosophies believe that the life force or vital energy that animates us also flows through, and is concentrated in, the soil, rocks and plants. Moreover, they believe that this also means that we share a subjective presence, soul, or consciousness with Earth. In other words it is more accurate to conceive of land as being part of the physical body of a living being than as an inanimate object. Indigenous peoples throughout the world believe that people belong to and are shaped by the land, rather than vice versa. This truth was once recognised by most, if not all, human cultures, but is now forgotten in the dominant human cultures. Indeed, conventional jurisprudence denies the mere possibility of land itself being sacred as opposed to being a place where religious rituals take place.

The land is our culture. If we were to lose this land, there would be no culture, no soul.

Kuna Elder, Panama

Whether or not you believe that land and Earth have sacred dimensions, the power that land exercises over the human mind and heart is undeniable. Our cultures are full of the heartbreaking songs of exiles lamenting their uprooting from the soil of their youth. Compatriots far from home renew their bonds by recalling the landscapes, smells and places of their homelands. Anthems, ancient and modern, sing of the beauty of the land that defines the nation. 'Soil' ranks with 'blood' and 'martyrdom' in the lexicon of the revolutionary.

You must teach your children that the ground beneath their feet is the ashes of your grandfathers. So that they will respect the land, tell your children that the earth is rich with the lives of our kin. Teach your children what we have taught our children, that the earth is our mother. Whatever befalls the earth befalls the sons of the earth. If men spit upon the ground, they spit upon themselves. This we know: the earth does not belong to man; man belongs to the earth. This we know.

Speech by Chief Seattle (Seatlh) in January 1854[1]

Since all land is part of Earth, the relationship between humans and land is of central importance to Earth governance and Earth jurisprudence. At present, the laws of the dominant cultures make it difficult for human communities to sustain an intimate relationship with land and hence with Earth. As discussed below, the understanding of land reflected in most laws reflects the myth that land is a commodity (despite the obvious fact that it was never manufactured for sale). By pretending that land is a form of commodity that can be owned and dealt with in a similar fashion to, say, a table, legal systems legitimise and encourage the abuse of Earth by humans.

LAND AS PROPERTY

The dominant cultures understand land as property. Land in the eyes of the law is therefore a thing, an object that may be bought and sold, and by definition devoid of any personality or sacred qualities. In the eyes of the law, revering land is idolatry — worshipping a thing. Caring for land may be economically prudent but is not an inherent attribute of ownership. In fact the owner may never even see the land he or she has dominion over, let alone enter into a personal relationship with it. Worse still, when the owner is a juristic person like a company, it does not even have the capacity to love the land.

Each one of us is intimately attached to the soil of this beautiful country. Each time one of us touches the soil of this land, we feel a sense of personal renewal.

Nelson Mandela (speech at his inauguration as President of the Republic of South Africa, May 1994)

Earth is transformed into this fictitious commodity by the process of being surveyed and demarcated to separate it from the surrounding land. Cadastral boundaries defining parcels and plots are marked on maps and hammered into the ground with iron pegs. Once it has been cut up and pegged down, land is sold on the market by the square metre or hectare. The extent and location of each demarcated portion of Earth and the details of its owner are then recorded in a registry of title deeds.

The title deed registry defines and circumscribes land as property both spatially and in time. It may record previous owners, but terminates their interest in the land from the date on which a new owner is registered. Future owners are not considered. Even a usufruct entitling someone other than the owner to use and enjoy the land during their lifetime or for a defined period, merely delays the owner exercising full rights, rather than seeking to protect the interests of future generations who will occupy it. Who the previous owners were, and how they used the land, usually does not directly affect the powers of the current owner, although it may have an indirect effect if there is legislation that requires that permission be obtained to effect a change in land use.

In many governance systems the current owner is given virtually absolute power over that land, including the power to transfer some or all of those powers to another either permanently or temporarily. The private landowner is usually also free to alter the physical characteristics of the land, for example by building roads, ploughing up vegetation or increasing or decreasing the fertility of the soil. In some countries these rights include the rights to mine minerals from the subsoil and rocks, while in other countries these rights are considered so valuable that they are reserved to the state.

Since conventional jurisprudence regards land as a commodity, in principle landowners are not under a legal obligation to care for land or for any other organisms that may inhabit it. In fact, the landowner is entitled, and sometimes encouraged with subsidies, to exploit the land for personal benefit. This may include not only cultivating crops and farming domestic animals, but also hunting and fishing for wild animals and harvesting the wild plants that inhabit that land.

Many countries have now imposed some indirect obligations on landowners, for example by prohibiting certain uses of the land (e.g. the use of agricultural land for industrial purposes), and certain practices such as unauthorised waste disposal or interference with endangered species of wildlife. Nevertheless, in most jurisdictions the fundamental principle is that the landowner may use land for any purpose and in any manner that is not prohibited. Consequently, in most countries the presumption is that the law should only intervene to restrict the powers of a landowner where it is absolutely necessary to do so, for example, to protect public health.

LAND AS POWER

Historically, land ownership has been associated with political power. The feudal systems that developed in the Middle Ages in Europe, for example, were structured around land tenure systems. At the apex of feudal systems was the monarchy, which derived most of its secular power from the fact that the Crown was the source of all land rights. The Crown rewarded those who were loyal with legal documents of title to land, while traitors had their lands confiscated. The barons and aristocracy to whom these lands were awarded, in turn gave rights to use the land to other 'landlords' loyal to them. In this way, each social class, from the serfs to the barons and princes, derived their ability to make a livelihood from the land, not from the land itself, but from their loyalty and obedience to those above them in the social pyramid.

Even today, ownership of land has other legal and political powers associated with it. For example, a landowner or occupier usually has the right to vote for local politicians, and enhanced rights to prevent others in the area using their land in an unreasonable manner. In many countries there are also laws that restrict the ability of foreigners to own or use land.

LAND MANAGEMENT SYSTEMS

As human occupation of land has intensified, societies have found it necessary to restrict the purposes for which land is used in certain areas. This is
done for a variety of reasons, for example to reduce the potential for conflict
between different landowners or to ensure that some land is kept for public
uses like parks, hospitals and schools. In most countries, land-use planning
legislation allows public bodies (typically municipalities) to indicate in broad
terms the human land uses that they think should prevail in a particular area
or zone. These are usually reflected in zoning schemes recorded in land use or
land management plans.

Land-use planning systems are typically linked with development control
systems that regulate how specific sites may be used. In many cases, constructing buildings and certain other uses of land, particularly those that have
the potential to affect the use and enjoyment by other landowners of their
land, require permission. In deciding whether or not to grant permission, the
decision-makers are usually guided by previously formulated land management plans and zoning schemes.

More and more countries are now requiring that the potential impacts of
proposed developments on the environment must be assessed and taken into
account when deciding whether or not to grant such permission. However,
even if it is desirable to impose a restriction on the use of a particular area of
land in order to protect the environment, the environmentally destructive
land use will frequently be permitted if it can be shown to yield short-term
benefits to humans. In other words, even in the area of environmental law, the
main factor in deciding whether or not to permit land to be used in an environmentally destructive fashion is the utility of the proposed activity to
humans.

THE EFFECTS OF PROPERTY-BASED
LAND GOVERNANCE REGIMES

Applying the laws of property to land reflects a worldview in which it is right
and proper for human subjects unilaterally to dominate all other aspects of
the Earth Community as objects. By defining land as a commodity, the dominant legal philosophies legitimise and facilitate our exploitative relations with
Earth. These philosophies also obstruct us from developing governance systems based on a respectful relationship with land or Earth, and prevent us
recognising that this is a reciprocal relationship between subjects with inherent Earth rights. In this way they increase our own alienation from nature.

The conceptual and legal transformation of a natural reciprocal relationship into a unidirectional exploitative relationship also creates imbalance. The law gives whoever owns or occupies land at a particular time very wide powers to manage or even destroy that land, as well as virtually unfettered rights in relation to living creatures who inhabit it. This represents a dangerously unbalanced force. The damaging consequences of this imbalance are plain to see in the wholesale and widespread destruction of the habitats of almost all species.

A CORE RELATIONSHIP

This relationship between humans and land is fundamental. It is a relationship that shapes the minds and hearts of individuals and the identity of nations. Changing how we understand and recognise this relationship is at the heart of shifting to a new governance paradigm. Not unexpectedly, it is also an area in which indigenous cultures and ancient wisdom offer us particularly valuable guidance.

Our resources came from the land because that makes us part of the land. It's a source of food that is created by that given area; that's what makes my life. Thirty thousand years of legends have been passed on orally as a teaching tool to maintain our existence on how we can live off this land. And how to maintain it is to make sure we do not disturb the resources.

David B. Andersen Gwich'in
Athabaskan, eastern interior, Alaska

The starting point is to recognise that this area of governance is concerned with the primary relationship between a component of the Earth Community (humans) and that part of Earth that provides us with both physical and psychic sustenance. As humans who live in intimacy with the land are fully aware, it is a reciprocal relationship which involves deep emotional, and even spiritual, connections. By choosing to characterise this relationship as one of master and chattel, we impoverish ourselves and prevent ourselves experiencing and benefiting fully from this most fundamental of relationships.

The relationship between humans and the land on which they depend is not a relationship between peers. It is a relationship that many cultures have compared to that between a nurturing mother and a dependent child, and as such needs to be characterised by respect. However, it is also one in which the 'child' is required to play an active role in caring for the land that provides for it. In contemporary times, those who care deeply for a particular part of Earth are increasingly being called upon to protect the integrity of that land from other humans. Resurrecting and adapting ancient notions of people and communities as guardians of land, with a sacred obligation to care for it in perpetuity, is likely to be an important part of the emerging Earth jurisprudence.

The human roles as land carer and guardian require personal intimacy between human and land. Intimacy of this kind requires real people: people

We think of ourselves as custodians of the land, and the land's not just soil and rock to us. It's the whole of creation—all the land, water, and air, and the life everywhere, people, too. All these things are related and linked together in the Dreamtime.

Pauline Gordon, Aborigine,
Bunjalung tribe, Australia

with bodies sensitive to the wind and the tingling dance of the morning sun on flesh after a cold night; people with minds that can share the consciousness and feel the pain of wounded Earth; people with tongues to taste poisoned water, noses that can run with the black phlegm of polluted cities and lungs that can expand with the joy of pure mountain air.

These are not the characteristics of artificial legal persons like corporations. The breakdown in the relationships between humans and Earth has been exacerbated by the fact that many landowners are incorporated persons that exist by virtue of legal fictions and are wholly incapable of forming an intimate relationship with the land. This lack of capacity means that they cannot connect and communicate with the Community and so are incapable of functioning as part of it. Unlike a landowner, a land carer needs a heart and empathy. Only real people with a real physical relationship with the land can fulfil this role.

THE LORE OF THE LAND

Caring for land is not a role for one person. This is a relationship or a communion that must be exercised in a community. Caring and protecting a place on Earth requires the timeless care of a community of people whose lives become interwoven with the sights and smells and texture of that place: people who bring up their children with its stories and introduce them to its creatures and special places, filling them with the lore of that land, until they know that they are of that land. The human-land relationship is never an entirely personal matter between one person and an area of land, no matter how intense the relationship. It always involves many other beings—those behind and ahead of us in time, and those whom we cohabit with on the land. Our means of governance needs to recognise that use by the current occupier of land should never be permitted to be at the expense of this much wider and larger community.

We sang songs that carried in their melodies all the sounds of nature: the running of waters, the sighing of winds, and the calls of the animals. Teach these to your children that they may come to love nature as we love it.

Grand Council Fire of American
Indians, 1927, Papua New Guinea

Respect and balance are central to this relationship. Indeed many would argue that it has a sacred quality which means that the relationship will flourish as it ought only when it is characterised by love, reverence and gratitude. It is not easy for respect, love or reverence to be commanded by law, but if we look at other cultures we can observe many techniques that can be used. For example, actions that are blatantly disrespectful may be prohibited. Celebrations remind humans of the food and nurturing bestowed by Earth, and other rituals which are designed to remind humans that they are humble in relation to Earth and to others, explicitly offer reverence and thanks. Perhaps most importantly, there are innumerable social practices used to increase the intimacy of this relationship, ranging from reciting short verses while doing daily tasks, to leaving fallow or uncultivated areas among the field to sustain wild creatures.

Perhaps we should be developing new rituals in which a community marries itself to land and publicly promises to love and honour it for as long as they exist as a community. City folk could forge links with a particular farming community from which they get food, and rediscover their links to the land. A bit romantic? Probably, but the point is that we need new mechanisms and social customs that recognise the fundamental importance of this relationship and that restore quality and soul to it. I have little doubt that if every person tried to heal just one tiny area of degraded and abused land in a way that strengthened their personal relationship with it, Earth governance and justice would soon flourish.

If we didn't do the ceremonies, it wouldn't mean the plants wouldn't bloom that year. It would mean we would stop having that respect and giving that praise. Then we stop having food to eat because we would lose respect and cut down the rain forest, pollute the water, and destroy the balance. That is the real truth behind this message.

Leandis, Mexican healer, northern Mexico

MOVING AWAY FROM LAND AS PROPERTY

In seeking to find a language and governance mechanisms that can adequately express the true nature of this relationship, we must also recognise that from a human perspective we need to emphasise the responsibilities that we have in relation to land, rather than the rights that we currently assert. In some cases we will also need to strengthen the rights of those humans who do live in intimacy with land to resist interventions by other humans who do not. For example, in many countries farmers and countryfolk are unable to prevent the introduction of genetically modified crops into their areas, or even to prevent companies buying up land and developing it in the most disrespectful manner.

Moving away from relating to land on the basis of ownership also means appreciating that we are concerned not with an absolute and unchanging relationship between a subject and an object but a dynamic relationship between different components of the same system. This also means that rather than focusing on the purposes for which land may be used, we must give attention

Others may laugh at our customs and how we are so closely related to the land and all things that grow on the land. But all the trees, animals, fish, insects, reptiles, and even mountains have special meaning for us.

West Papuan Elder, Papua New Guinea

to the quality of the relationship. Asking whether or not land is being used for agriculture in an agricultural zone is not as important as asking if the occupier is conserving, protecting and utilising the land in a manner that is beneficial, not just to humans but to Earth. In particular, what is becoming of that little Earth Community that inhabits the land? Is the trend towards or away from integration with the whole?

Only by accepting what was once a sacred responsibility to care for the land and by constantly deepening the intimacy of that relationship and restoring it when it is damaged, can we be fully human. The costs of continuing to maintain our current ideas of property rights are expatriation and virtual excommunication from the Earth Community as well as alienation from our deeper selves. Radical as completely rethinking property law may seem, on a wider evaluation of the costs and benefits, it seems fully justified. The challenge that now faces us is how to begin the process of undoing the property systems that impede a proper relationship with land, and to build a workable alternative in its place.

Chapter 13
A communion of communities

HOLONS AND HOLARCHIES

Have you ever gone walking and stopped to look at a fern frond or a compound leaf like the leaf of an Acacia thorn tree? As one looks more closely, one can see that the whole is composed of a pattern, repeated at different levels. A bracken frond, for example, is made up of what look like tiny leaves, each constructed around a central line off which little veins branch. The structure within the leaf is repeated in the arrangement of the tiny leaves around the thinnest stems of the frond. These little Christmas trees of leaves in turn are arranged in a similar configuration around thicker stems to form the whole frond. The whole is effectively created by repetitions of the pattern of a central stem and branching veins, which is apparent in the smallest part of the leaf. Each part is simultaneously part of a coherent substructure and part of the whole.

The whole is also greater than the sum of the parts, in that as one goes up each level additional properties emerge. The smallest leaflet of an Acacia can only respond to the touch of the breeze by moving in one plane. However the whole composite leaf can move and align itself in different planes simultaneously. The leaves of some plants in this family can even shrink away from human touch and rapidly close up.

Nature, it seems, has a penchant for producing complex shapes by repeating the same patterns over and over at different levels of scale so that the parts, at different levels of scale, have a similar shape to the whole. This had been described mathematically by the French mathematician Benoît Mandelbrot, author of *The Fractal Geometry of Nature*.

Everything in nature can be seen as belonging to such [holarchical] arrangements—molecules within cells within cell communities within ecosystems, or molecules within cells within organs within organisms within families within communities within species within ecosystems. . . . This kind of understanding shows clearly that embedded systems, or holons, must contribute to the health of the holarchies embedding them if they are to remain healthy. They must continually balance their independence with inter-dependence, their autonomy with their holonomy, or membership in the holarchy. . . . In short, simultaneous self-interest at every level of a living holarchy leads to co-operation by way of dynamic and continual negotiation among all levels.

Liebes, Sahtouris and Swimme, *A Walk Through Time*, pp 166–7

Capra (1996) describes how Mandelbrot demonstrates this by breaking the head of a cauliflower into smaller and smaller pieces (which he calls 'fractals'), each of which is similar in shape to the whole head.

Ecologists have identified that living entities and systems evolve in a similar way, creating wholes from pattern of smaller wholes. Even the complex whole of the termite mound I described in Chapter One is made of smaller wholes. Within the gut of each termite live protists (tiny unicellular organisms) called *Mixotricha paradoxa*, and within each protist live millions of bacteria. There may be hundreds of termite mounds within an ecosystem, each containing many thousands of termites, each of which provides a universe for ten million protists, which in turn contain a trillion bacteria. Arthur Koestler describes these structures as 'holons in holarchy'.[1] The whole of nature, it seems, is arranged in this way. The fact that there are 'wholes' or holons at each level that are simultaneously part of larger wholes creates tension between the self-interest of holons at one level and the holarchies in which they are embedded. This tension can only be resolved by co-operation and ongoing 'negotiation' if the whole ecosystem is to remain healthy.[2]

EARTH COMMUNITIES

The 'Earth Community' then can be understood as being made up of all the smaller communities at different levels that are embedded in the whole system that we call Earth. I may simultaneously be a member of my family, the ecological community of the river basin that I inhabit, my country and an international community of environmentalists. However, since we are talking about governance, I will focus more specifically on communities that include humans and that define themselves in relation to the area that they inhabit. However, the 'local communities' to which I refer in this chapter incorporate not only humans but also the soil, air, waters and what might be termed the 'biotic community' of that area. In other words, it is a local community of the Earth Community rather than of human society.

There are a number of reasons for devoting specific attention to communities in a discussion on a new governance paradigm. Firstly, strengthening the bonds of which local communities are made means strengthening the Earth Community and so the health of the whole. The relationships between the many smaller communities of Earth form the whole Community. Without this 'communion' between them there is no Community.

A community is an intimate relationship with all living things both animate and inanimate.

Mike Bell (2001), quoting an aboriginal definition of community

Secondly, governance systems require structures, and local communities seem to provide an instructive model. Local communities typically manifest

*Individuality, not individualism, is
the cornerstone of community.
Individuality is synonymous with
uniqueness. This means that a person
and his or her unique gifts are
irreplaceable. The community loves to
see all of its members flourish and
function at optimum potential. In
fact, the community can flourish and
survive only when each member
flourishes, living in full potential of
her or his purpose. To honour and
support its members is in the
self-interest of any community.*

Malidoma Somé, *The Healing Wisdom
of Africa*, p. 92

the principles of differentiation, diversity and self-regulation referred to in Chapter Six. Looking at it from a human perspective, the people in the local community will typically identify themselves as being, to a lesser or greater degree, culturally different from neighbouring communities and will assert the right to govern themselves to a degree in accordance with their own customs or world-view. In short, they will have a group identity that they wish to maintain. From a biological perspective, the community would be com-posed of different components (animals, plants, soil, water, air etc.) that interact with one another in a manner that gives rise to a distinctive ecosystem. From both perspec-tives the community exists only by virtue of the interrelationships between the members. If these are not 'whole-main-taining', the community will deteriorate and may die, creating an opportu-nity for others to arise.

Thirdly, the rights of local communities and perhaps even their contin-ued existence is under threat almost everywhere by the vast homogenising forces of the dominant cultures. This force is most clearly visible at present in the range of phenomena referred to as 'globalisation'. In this sense, re-affirm-ing the right of communities to exist and to self-regulate is part of the strug-gle to maintain the diversity necessary for stable and sustainable governance structures.

*The individual parts [of the maloca]
are associated with cosmological
models, astronomical phenomena,
anatomical and physiological
functions, kinship notions, ritual
dimensions, and landscape features, in
short, with all spheres and scenarios of
human experience. The maloca is a
cosmic model, it is a forest, an
assembly of kin and allies, a womb,
a grave, a tortoise, a microcosm in
which every part is named and every
relationship between parts is seen as a
link in a coherent whole.*

Reichel-Dolmatoff, *The Forest Within*,
p.49

Finally, healthy communities provide an environment that is conducive to people achieving their true potential. Yet again there is much to learn if one looks at indigenous peoples. Malidoma Somé's description of the role of the individual within a traditional West African community not only expresses the value of human communities but could be a description of a healthy Earth Community. Similarly, Reichel-Dolmatoff's description of how the multi-family long-house (*maloca*) of the Tukano Amazonian Indians is also a model of life and the uni-verse, presents a beautiful example of the degree of integration between those human societies and the Earth Community in which they are embedded. Imagine the effect on one's worldview of growing up in a communal house with your ancestors buried under your feet, your family around you and the structure itself modelling the wider universe that is your home.

COMMUNITIES IN THE CURRENT GOVERNANCE PARADIGM

The legal theories of the dominant cultures have had a particularly pernicious effect on local communities. Their jurisprudence vests rights in individuals and artificial legal persons like corporations, and does not, with limited exceptions, recognise collective or group rights. The notion that certain rights and obligations are held and exercised as a community for the common good is at the heart of the concept of community. Attacks on these rights, such as the enclosure of common land in the United Kingdom so that it could be used for the exclusive benefit of private sheep farmers, have always undermined the health of communities. Removing these rights often deprives the community of its means of creating a livelihood. Perhaps more significantly, it undermines the relationships that create the community by encouraging competition rather than co-operation among different members of the community.

This conflict between the dominant governance paradigm and the community-based approach is clearly apparent at the present time in relation to access to so-called 'genetic resources' and to the traditional knowledge associated with their use. Communities living close to nature have developed and nurtured an intimate knowledge of the Earth Communities to which they belonged, including extensive knowledge of the medicinal and other uses of plants. They have also developed, through thousands of years of careful selection, breeds of crops and domesticated animals specifically suited to local environmental conditions, and the husbandry techniques to enable them to flourish. This knowledge and the associated skills were simply a part of the culture of that community. Some aspects were secret and only divulged to a few, others were widely known and freely shared with others.

The problems arose when members of the dominant cultures in far-off places recognised that these cultures, previously despised as 'primitive' and having nothing to offer, in fact had knowledge that could be commoditised and sold in the markets of the developed world. The problem was that this knowledge was not in the realm of commerce, because the holders did not define it as property and did not buy and sell it. Although this could be useful when acquiring the knowledge for the first time, it also meant that it would be harder to make large profits because there was no way of ensuring that others didn't do the same.

Therefore it was necessary first to define this indigenous knowledge as property that could be privately owned. This was achieved by expanding and distorting patent laws. These laws had been designed to encourage people to invent socially useful artefacts by giving the inventor an exclusive right to use the invention for a limited period of time (usually 15 to 20 years). However, for a patent to be granted the invention had to be novel (i.e. the inventor had to have created something original and not merely discovered something that already existed), that was non-obvious and useful in the sense that it was capable of industrial application. Changes to patent laws in America and other countries have altered the criteria for granting patents to allow the patenting of certain life forms [3] (hardly 'inventions') and of specific uses of natural compounds. Many of these herbal compounds have been used in various forms by communities for thousands of years and can in no way be considered to be new uses. The dominant cultures then used international legal instruments and international organisations such as the World Trade Organisation (WTO) and the World Intellectual Property Association (WIPO) to impose this approach on most of the rest of the world.

The effect of these legal changes made by distant decision-makers was to allow outsiders to obtain valuable information from communities by fair means or foul, to transform it into a form that the dominant legal system recognised as property. Users can then legally be obliged to pay royalties to the patent-holder (almost invariably a corporation). For example, if a corporation isolates a specific plant compound from a plant traditionally used for medicinal purposes and then patents it for use in treating certain medical conditions, it is legally entitled to prevent even the member of the community who supplied the knowledge from using it in this way.

The genetic engineering of crops by corporations represents a particular threat to local communities in many parts of the world. In addition to the potential dangers that these genetically modified organisms may pose to the health of the Earth Community, since corporations own the patents to the seeds (which are usually designed to be used in conjunction with pesticides and fertilisers), their use makes the communities dependent on external inputs, and subject to corporate control. This not only weakens the autonomy of human local communities, it also undermines traditional regenerative systems of agriculture and the sustainable use of biodiversity.

LOCAL COMMUNITIES AS HOLONS WITHIN AN EARTH GOVERNANCE HOLARCHY

As discussed in Chapter Six, Earth jurisprudence and Earth governance requires us to respect and observe the principles of the Great Jurisprudence. It seems that by looking at how the universe functions, we can discern certain principles of organisation that would be immensely helpful for us to apply to human governance. The concepts of holons and holarchies, in particular, could be very useful in choosing which social structures to support and which not to, and in structuring governance systems, including our legal systems.

It may also be helpful to turn the conventional model of structuring governance systems on its head. Instead of adopting an architectural model based on designing the overall architecture for the governance structure, we could consider what a governance system might look like if it were created organically. From our knowledge of natural structuring, we can hypothesise that a successful 'organic' structure (as opposed to a structure that is imposed on Earth) is likely to incorporate small 'patterns' which are repeated in a manner that allows more complex patterns of organisation to emerge. It seems possible that if we start at 'grass roots level', where there is a greater degree of intimacy in relationships, we might find appropriate or inspirational models. However, in many places useful models may no longer exist, and we will need to begin consciously to weave these small patterns. Since successful small patterns may combine to form a similar larger pattern, the shape and form of the smallest pattern (i.e. how we make it) is of the utmost importance. This could also be regarded as another way of saying that the means are the end in the making. It is not that what we do is not important, but rather that how we do it is crucial because it is this that will give form to the pattern. Such a pattern, if successful, may become self-replicating and combine to form a larger whole.

This may sound very theoretical, but there are precedents in other areas. For example, during the struggle against apartheid in South Africa, the United Democratic Front (UDF) was formed as an alliance of many separate and diverse organisations such as trades unions, youth clubs and civic associations. The UDF was trying to bring about a non-racial and democratic country. At that time most people had very little experience of either democracy or a non-racist society. One of the ways in which the UDF made these concepts real and ultimately helped bring them about, was by requiring each component organisation to organise itself democratically. In this way, the election of office bearers in a township youth group not only strengthened relations within it, but also contributed in a very real way to democracy taking root in the whole country.

What characteristics might we be looking to find or create in order to help Earth governance grow? For a start I think that each of the smaller patterns of social organisation must have a certain quality of integrity. In other words they should be self-organising, able to sustain themselves over a long period of time, and be beneficial in the sense that the benefits which the participants derive from the system exceed the energy required to maintain it. Furthermore, in order for the social group to function properly, it must be based on a certain common intention, which unifies, directs, and hence structures the activities of the participants.

It also means that within these social structures how the individual lives is crucial. (This is, of course, hardly a startling insight since it forms part of probably all ancient traditions of wisdom and religions.) In the context of Earth governance, it is clearly important that as many individuals as possible live in accordance with an intention to be productive and responsible members of the Earth Community. This means that the development of widely accepted environmental or earth-centred ethics is of crucial importance. It also means that we should strive to incorporate practices in our lives that we find to be beneficial both to ourselves and to Earth, and that are sustainable in the sense that we can maintain them. So doing very small Earth-caring things on an ongoing basis is probably far more important than the odd grand gesture (or World Summit), though both have their place. Communities, in the sense of groups of like-minded people bound together by mutually supportive relationships, should then provide the mechanism whereby these individual patterns can be scaled up into collective patterns.

We should come a lot closer to arriving at more appropriate governance systems if we favour those policies and forms of organisation which display two key characteristics. Firstly, they must promote stronger and more intimate relationships between the members of a local Earth Community (including inter-human relations). Secondly, they must contribute to the health of the wider system of which they form part (i.e. they must help to maintain the whole).

I am not suggesting that transforming the governance systems of most of the dominant societies will be easy or quick. However the good news is that we don't have to start at the top, we can start with ourselves and with those around us and aim to make small, manageable, replicable changes which are beneficial to us.

THE QUESTION OF SCALE

If we see the daily living practices of an individual and his or her inter-relationships as a holon, then replication at a higher level can occur when this person functions as part of a human community that is bound together by mutually supportive relationships and a degree of common commitment to the same principles. As Malidoma Somé points out (see page 148), a healthy relationship between the individual and the community enhances both.

Most people can conceive that this might be possible in a village or a city neighbourhood. Community, the touching of those around you, is a very personal thing. It cannot be scaled up massively without becoming shallower and less intimate. This may be the reason why the sense of connectedness and belonging that characterises healthy communities seems to break down as one moves upwards in our governance hierarchies. At the level of the 'international community', which is populated with yet more artificial legal persons (states and international organisations), the sense of intimacy and common purpose may have disappeared altogether. One of the challenges of implementing Earth governance will be to explore ways of allowing the positive aspects of community organisation to be replicated within larger social systems.

The idea of adopting a bio-regional approach to governance may be particularly useful. This approach advocates orientating decision-making towards a particular bio-regional community. Certainly one can imagine that if the patterns of social organisation were scaled up not from individual, to local authority, to provincial government, to national government, to international community, but instead were scaled up with reference to ecological communities, the result would be very different. For example, one can imagine the human inhabitants of a small valley taking decisions as a community to preserve the integrity of the Earth Community within that valley. As a community they could then participate in the decision-making of the body concerned with, say, the entire catchment basin of a river system. This body might then be part of a community that is characterised by a particular climatic or biophysical region, or perhaps a larger community which has close relationships with the ocean into which the river flows, and so on.

One of the advantages of a bio-regional approach to governance structures is that it would allow small patterns of organisation to build seamlessly into larger, consistent structures of governance, in the same way as fern fronds are formed. Interdependence and relationships would be built into the structure of governance, giving it greater stability and promoting co-operation. Within such a pattern of governance, the idea of fighting other communities for their resources or, for example, transferring large amounts of water from one catchment basin to another, would appear more obviously inappropriate. It would be clear to all that the proper functioning of the whole and the well-being of each person depended on each community caring for 'their' part of Earth and contributing to the health of the local Earth Community. If each human community is able to do so, this will automatically improve the functioning and health of the next higher order of organisation, and ultimately the health of the whole.

This type of governance structure would tend to create positive feedback loops in the sense that the improving health of the whole would also make it easier for the smaller units to function effectively. Healthy catchments would mean less destructive erosion along the lower reaches of the river system. At the moment, we see the converse in the world. As a result of the profligate burning of fossil fuels in certain areas, Earth's climate is being affected in ways which are jeopardising the ability of communities everywhere to provide their own livelihoods. This means that their ability to live harmoniously as part of a local Earth Community is being undermined by factors beyond their control. These factors need to be addressed at the highest levels in the international governance system. However, as we so often see, the organisational structure and philosophies of that level of governance make it extremely difficult to address such issues as effectively as a true community would.

In the short-term it would also help to reduce the distance between decision-makers and where the effects of the decisions are felt. This has been recognised to some extent by the application of what the European Union refers to as the principle of 'subsidiarity'. This principle essentially postulates that decision-making should be devolved to the lowest appropriate level. It recognises that the nature of the decision may determine the level at which it should be taken (e.g. questions of international relations are not to be decided at village level). If properly applied, such a principle would mean that most decisions would be taken by the community most directly affected and most intimately concerned with the issue, unless there was a good reason why it should be taken at a higher level. Although giving effect to the principle of subsidiarity has a long way to go even in the countries that subscribe to it, from the perspective of Earth governance it makes sense for decisions that affect a local Earth Community to be made by members of it wherever possible. This approach should also facilitate the evolution of governance systems that are more responsive to feedback and better adapted to the nuances of the local Earth Community.

NEW EARTH COMMUNITIES AS A SOURCE OF EARTH JURISPRUDENCE

When I advocate that our governance systems should be structured around communities, and communities of communities, I am not necessarily advocating a return to a romanticised pre-industrial world in which the countryside is dotted with small villages, and governance is by autonomous tribal groups. Such a world may have much to recommend it, and I certainly support the continued existence of those remaining tribal cultures and communities. However I do not think that turning the clock back is an option that is available to us. The world has changed too much. We need to learn from our tribal pasts and from the history of Earth that lies beyond that, in order to gain wisdom and inspiration to guide us to becoming Earth-centred peoples once more.

Already new social movements based on Earth-centric or eco-centric worldviews are emerging. The Earth Democracy movement in India (which is discussed briefly in Chapter 14) is one example, while South African community activists have linked up with groups from several other countries to form an Earth Justice Movement (EJM). The EJM is not a nongovernmental organisation or even a confederation of organisations, but a community: a community based on a shared worldview within which different groups and individuals can support one another to restore healthy relationships between humans and the rest of the Earth Community. Therefore its emphasis is on establishing and strengthening mutually supportive relations that enable the members to be more effective in what they do, rather than on carrying out any particular action plan. It is too early to predict whether or not these particular social movements will have any significant impact in promoting Earth governance as described in this book. Nevertheless, they are examples of the emergence of 'communities of communities' that are organised around a common approach and Earth-centred philosophy rather than around specific issues.

The EJM, as might be expected, has experienced some difficulties in creating itself as a community without having offices, office bearers and all the trappings of organisations. It has wrestled with how to make democratic decisions as a movement and yet remain efficient, and has agonised over means of resolving minor disputes. One of the things that has fascinated me about participating in the emergence of a new type of international, proto-community has been observing the development of small practices that gradually develop and harden into shared approaches. In the process of coming into being, these new forms of social organisation are creating their own specific forms of Earth jurisprudence and Earth governance. Hopefully there will be many more such experiments all over the world (I suspect that there are already thousands). Some will flourish and grow, others will flower briefly before disappearing. Collectively they represent the kind of diverse social experimentation that human societies need in order to explore and evolve workable models of Earth governance.

EARTH JURISPRUDENCE
AND COMMUNITY RIGHTS

Communities all over the world have been fighting to survive in a world that has become increasingly hostile to them. The dominant cultures are increasingly interacting with different cultural minorities in a manner that creates enormous pressures on them to abandon their languages and cultures. As discussed above, the pressures on cultures all over the world to discard their traditional ways in order to become simply consumers and producers in the global market is intensifying.

Many developing countries that are still rich in biological diversity and cultural diversity saw the Convention on Biological Diversity (CBD) as a very important safeguard. The CBD recognises "the close and traditional dependence of many indigenous and local communities embodying traditional lifestyles on biological resources, and the desirability of sharing equitably benefits arising from the use of traditional knowledge, innovation and practices relevant to the conservation of biological diversity and the sustainable use of its components".[4] However, in practice there are very few successful examples of 'benefit sharing'. Most involve foreign companies paying sums of money to governments (and sometimes also to indigenous peoples) in order to undertake bio-prospecting guided by the use of indigenous knowledge. Several such agreements also hold out the promise of significant royalties if the research produces any product that is commercially successful. In my view, in most cases it is highly unlikely that this will occur because the relevant contracts would be very difficult to enforce. Even if it did, paying large sums of money to indigenous groups may well hasten their destruction in some cases.

However the benefit-sharing provisions of the CBD could still be useful if they are interpreted from an Earth jurisprudence perspective. For example, instead of focussing on the exchange of money or technology as the main 'benefits', the focus would shift to asking what arrangements would most promote strong relationships between all the people involved and the local Earth Community from where the 'resources' were obtained. One objective might be to forge close personal relations between the indigenous communities who discovered the healing properties of a certain plant and the human community involved in making drugs derived from that plant, with both seeking ways of preserving the local Earth Community that had given them this livelihood. The end results would be very different from those achieved by the usual cascade of intellectual property licences from one multinational to another.

Chapter 14

Transforming law and governance

Up until now I have focused mainly on why we need to re-think our ideas of governance and how we could approach the challenge of re-conceptualising the nature and purpose of governance. I have argued that contemporary societies must recognise that we are operating within a larger system or context that we need to pay heed to, and that our governance systems need to observe, the principles of what I have called the Great Jurisprudence. I have also suggested that we will need to articulate a new philosophy of law (Earth jurisprudence) to guide us in transforming our governance systems, and have sketched some of its features. I have not, until now, made much reference to how adopting an Earth jurisprudence approach might provide practical guidance in transforming existing legal and political systems. In this chapter I discuss whether or not it is realistic to hope to achieve such a comprehensive transformation, how such a transformation might happen, and a few ideas about small changes that could be made now in order to begin moving towards Earth governance.

DELUSIONAL OR PRACTICAL?

Several people who have encountered the idea of Earth jurisprudence over the past year or so have been dismayed at the prospects of attempting such a radical revisioning of legal theories and governance systems. Others have questioned the wisdom of a frontal assault on the bastions of the homosphere when there are so many urgent tactical battles to be fought. Certainly in the face of the arrogant self-belief of the most powerful human institutions, the idea of winning widespread acceptance of Earth jurisprudence can seem farfetched at best, and at worst dangerously delusional. Faced with the enormity of the task, and the power of those with vested interests in the status quo, some lose heart and reject these ideas out of hand as impractical.

It *is* very difficult sometimes to retain faith in the ability of humans to alter course and to stem, let alone reverse, the wholesale destruction of natural systems and human cultures and communities. When I get too gloomy,

I remind myself that the modern world as we know it, and in particular the belief that humans are separate from nature, is a very recent (and hopefully transient) phenomenon. If one views contemporary societies and beliefs within the context of human history over the last two million years or more, then what appears to be 'normal' shifts dramatically. In fact, from a long-term perspective, the worldview on which Earth jurisprudence is based seems more mainstream, and it is our societies that seem out of step. A long-term view of the development of human cultures also reminds us that even civilisations that were enormously powerful in their day have passed into history. (Interestingly, as mentioned in Chapter Seven, more evidence seems to be emerging that in some cases the decline may have been precipitated by the degradation of the environments on which the society depended.)

Some people have understood the argument for re-thinking the entire philosophical approach to governance, both nationally and internationally, as a call for the wholesale abolition of existing legal and political systems. This is not the case. They are two related, but separate issues. In other words, when I argue in Chapter Twelve that treating land as any other commodity is mis-conceived, I am not proposing that property laws be abolished overnight. I am under no illusions about the short-term chaos that would ensue if this happened. My argument is simply that Thomas Berry is correct when he points out that the present forms of law and governance are not only unhelp-ful but positively obstructive, and that an entirely new philosophical approach is needed. There is clearly no point in developing a new Earth jurisprudence approach unless it is going to be implemented by developing wild law. How that is done is another matter. It will undoubtedly take time, and I suspect that much of the wild law that grows will be specific to particular locations and will not be suitable for general application. It will nevertheless be recog-nisable as wild law, because it is based on common Earth jurisprudence and Earth governance approaches.

My purpose in giving a few examples in this chapter of how to start intro-ducing wildness into existing governance systems is to show that these ideas are capable of practical application. Indeed there is more and more evidence that many legal systems already contain elements of wild law, and are show-ing some signs of recognising the importance of an ecocentric approach in some areas, albeit rather haphazardly. The particular prescriptions that I sug-gest may not work. No matter: the point is that we must consciously initiate this process of transformation so that we can develop and refine ones that will.

THE DYNAMICS OF CHANGE

Sometimes one can be convinced of the need for radical change but not be able to see how it can possibly happen. This doesn't mean that the desired change won't occur. For example, many people had for many years deeply desired the demise of apartheid in South Africa. When the transition eventually happened, it was surprisingly quick, and the way in which it occurred was not foreseen by most commentators, or even by many participants, until shortly beforehand. Yet it is also true to say that the change would not have occurred had there not been a long struggle for liberation founded on the basis of a vision of a democratic society that rejects discrimination on the base of race.

It is also important to bear in mind that societies, as with everything else, are constantly changing and evolving anyway. The issue is not whether or not we can change societies and legal and political structures, but how they will change and in which direction. This means that it is more important to focus on the process of becoming (i.e. what is influencing the nature of the change) rather than on working out any detailed prescription for changing the status quo. The challenge for thinkers and leaders is to remind people where we come from and to inspire them as to what we may yet become, as Brian Swimme and Thomas Berry do in *The Universe Story*.[1]

ECOZOIC OR TECHNOZOIC?

My own view is that, sooner or later, most humans will support the idea that societies should change their governance structures so that we strengthen rather than weaken our relationships with our evolutionary partners in the 'natural world'. In other words, as the current Cenozoic age draws to a close, there will be growing support for a transition to what Berry calls the 'Ecozoic' age and for 'Ecozoic governance', rather than to a 'Technozoic' age. However, I may well be wrong. Certainly, on the basis of the evidence of the last few hundred years, it is entirely plausible that our societies will continue to place their faith in improving our technological ability to manage the planet until it is too late to prevent massive environmental degradation.

The main reason for my optimism is that we have Gaia in our corner. If one accepts the Gaia Theory that Earth functions as a self-regulating entity capable of maintaining itself in a state of homeostasis, it seems to me entirely plausible (but possibly not capable of scientific verification) that the Earth system will respond to assaults on its integrity. One could take a pessimistic view and say that since humans are the problem, we can expect Earth (or God) to devise some particularly nasty new diseases or disasters that will wipe us out.

A more benign interpretation, and one that seems more plausible, is that because we humans are ourselves an aspect of Earth, we might be part of the cure. Scientists such as James Lovelock and Lynn Margulis, among others, have provided strong evidence that Earth (Gaia) functions as a kind of 'super organism'. As discussed earlier, some sort of consciousness appears to be inherent in all living systems (see Chapter Six). If this is so, it does not seem unreasonable to speculate that at least some humans would begin to pick up on and respond to increasing levels of 'distress' within the systems of which they are a part. Certainly the teachings and writings of people like Joanna Macy and Molly Young-Brown provide powerful testaments that this is so.[2] Therefore, to the extent that we respond in a manner that addresses the cause of the distress, we humans would be functioning as part of Earth's self-regulatory and self-sustaining response.

CHANGING GOVERNANCE SYSTEMS FROM WITHIN

In addition to developing a vision of Earth jurisprudence, we can also begin to work on changing our existing governance systems from within. Indeed, there are already a few symptoms of wildness breaking out in the world's governance systems. Germany and Switzerland already recognise that animals are 'beings'; while the constitution of Ecuador recognises the rights of Nature (see Postscript).

Environmental laws all over the world are giving increasing attention to how our societies make decisions that affect the environment — in other words they are focusing on the process of change. Many countries now require environmental impact assessments of proposed projects to be done before a decision is taken whether or not to authorise them. Some require strategic environmental assessments of public policies, programmes and plans, and others prescribe principles that officials must give effect to when making decisions affecting the environment.

This is not the place to attempt a proper assessment of the extent to which proto-wild law provisions already exist. Certainly, most legal provisions and other governance mechanisms that could be seen as reflecting Earth jurisprudence have almost certainly not come about as a result of any conscious desire to implement a new Earth-centred jurisprudence. They are probably more the result of intelligent and informed responses to particular problems. Nevertheless, experiences with these techniques are likely to prove valuable in further developing Earth jurisprudence. Some further ideas about what could be done are given below.

OPEN SPACES WITHIN WHICH EARTH-CENTRED CULTURES CAN FLOURISH

In the 19th Century in Britain, as a result of the so-called 'enclosures', much of the common land was fenced off and given to private landowners, primarily to farm sheep. Communities had used these spaces from time immemorial, not only for grazing their animals and generating livelihoods, but also to enjoy nature, and to celebrate an array of diverse carnivals and rituals. Depriving them of access to the commons had a devastating effect on community life, and radically altered British society. A similar process of enclosure has fenced us out, both physically and mentally, from the Earth Community. The intricate and glorious diversity of relationships that previously existed between people and their environments is rapidly disappearing under the sterile, global uniformity of parking-lot culture.

One of the things that we can begin to do in order to express Earth jurisprudence is to consciously open spaces within the dominant legal systems within which communities can begin to give expression to an Earth-centred worldview. This might take many different forms, including: supporting the rights of indigenous people to live in accordance with their own cultures; reclaiming the right to grow crops that are not 'approved varieties'; and claiming the rights to keep areas free of genetically modified organisms.

EXPAND HUMAN-CENTRED DECISION-MAKING PROCESSES

One of the ways of influencing the direction in which our societies develop is to change decision-making processes so that they make it more likely that decisions will reflect an Earth-centred worldview. For example, in the dominant legal cultures many decisions of public bodies must be made 'in the public interest' or 'for the public good'. The relevant legislation could be changed or reinterpreted so that the decision-makers are required to refer to the interests of the whole Earth Community instead of only to human interests (narrowly interpreted). We would then have begun to move towards self-regulation in a manner that maintains the whole. Even if such a change did not have much impact on the decisions that are made at first, it would serve a valuable educational and consciousness-changing function.

Once there was more acceptance of Earth jurisprudence, one could begin to revisit and re-interpret other common legal phrases. For example, many legal systems have provisions that permit the normal legal rules to be overridden 'in the national interest' or in the interests of 'national security'. Why shouldn't the taking of special measures to be justified on the basis of 'biosecurity' (protecting the biodiversity of an area from threats, usually invasive alien organisms) or even 'Earth integrity'?

Other useful techniques for making decision-making less anthropocentric include requiring the decision-maker to look at a wider range of information (e.g. studies relating to the long-term cumulative impacts of a human activity), or to apply certain principles (e.g. that all living creatures have intrinsic value irrespective of their usefulness to humans). In both instances this will help to dilute the influence of purely commercial, and other exclusively human-oriented factors, on the decision.

LIMITING THE AMBIT OF HUMAN POWERS

Humans have had a very profound impact on the physical aspects of Earth within a very short space of time, particularly during the 19th and 20th Centuries. However in the course of expanding the considerable ambit of our physical and technological powers we have also convinced ourselves that it is proper for us to be governing that over which we have power. Our notable lack of success in governing the natural world is now reflected in the growing emphasis on improving 'environmental management' techniques in order to ameliorate the worst excesses of the dictatorship of our species.

In fact, just because we can change virtually all aspects of our environment does not mean that we ought to govern and legislate for all these aspects of Earth. Instead of trying in vain to perfect our environmental management techniques so that we may better manage Earth, we should focus on the proper province of human jurisprudence and law — the self-regulation of human beings.

This also involves accepting that there are certain limitations to the ambit of what it is appropriate for humans to control — such as Earth's climate. Certain human interventions, such as consciously effecting radical alterations to Earth's climate, or destroying the habitat of another species to the extent that its extinction is inevitable, must not be capable of having legal legitimacy under human jurisprudence. From the perspective of the Community, such a decision would be illegitimate and invalid in the sense that it cannot be justified on the basis of the Great Jurisprudence. We need a jurisprudence that says to those who wish to undertake such actions, that humans do not have the power to authorise actions that strike at the heart of the Earth Community of which we are a part. On the contrary, every human has a duty to resist practices that betray our most fundamental obligations to the Earth Community.

These limitations on the extent of human powers to govern must be reflected in our governance systems in a fundamental way that ensures that politicians engaged in determining national policies with an eye to their short-term political careers cannot override them. If this were done, any law or authorisation that had the effect of allowing Earth-threatening activities would be regarded as being null, and of no legal effect.

MOVING FROM MANAGEMENT TO DEMOCRATIC PARTICIPATION

As discussed in Chapter Eight, humans need both to recognise that other members of the Earth Community have a 'right to self-determination' and to restrain ourselves from impinging on these rights. However, we need to go beyond that, and to recognise that in relating to other subjects within the Community, we need to abandon a dominating management model in favour of an approach that is more analogous to democracy. I do not mean this in a literal 'one-species-one-vote' kind of way. However, an Earth democracy, like a human democracy, would recognise the right of all to be heard, and that it is legitimate to restrain the interests of a particular group in order to promote the greater, democratically determined good of the whole Community.

This may not be realistic to achieve within our present cultural frameworks, but grassroots social movements based on a recognition that humans must protect the interests of other members of the Earth family within an 'Earth democracy' are already growing. For example, the Earth Democracy Movement in India is based on the understanding that:

- the freedom of all life forms on Earth is indivisible;

- justice, peace and sustainability are indivisible, because true justice cannot exist without sustainability and fair access to the earth's bounties, and without justice there can be no peace;

- every form of life is intrinsically valuable, and diversity is to be prized because it signifies freedom, whereas monocultures are produced by the dominance of one species, variety, race, or religion, and the exclusion of others.[3]

ENCOURAGE PRACTICES THAT HONOUR AND RESPECT THE EARTH COMMUNITY

As with any community, harmonious co-existence within the Earth Community requires the observance of a certain etiquette based on an understanding and respectful recognition of the needs of other members. Our cultures once embodied ritual practices that reminded humans that they did not have an unqualified right to kill or use other members of the Community. Respect for the sanctity of other forms of life, and the honouring of the sacrifice of the lives of other animals and plants so that humans might live, were woven into the fabric of social life through ritual offerings, sacrifices and thanksgivings. Often a strong sense of the importance of maintaining a balance of energy or of other forces, meant that these societies consciously considered whether or not their activities would result in an imbalance, or infringe on the rights of other beings, and where appropriate, they took corrective action.

Today, although many international declarations and conventions call for nature to 'be respected', the rituals and other mechanisms for doing so have disappeared. Humans within the dominant societies no longer observe any etiquette or ethics in relating to the rest of the Earth Community, and instead base most 'environmental management' decisions on a combination of scientific models and economics. Once one shifts perspective out of the homosphere, it is clear that a theory of economics that is designed to allocate 'scarce resources' among humans as efficiently as possible, cannot possibly provide a sound basis for a respectful relationship with Earth. Indeed, we know that those human relations that are based solely on economic considerations tend to be characterised by an absence of mutual respect and true intimacy. Even concepts such as sustainability tend to be focussed on determining the maximum level of exploitation that can be sustained, rather than on maintaining a healthy balance.

DO AWAY WITH DEGRADING LAWS AND PRACTICES

People look to laws as an indication of what is right, and the role of laws in shaping people's ethical attitudes is often as important as the reverse. In the South Africa that I grew up in, the apartheid worldview found expression in a body of laws that prevented people from different ethnic backgrounds living in the same areas, going to school together or even having sexual relations with one another. These laws helped to perpetuate and legitimise the falsehoods and misconceptions inherent in apartheid, and made it difficult or impossible for those who believe in non-racialism from living in accordance with those beliefs. When democracy finally dawned in South Africa in 1994 and the discriminatory laws were repealed, it did not result in the immediate emergence of a non-racial community. However there is no doubt that removing those laws did a great deal to create the conditions under which a more just society was possible, particularly when reinforced by a Bill of Rights that specifically forbids discrimination.

One of the best ways of beginning to change towards a more Earth-centred governance system is by beginning a process of systematically identifying, modifying and replacing those legal doctrines and theories that obstruct or prevent people playing a responsible role in the Earth Community. Legal recognition of the fact that living creatures are not objects and must be respected, is a start. Another example might be placing new obligations on self and all other living things that inhabit it. This would be an important and educational step forward, particularly if anyone who failed to do so was required to spend time restoring the damage in person, and so have an opportunity to reconnect with land.

DEVELOP NEW REGULATORY MECHANISMS

It is also important to bear in mind that though it may be difficult, it is vitally important for our species to develop effective ways of preventing humans and legal persons from continuing to violate the Earth rights of other aspects of the Earth Community. One of the striking differences between modern societies and tribal communities that live in a close relationship with the natural world, is that tribal communities generally do not use prisons to regulate human behaviour. Mostly the members of the Community place such a high value on their membership of it and the maintenance of mutually respectful relations within it, that they take great care to observe the Community's customs and laws. When they fall short, rituals and other social mechanisms are used to restore damaged relations.

Today many of us live in a global society that has been 'de-socialised' in many respects, and this is even more true of legal persons such as companies and nation states, which do not function within true communities. This is one of the reasons why the governance techniques that worked in traditional societies no longer seem to assist us. As discussed in Chapter Thirteen, creating and strengthening new communities based on shared values will be an important step in re-establishing 'social sanctions' as a potent force in regulating human societies. Reawakening a sense of the sacred dimension of Earth is likely to be an important part of this. If one compares modern governance structures with those of tribal communities in relation to their effectiveness in regulating human relationships with the Earth Community, it suggests that sanctity, and not sanction, works best.

RE-PRIORITISE

Sometimes it seems as if we have forgotten that some legal rights and issues are more important than others and require different treatment. For example, the current international debate about whether or not the trade rules of the World Trade Organisation should take precedence over obligations to protect the environment contained in multilateral environment agreements like the Convention on Biological Diversity, would be ludicrous were it not so tragic. The idea that legal rules designed to foster free trade (which will only bring significant benefits to a few of the wealthiest humans) should be treated on a par with obligations intended to preserve absolutely fundamental aspects of the Earth Community, is absurd and wrong — as is the notion that a corporation's 'right' to profit from its manipulations of plants that co-evolved over millennia should take precedence over the rights of poor farmers to save and propagate seeds. It is time for the governments of the world to set aside their obsequiousness to the corporations, and make it clear that there can be no balancing of the fundamental Earth rights of the Earth Community and the 'rights' derived from human laws, such as freedom of trade or freedom of contract.

BRING WISDOM BACK

One of the toughest challenges may be to find a place for wisdom at the governance table. There are of course, wise people in government all over the world. However we need to face up to the reality that the institutional arrangement of our governance systems and the incentive systems incorporated within them, are not designed to promote or reward wise decision-making. In fact, wisdom of the kind needed to begin healing our relations with Earth is not only undervalued in the corridors of power; it has been absent so long that the very word has a strangely archaic ring to it. Again, this is an area where it would be helpful to consult ancient traditional practices for inspiration and guidance.

REDUCE THE DISTANCE BETWEEN THE DECISION AND THE IMPACT

It seems that the more 'sophisticated' our political and regulatory systems become, the more complex the instructions to be transmitted, the more layers of bureaucracy to be negotiated, and the greater the distance between the decision-makers and both the issues concerned and the consequences of their decisions. The longer this chain, the more likely it is that decisions will be made for communities (both human communities and ecological communities) by outsiders with little or no experience of the community. I am well aware that, for example, the environmental authorities of a central government can play a vital role in restraining local communities from making environmentally harmful decisions, particularly under the influence of powerful individuals or corporations. However, in the long term it will be important to consciously build the ability of stable communities with long-term relationships with particular ecosystems to regulate themselves as far as possible. If our governance systems are to evolve to higher levels of sophistication, they must be able to be adapted and fine-tuned for local conditions.

PART 5

The terrain ahead

The silence of landscape conceals vast presence. Place is not simply location. A place is a profound individuality. Surface texture of grass and stone is blessed by rain, wind and light. With complete attention, landscape celebrates the liturgy of the seasons, giving itself unreservedly to the passion of the goddess.

John O'Donohue, *Anam Cara*

Chapter 15

The mountain path

RETURNING TO THE MOUNTAINS

In Chapter Six I likened the Great Jurisprudence to the mountains of the Cape Peninsula that I can see from my window. The mountains have been my constant companion during the winding turns of this story. Constant, but ever changing. Dark and still in the grey of morning. Now, in the first slanting light of a mid-winter's morning, the ridges cast dramatic profiles across the steep face, the ravines still deep in shadow. In an imperceptible moment the sun breathes browns, ochres and greens into the landscape. The hadedas appear flying high, pairs of white-winged Egyptian geese hiss past on their way to the feeding grounds and the calm quickens into life. The sun climbs and the dark patches on the cliffs begin to retreat into the ledges and overhangs, and to soak into the patches of forest.

Yesterday the mountains were lost in mists, but today they are still and clear and calm. Beauty reaches across the space between us to touch my heart and to call my imagination out from between the books. Hard-ridged, but weathered by the millennia into slopes up which the forests and fynbos shrubs creep like quiet supplicants. Advancing respectfully with crowns bowed to be nearer, but not presuming to cover the mountains' craggy visage. The mountains do not do things, they simply are. Yet through their being and the slow geological changes of their becoming, they give much to the biological communities that throng the slopes. Satisfying their thirst with amber waters drawn down from the clouds rolling over the summit. Replenishing also those like me who raise their eyes to contemplate the grandeur of the ancient granite and sandstone faces.

I hope that we will remember once more that, like the forests, we live on Earth's flanks, that we will understand again the necessity—and beyond that, the great purpose—for adapting ourselves to the mountains: for adapting our civilisations to its form, and rooting ourselves deeply in its soil until no-one can say where one ends and the other begins. Nature, human nature and culture will then be recognised once more as an indivisible continuum.

In this book I have journeyed far across a landscape that sometimes fades away into the dusk and sometimes stands out clearly in my imagination.

Often I have stumbled and sometimes I have found gaps through the boulders. In this last chapter I want to glance back for a moment at the landscape that we have traversed, before looking at what might lie ahead for us, as always trying to remember to look with both intellect and heart.

THE LOGIC

I believe that there is a strong logical argument for fundamentally changing the governance systems of most (if not all) countries, as well as the international legal and political order. Earth is deteriorating rapidly. The apparent economic successes of the dominant cultures are built on consuming and wasting the natural 'capital' of Earth, and on increasing the inequalities between people, and between people and the other members of the Earth Community. Every year the warning signs become clearer and the irreversible loss greater. This cannot continue indefinitely. It is also tragic, particularly for our descendants and other members of the Earth Community. Even from an entirely human-centred perspective, humans ought not to continue on this destructive path.

If we are to halt and reverse the process of degrading Earth we *must* completely revise how we govern ourselves. Thomas Berry and others are correct when they draw attention to the fact that this will require us to move away from some of the fundamental beliefs and the mythologies so dear to the cultures that currently dominate world society. In particular, we must reject the misperception that humans are separate from Earth, and recognise that every aspect of our well-being is derived from Earth. The conscious reintegration of human societies into the Earth Community will not be possible until we can conceive of an Earth jurisprudence that allows us once more to assume our rightful place as an integral part of the larger community of beings.

In the legal and political sphere, the challenge for those who wish to respond to Thomas Berry's call "to assist in establishing a mutually enhancing human presence upon the Earth"[1] is to develop a coherent philosophical foundation for the development of more appropriate laws to govern human behaviour. Laws must contain within them an element of 'wildness'. In order to develop Earth jurisprudence, wild law and functioning Earth governance systems, we must consciously attune ourselves to the wider context of nature. We need to draw on the wisdom of those communities that have successfully adapted to Earth, and to remember to temper our theories in the heat of experience.

This is a challenging task, particularly for those of us who have been brought up within the 'homosphere', that mythical world of human separation, mastery and superiority. It requires us to learn how to think without being constrained by how our cultures understand the world. The worldview of these cultures is now so pervasive that it has soaked into virtually every aspect of our social lives. It has affected our understanding of ourselves, of time, spirituality, meaning, and of our purpose and role as humans. Discussing these issues is often difficult, because even the language that we use is stained with this worldview. Words and concepts that we use to think about and express core ideas about governance such as 'rights' and 'justice' are deeply embedded in our current culture, and are burdened with unhelpful meanings and associations from the existing systems.

The task is urgent. Changing governance structures is usually a slow process. As the GEO-3 report observes, "Much of the environmental change that will occur over the next 30 years has already been set in motion by past and current actions . . . many of the effects of environmentally relevant policies put into place over the next 30 years will not be apparent until long afterwards."[2] Meanwhile the Community is being irreparably damaged at a rate that is accelerating in many cases. This is reducing the options available to us, and dramatically increasing the sacrifices that will have to be made eventually if our civilisations are ever to become ecologically sustainable.

Activists, policy-makers, public sector decision-makers, legislators and concerned people everywhere desperately need a coherent philosophy that can provide a rationale for, and guide to, the reorientation and reconstituting of human societies. Unless we articulate a vision for regulating human behaviour in a manner that promotes the integrity of Earth, the worldview of the homosphere will continue to dominate by default. This means that, despite the inadequacies of the current systems, the form of the laws and institutions that profoundly affect the health of the whole Earth Community will continue to be determined by an acquisitive and destructive minority within the dominant societies of a single species.

From a logical perspective, one could say that the argument that I have presented in this book goes more or less as follows.

1. We humans are an integral and inseparable part of the Earth system.

2. This essential unity means that humans and our social systems are inextricably embedded within and influenced by the context of the larger Earth Community.

3. Therefore, the way we govern ourselves must of necessity be consistent with this context and must have as its purpose to ensure that the pursuit of human well-being does not undermine the integrity of Earth, which is the source of our well-being.

4. Human fulfilment is unattainable outside of a web of healthy relationships with the wider community of life on Earth.

5. Only by creating a jurisprudence that reflects the reality that human societies are part of a wider Earth Community and must observe certain

universal principles, will we be able to begin a comprehensive transformation of our societies and legal systems.

6. In order to reorient our governance systems to reflect this Earth jurisprudence we need to establish laws that are 'wild' at heart in the sense that they foster, rather than stifle, creativity and the human connection to nature.

7. To implement wild laws effectively, we will need to cultivate personal and social practices that respect Earth, and social structures based on communities, and communities of communities, as found in nature.

THE SOUL

This logical argument is not the whole story. Perhaps more importantly, I am pleading for the recognition that what we call 'governance' needs soul. Not 'soul' in the sense of an immortal soul (although there are parallels) but in the sense of a quality of depth, connection, and emotional and intellectual substance. This depth and connection is closely associated with the wild creativity that runs through the heart of humans back into the wild spaces and times that are our heritage and the context within which we belong.

When we connect our ideas about how to constitute and 'govern' society with a clearer understanding of our role as people and how we 'govern' our own behaviour, the continuum of being and acting in the physical world becomes clearer. We define who we are as individuals by how we act in relationships with others. For example, we are only honest if we behave honestly in our relations with others. Honest behaviour is the result of consistently choosing to act in a manner that accords with certain values rather than any of the many other different courses of action available to us. Therefore a person can only be honest by choosing over and over again to relate to others in a certain way. The same can be said for a society. If the society does not make repeatedly consistent choices to fight corruption it becomes corrupt, and so will many of its members.

Earth governance is concerned with who we are as individuals, as communities, as human societies, and as a species. It is not something that can exist solely in the external legal and political realm. I am also increasingly convinced that it is not something that is divisible. In other words, we need to understand that the systems that we establish to govern ourselves at every level both reflect who we are, and play an important role in shaping who we become. Whether we are choosing to separate our household waste, or to enact legislation holding polluters liable for environmental damage, we are demonstrating what we value (i.e. who we now are) and choosing to influence who we will become. One of the difficulties is that the more distant and detached our governance systems become from ordinary people, the more we feel that it has very little to do with us or who we are as individuals. Indeed, many of us have made the mistake of thinking that we could leave protecting the environment up to governments. The years since the environment was first put on the international governance agenda at the 1972 Stockholm Conference on the Human Environment and then brought to the fore at the 1992 Earth Summit,[3] have demonstrated that this is insufficient. How we relate to the rest of the Earth Community is so central to who we are that we all need to take personal responsibility for ensuring that our conduct helps the growth of Earth governance instead of negating it.

One of the reasons why these global issues are also so personal is because degrading Earth also degrades our inner souls or deeper sense of self. As Thomas Berry points out, whatever we do to the exterior world we do to our interior world. Stopping to experience a sunset recharges the soul, suffuses the mind with beauty and fills us with the breath of life. Scraping topsoil, plants and the rich community of life off land and covering it with concrete is also an assault on our inner world. If we continue too long on this course our consciousnesses, and those of the generations who follow us, will no longer be shaped through interaction with the beauty, diversity, and sheer unexpectedness of nature. Concrete parking lots breed parking-lot minds: uniform, barren, predictable and devoid of any sacred or transcendental meaning. How many great works of art or literature do you suppose our parking lots will inspire? How many laws on our statute books *are* inspired by this outlook?

However, if you ask a lawyer in most contemporary societies whether or not a law or a system of governance has 'soul', you are likely to get a very strange look indeed! This question does not make sense within our paradigm. It is irrelevant and consequently inadmissible within the court of logic. Yet this is a question that ought to be considered. It is a matter that deserves serious attention and should not be dismissed out of hand as romantic extravagance.

One way to begin the process of assessing the deeper substance and purpose of a particular aspect of a governance system is to consider whether or not it contradicts the Great Jurisprudence or the principles of Earth jurisprudence in any way. For example, one might ask whether the law creates rights for humans in relation to other beings that are not balanced with appropriate responsibilities? Does it interfere with other Earth citizens' Earth right of 'self-determination'? What is the purpose behind a particular law or legal rule, and what is its actual effect? Is this consistent with the overall purpose of our governance system? What effect is the purpose behind the particular law and the greater purpose behind the governance system likely to have on who we are becoming as individuals and as a society? Is this what we want?

It is important to consider not only in which respects the governance system falls short of the requirements of Earth jurisprudence, but also the extent to which it promotes Earth governance. In other words, does the law, rule or governance system help to create an appropriate environment within which wildness can flourish and communities can thrive? This means enquiring into the extent to which the law allows for the development of diverse approaches to meet the needs of different places, times and communities. How might it affect how local ecosystems and human communities change over the next few hundred years or more? Is it something that is capable of being integrated into a way of life?

When looking for the presence of this kind of soul in law and governance, it helps to ask questions about connection. Ask yourself whether or not the effect of a particular aspect of a governance system is likely to increase or decrease the intimacy of relationships. Will it promote community and a sense of belonging? For example, these questions will yield very different answers when asked in relation to a dispute resolution system based on the idea of restorative justice (discussed in Chapter Five) and when asked in relation to a typical, revenge-oriented criminal justice system.

Soul, or the loss of it, is a very real issue in many societies. So many people now have a great, often inarticulate, sense of loss and being lost. It is felt in shanty towns as well as penthouses. It stems from the detachment in heart and soul that comes from having become strangers to our wider Earth Community. We are made of the same earth and breathe the same air. Yet many of us humans have wandered so far from Earth that we do not even recognise those with whom we co-evolved in intimacy, as family. Speaking of this kinship now sounds crazy to many people. It sounds even stranger to mention detachment and 'loss of soul' as an issue that governance should be concerned with. It is time to stop ignoring these issues. Those in governance can no longer ignore soul issues any more than biologists can ignore the creativity and consciousness inherent in life. Our governance systems must become sophisticated enough to be sensitive to how we do things and conscious of the need to express the purpose of adapting ourselves to play our role within the Earth Community.

THE PRACTICE

Simply recognising the need for 'soul' is not enough. Earth jurisprudence is not merely a theory, it must be a living practice, a way of life. We must also learn to observe Earth jurisprudence personally by including in our lives little rituals and practices that respect, honour and celebrate Earth and rededicate ourselves to deepening our connection with the whole. As so many religions and ancient philosophies teach us, practising small acts of observance and respect are a way of deepening and adding meaning to our lives. In this case, for Earth's sake and our own, we need to weave Earth-centred practices into who we are as people.

We are told today that Innuit never had laws or maligait ('things that have to be followed'). Why? Because they are not written on paper. When I think of paper I think you can tear it up and the laws are gone. The maligait of the Innuit are not on paper. They are inside people's heads and they will not disappear or be torn to pieces. Even if a person dies, the maligait will not disappear. It is part of a person. It is what makes a person strong.

Innuit elder, Mariano Aupilaarjuk[4]

In this way they will also become woven into the fabric of our communities and be part of who we become as a species.

We also need to consider the practices of our societies. What ceremonies and practices characterise, for example, decision-making concerning our relations with the Earth Community? Do these practices support or hinder us from becoming what we wish to become as societies? If we ask these kinds of questions, it is soon apparent that most decision-making is done in a manner that obstructs connection with the reality of Earth. We decide the fates of local Earth Communities on the basis of documents, in distant, sealed rooms where we cannot hear their songs, and their beauty is forgotten. We rush through the papers in obedience to timetables and in fear of inefficiency, yet leaving an eternity to regret our follies. In extreme instances, like the dispute resolution proceedings of the World Trade Organisation, we make rules to keep people out and to ensure that issues more weighty than economic efficiency (like the protection of the environment) cannot be fully considered. Should we really be surprised when the consequences of WTO jurisprudence is destructive of Earth and its communities, when the legitimacy or otherwise of national laws and other measures are allowed to be decided by remote, undemocratic bodies on the basis of what is least burdensome for international trade, with no consideration of their effect on burdening Earth, and when there is no superior body to overrule trade rules for Earth's sake?

It is also time to make time and space for wisdom in our governance systems. Instead of always prioritising the things that seem most urgent, we must now look at what is most important. Ironically, protecting Earth is also extremely urgent, but this is not so apparent because most decision-makers who operate on short political cycles are insensitive to the longer cycles and rhythms of nature. There are very many ways in which this could be done. A useful start would probably be for groups of public officials and other concerned people to stop doing what they usually do, go on a retreat and begin to consider some of these issues.

When we remember the wildness that connects us with all life, we will belong again. When we experience our role within the Earth Community once more, we will be able to see that we cannot separate how we govern our societies from who we are. As indigenous people know, it is our 'laws' and practices that make us who we are, as societies and as individuals.

THE PATH

Earth jurisprudence is also a path. I draw confidence from its existence, not only because I can see it flowing from under my feet into the future, but also because I imagine it as a mountain path. It is a path that connects the busy city lowlands with the quiet wisdom of the peaks, a wild path that leads toward life and away from the destruction of the Community of Earth.

Anyone who walks down a particular path chosen among many possible paths is also choosing to live with purpose. Walking this particular mountain path is also about choosing a particular role for humankind within the Community. Many of us have been searching for a role for our species that we can identify wholeheartedly with. Watching your own community playing a destructive role can be hard to bear if you cannot see any way out of the situation except by rejecting your culture and people. (In similar circumstances, the self-esteem of many young white South Africans was corroded away by internalised guilt and resentment during the apartheid regime.) One of the most positive aspects of exploring the path of Earth governance is that it also involves embracing the whole Earth Community and the special responsibility of our species within it. Humans are unusually gifted members of the Community. Our technologies and arts demonstrate our amazing powers to imagine and then to focus the power of will to transform these visions into physical creations.

But our responsibility to the Earth is not simply to preserve it, it is to be present to the Earth in its next sequence of transformations. While we were unknowingly carried through the evolutionary process in former centuries, the time has come when we must in some sense guide and energise the process ourselves.

Thomas Berry, *The Great Work*, p.173

Imagine what might happen if we consciously set out to play a constructive part in co-creating the future of Earth and applied these abilities for the benefit of the whole Community.

Practical-minded readers may by now be frustrated with the absence of a set of prescriptions and next steps to 'solve' the governance crises that I have referred to. Although I have alluded to some specific things that could be done, I have tried to avoid being too specific or prescriptive in the belief that at this stage the most important task was to convey my sense of what Earth governance, Earth jurisprudence and wild law is about. Nevertheless, it is appropriate to end by giving some sense of what some of the next steps down this path might be.

The main imperative is to widen the discussion of these ideas so that more people, each with different insights and perspectives, can begin to contribute to the development of these approaches. We will also need to deepen our enquiries. My discussion of many crucial issues, including what we can learn from indigenous cultures and the deeper significance of scientific discoveries,

Like us, competitive ancient bacteria created cities, pollution crises, genocide, and gross inequities. But eventually they learnt to share their remarkable technologies in huge cooperative multicreatured cells. Is it now up to us, among the most recent of multi-celled creatures, to recognise Earth as the giant cell within which we must live together—with each other and all other species?

Liebes, Sahtouris and Swimme, *A Walk Through Time*, p.191

particularly those relating to the nature of living systems, has been superficial.

There are many areas in which people have already done in-depth studies that could be enormously valuable in refining our ideas about Earth governance.

There is vast potential for humanity if we consciously begin governing ourselves and our societies for Earth; if we participate willingly as good Earth citizens in the co-evolution of our planet, and use our abilities for the benefit of the Community. We also need to act: the critical condition of so many ecological communities on Earth and of some of Earth's life supporting systems demand it. The perspectives offered by Earth jurisprudence, even in its present rudimentary form, can be of great practical value to social and environmental activists, particularly those who work in communities. This approach can facilitate the development of a common framework that links many different social and environmental campaigns. In many cases the different issues are simply different symptoms of the same deficiencies in governance. However, earth jurisprudence is not only a useful basis for critiquing current systems, it also provides guidance on how to develop alternatives. I hope that the ideas discussed in this book will help those involved in the mainstream of law to understand that 'the environment' cannot be adequately dealt with simply by creating a new category of environmental law. Ultimately, all law must be based upon and reflect Earth jurisprudence, as must all the institutional structures of our societies. For all of us it represents a challenge to look deep into ourselves and to discover or invent Earth-centred practices that we can use to deepen our connection to Earth and to grow Earth governance from the inside outwards. A good next step would be to get people who are concerned about the current direction of our societies to begin to talk about these ideas. Perhaps to convene meetings at which groups can explore the ideas more fully. To build networks of collaborators and to share examples of 'best practice' so that we can all expand our vision of what is practically possible and benefit from the great diversity of human experience and knowledge, remembering always to ground our emerging theories in the reality of Earth and to check them against the pulse of experience.

When we feel confused or become lost in complex abstractions, it is important not to forget to go back to the beginning and connect once more with our common ground. To walk wet-footed in the cold grass of dawn, to breathe clean air, and turn the rough surfaces of a stone in our hands, until we remember who we are and why this is important. May we all find our paths home to the intimacy of the Earth Community.

Postscript:

The emergence of Wild Law

A BUDDING COMMUNITY

There is something insurrectionary about buds. They are by nature secretive, and I never notice them emerging. It is only when the lengthening days draw my eyes to the bare branches in search of signs of spring that I see the small, hard, brown nodules already gathered on the thin, wet, winter branches. It seems improbable then that each tight pellet will swell and burst into leaf, but they do. Quite suddenly a sunny spell charms them into abandoning caution, and they arch into silky catkins or burst into fragile leaflets. Secrecy and protection is cast aside by the intoxicating promise of photosynthesis. Caution is abandoned to float soft lime-green canopies into the risky open air – living kites to catch the precious rays and breathe in the carbon-laden air. Urgently unfurling, they spread palmate veins and soft sails which thicken greenly as they alchemise the dark powers of the soil, the invisible structures of air and the glorious radiance of sunlight into new life and food. Magically, last week's buds now provide food for caterpillars and aphids, for the predatory larvae and insects that follow and for the chicks which fatten and fledge on the bounty which their parents stuff into their orange gapes.

The forest has been plotting this moment all winter. Even as the trees withdrew their sap from the dying autumn leaves they were preparing for this. Last season's fallen leaves laying down their nutrients in the humus were already preparing for their return. Forces were gathering in the silence of the soil, stirring in hidden roots and establishing clandestine cells for the time when Earth inclined her face again to the sun and the warmth tipped the balance in favour of new growth.

Ideas are like buds. Some emerge too soon and quickly wither in inhospitable times; some flower gloriously but briefly. Others that push slowly up from the humus of collective consciousness are deceptively innocent at first. Their emergence may be unremarkable – their full meaning, power and potential form still tightly bound in dense forms until the turning of some great tide begins to draw the flow of thought through them. Under the influence of some mysterious field they begin to thicken with energy, and new dendrites fan out out like brambles connecting vast new webs of thought in our collective consciousness.

It is only now becoming clear to me that the ideas of wild law and Earth jurisprudence are buds of this kind. They have grown quietly and unremarkably for the most part, drawing on the rich nutrients laid down by many earlier thinkers and writers and spreading by word of mouth from one small group to another. However deep underground in the darkness of the collective unconscious something is stirring and the buds are quite suddenly beginning to swell and thicken with energy. Suddenly there are buds everywhere and I can feel a new *Zeitgeist* rising like sap, a wild flow that is stretching and popping the old veins. It is as if when the timing is right, new ideas attract one another and cohere in narrow channels to create a powerful capillary action that draws them up into the collective consciousness despite the mainstream inertia.

Writing *Wild Law* was a political act of sorts, in the sense that I was motivated primarily by the desire to create a means of spreading the ideas more efficiently. I found them difficult to explain to someone in a brief conversation and thought that a book might help to broadcast the ideas more widely – in other words be a communication tool. What I didn't then fully appreciate was that this book was itself a small bud of something far larger – that others all over the world were tapping into the same wild sap that fed my writing and making sense of it in their own ways. Today I am clear that far from *Wild Law* driving these ideas, it is but one expression of a new *Zeitgeist* that is rising everywhere. A wild consciousness is swelling rebellious growth all over the world. And this is happening just as the energy and promise of a better future that drove the growth of the industrial civilisations drains away and they begin to circle in confusion – perplexed at how to respond to converging crises. How does a society built on consumerism, incessant economic growth and the profligate consumption of fossil fuels deal with potentially fatal challenges, such as climate change, which are driven by those same forces? The psychic and physical energies that fuel industrial civilisations are also fuelling the forces that will destroy them. These challenges cannot be addressed successfully from within the worldview that gave rise to them. Consequently the solutions remain invisible to all who will not step into a new perspective.

In a few short years Earth jurisprudence and the idea of wild law have gained wide acceptance and there is now a growing number of people all over the world who are committed to finding ways of governing themselves and their communities as a part of the Earth community. These people are also part of a wider community of millions who are actively seeking ways of bringing into being new societies based on social justice and ecological health. Organisations and individuals dedicated to these ideals have been around for decades (and longer in some cases), but this community is only now birthing itself as it begins to reflect on itself as a whole and to notice that many of these groups share a cultural DNA of common values and aspiration which has the potential to enable them to combine into a whole that is much greater than the sum of the parts.

Some have tried to catalyse the emergence of this community by trying to help those within it to see that they are part of a greater whole. (The work of Paul Hawken, who has established the Wiser Earth website to enable organisation and individuals in the community to describe themselves and map their location and make themselves visible to one another, is a particularly good example of this). I believe that developing this self-consciousness, or sense of self, is an essential step in the birthing of a community that is able to function consciously as such. However, for such a community to be able to function effectively it will also have to articulate the core of shared values and beliefs that gives it form – no easy task in a world of great cultural diversity. I believe that despite the substantial cultural, philosophical, religious and political differences among the people in this emerging social movement, there is already a high degree of consensus about certain fundamental issues. Most would accept that humans exist within a larger community of life on which we are wholly dependent, and would like to see the establishment of societies that are not destructive of Earth, that respect the fundamental rights of its members and are motivated primarily by mutual empathy, caring and love – rather than fear, domination and competition. These values may seem trite, but there can be little doubt that the legal, political, economic and other societal structures of contemporary industrial civilisations were not designed to reflect or promote them. On the other hand, a governance system based on Earth jurisprudence principles would promote these values.

Perhaps in the longer term the greatest contribution of Earth jurisprudence will not be in the area of law but in demonstrating how we may be guided by the common language of the Earth community to redefine each aspect of society to align it with the fundamental principles of Earth's systems. This approach can take us beyond the multicultural ideological and religious minefields which bedevil attempts to formulate common values and approaches, to a common language that we can all understand and a community to which we all belong – that of Earth. If we want to articulate the common vision, values and principles that will animate and direct this emerging community, we must turn back to Earth and consciously adopt and seek to conform to Earth's preconditions for well-being. In this sense, Earth jurisprudence can be understood as part of a greater understanding that the pursuit of human happiness is best guided by attending to the fundamental wisdom embodied in Earth.

For me, probably the best thing about writing *Wild Law* has been the wonderful people it has brought me into contact with. They have encouraged and inspired me, argued and laughed with me, in the process convincing me that this is a company I want to be part of. Some are lawyers, other are conservationists, environmental consultants, farmers, psychologists, parents, students, artists, writers, film-makers or business people, but all are deeply concerned about the direction in which the dominant civilisations are heading and want to do something to change it. They are the people who are individually and collectively carrying the Earth jurisprudence message across the globe and pioneering ways of bringing wild law into being.

RECONNECTING WITH CUSTOMARY LAW ROOTS IN AFRICA

In Africa, the idea of Earth jurisprudence and its emphasis on deriving inspiration from indigenous customary law systems has been enthusiastically received by legal scholars, practitioners and community activists. The African Biodiversity Network, with support from the Gaia Foundation of London and from traditional healers and teachers of African customary law such as Colin and Niall Campbell, has played an important role in awakening lawyers and activists to the potential of drawing on centuries of indigenous wisdom to heal damaged relationships between people and their land.

Professor Melesse Damtie, who teaches law at the Civil Service College of Ethiopia, has inspired government officials to return to their regions and rediscover the ancient and almost forgotten wisdom of African customary law systems with a view to inspiring the development of more effective governance system that are consistent with both people and place. In Kenya, the late human rights lawyer Ng'ang'a Thiong'o and the NGO Porini were inspired by reconnecting with ancient African legal lineages to recover indigenous practices that teach people to respect and care for the Earth community. This has lead to renewed interest in the wisdom of tribal elders and to a successful application to court to restore to a community the right to conserve and manage sacred sites. In many other African countries, young social and environmental activists have began to seek advice from elders and to work on developing what they term 'community ecological governance'[1] which is based on a similar approach.

EARTH DEMOCRACY IN INDIA

In India, the celebrated environmental activist Dr Vandana Shiva coined the phrase 'Earth democracy' to describe a world view and political movement promoted by Navdanya (an organisation which she founded).[2] As Dr Shiva explains:

"Earth democracy is both an ancient worldview and an emergent political movement for peace, justice and sustainability. . . . It incorporates what in India we refer to as *vasudhaiva kutumbkam* (the earth family) – the community of all beings supported by the earth. . . . Earth democracy is not just a concept, it is shaped by the multiple and diverse practices of people reclaiming their commons, their resources, their livelihoods, their freedoms, their dignity, their identities, and their peace."[3]

The Earth democracy movement in India was started by Navdanya to provide:

"an alternative worldview in which humans are embedded in the Earth Family, we are connected with each other through love, compassion, not hatred and violence and ecological responsibility and economic justice replaces greed, consumerism and competition as objectives of human life."[4]

One of the reasons for the success of the Earth democracy movements is because they have reconnected people with pre-consumerist cultural understandings of the sacred dimensions of seeds, food, water and land. Navdanya have also drawn on traditions of resistance to colonial authority, for example, by employing the strategies of Mahatma Gandhi's salt *satyagraha* to resist legislation which allowed the patenting of seeds and other life forms.[5] As in Africa, the ideas of Earth jurisprudence are being carried forward by new organisations and approaches that reconnect people with an ancient sense of identity and fulfilment within a sacred community of life.

WILD WEEKENDS IN THE UNITED KINGDOM AND AUSTRALIA

For me these ideas took root in the United Kingdom, when a former colleague of mine, Donald Reid, organised a wonderful expedition led by David Key into the wilderness of the remote Knoydart Peninsula in Scotland. We explored and debated these ideas as we climbed through the hauntingly beautiful glens, long cleared of human habitation, and around the fire in the bothy in which we sought refuge from the tumultuous weather. As always, the wild place began to exert its influence and to draw us into its presence. The sense of the hardy clans unjustly cleared from their homes, the wild creatures of that place – the great shaggy stags and Cernunnos, the horned Celtic god which their discarded antlers evoked – rose into consciousness. We began to feel again what it must be like to belong, to be the kin of that place and all who dwell there, part of the timeless lineage of landscape and clan.

Later the idea of wild law captured the imagination of Elizabeth Rivers, who introduced it to Simon Boyle and others who brought it into the heart of the United Kingdom Environmental Law Association (UKELA). An initial conference on Wild Law and Earth Jurisprudence was held in 2004 at the University of Brighton and quickly metamorphosed into annual 'wild law weekends' held in the countryside. In 2008 UKELA established a formal Wild Law working group which arranges wild law weekends and other events, undertakes research and promotes the teaching of Earth jurisprudence at universities. The Gaia Foundation of London has also made Thomas Berry's *Great Work* and Earth jurisprudence central to its work, and promotes these ideas through talks, discussion, research and an online resource centre. The Gaia Foundation has also initiated courses on Earth jurisprudence and related subjects at Schumacher College in Devon.

Wild law conferences have also taken root in Australia. In October 2009 Peter Burdon organised the first conference in Adelaide; the following year Alex Pelizzon organised another near Sydney, and planning for the 2011 conference is already underway.

EARTH JURISPRUDENCE AND LOCAL DEMOCRACY IN THE UNITED STATES OF AMERICA

The first institution dedicated to Earth jurisprudence was established in Florida in 2006 as a joint project of the law faculties of the Catholic Universities of Barry and St Thomas. Inspired primarily by the work of Thomas Berry, sisters Patricia Siemen and Margaret Galiardi succeeded in securing grant funding to establish the Center for Earth Jurisprudence (CEJ) and to offer the first Earth jurisprudence seminar at the Barry Law School in Spring, 2007. The CEJ adopts a multi-disciplinary approach in seeking to develop a philosophy and practice of law that respect the rights of the natural world and recognise humans as an integral member of the Earth community. Its mission is to re-envision law and governance in ways that support and protect the health and well-being of the Earth community as a whole.[6]

An exciting new vista on Earth jurisprudence opened up for me when I connected with Thomas Linzey of the Community Environmental Legal Defense Fund (CELDF) of Pennsylvania in the United States of America. I had been asked by *Orion* magazine to write an article look at the contribution of Christopher Stone's seminal article 'Should Trees have Standing?' (which is discussed in Chapter 8). The features editor gave me Thomas Linzey's email address and suggested that I contact him as he was a lawyer who was working on rights for nature. I immediately emailed Thomas, and the next morning received his response saying that the evening before the Borough Council of Tamaqua County had become the first local government body in the USA to adopt an ordinance with recognised legally enforceable rights for natural communities and stripped corporations that unlawfully deposited sewage sludge on farmlands of their civil rights as juristic persons. I was amazed and thrilled to find that a contemporary example of wild law already existed in the United States, despite the fact that Thomas had not previously heard of Earth jurisprudence or read *Wild Law*.

A fruitful correspondence followed and after reading a copy of this book, Thomas invited me to accompany him in 2007 on a 'Rights for nature' speaking tour to about eleven law schools across the USA. We met for the first time at the second Earth jurisprudence conference convened by Sister Pat Siemen of the Center for Earth Jurisprudence in Florida, and immediately started a conversation which continued more or less unabated from Florida to Spokane and back to Pennsylvania. I was delighted and encouraged to find that a brilliant lawyer and community activist like Thomas and his colleagues in CELDF had arrived via a very different path at conclusions that were strikingly similar to my own. For them, the primary motivation had been the realisation that the current legal system in the USA favours corporations and that the odds are heavily stacked against local communities that wish to preserve healthy environments for themselves and their descendants. A careful analysis of how the original ideal of the American republic – that "the people shall govern" – had been displaced by a system that favoured the interests of corporations and those that control them, led the CELDF to conclude that local communities could only defend themselves successfully if they developed local laws that ensured that the fundamental rights of local people and ecological communities could trump those of corporations instead of vice versa. Thanks to the hard work and dedication of the CELDF and those who have passed through its democracy schools, a growing number of municipalities across the USA are adopting local ordinances and charters that recognise rights for nature.

LATIN AMERICA

One of the most significant advances to date has been the adoption in September 2008 by the people of Ecuador of a constitution that commits the state and citizens to seeking well-being in a manner that is harmonious with nature and that recognises the rights of nature. The preamble to the Constitution explicitly refers to the intention of the people of Ecuador "to build a new order of cohabitation for citizens, in its diversity and in harmony with nature, to achieve well being (which is defined by using both the Spanish term '*el buen vivir*' and the indigenous Quichwa term '*sumak kawsay*'). The

Constitution explains that "*El buen vivir* requires that individuals, communities, peoples and nationalities shall effectively enjoy their rights, and exercise responsibilities within the framework of inter-culturality, respect for their diversity and harmonious cohabitation with nature." (article 275).

The fundamental rights of nature are set out in Chapter 7 of the Constitution which provides that: "Nature or *Pachamama*, where life is reproduced and exists, has the right to exist, persist, and maintain and regenerate its vital cycles, structure, functions and its evolutionary processes." (article 72). It also provides that Nature has a right to be rehabilitated or have its integrity restored which is independent of any rights of compensation which may be claimed by people or groups that depend on the natural systems that have been impaired.

Importantly, the Constitution places specific obligations on people, legal entities like companies, and the State, to respect and uphold the rights of nature, and provides that these rights are legally enforceable. A duty is also imposed on all Ecuadorian men and women "to respect the rights of nature, preserve a healthy environment and use natural resources in a rational, viable and sustainable manner" (article 83(6)), and every person, people, community or nationality may require public bodies to recognize rights for nature.

The Constitution mandates the State to actively promote *buen vivir* including by guaranteeing the rights of nature (article 277), promoting "forms of production which will ensure quality of life for the people and shall discourage those which threaten those rights or those of nature ..." (article 319) and guaranteeing "a sustainable model of development, environmentally balanced and respectful of cultural diversity, which protects biodiversity and the natural capacity of ecosystems to regenerate, to ensure the needs of present and future generations will be met." (article 395(1))

These provisions effectively commit Ecuador to pursuing human well-being in a manner that does not threaten the rights of nature, rather than joining most other countries in pursuing the unachievable and socially and environmentally harmful goal of infinite growth in Gross Domestic Product.

These remarkable provisions came into being as a result of the collaboration between indigenous peoples and environmental organizations in Ecuador, supported by the CELDF of the USA and championed by Alberto Acosta, the president of the Constitutional Assembly charged with drafting the new constitution. The Fundacion Pachamama (a non-governmental organization working on environmental and indigenous rights issues in Ecuador) brought Thomas Linzey and Mari Margil of CELDF to Ecuador, where they found that the idea of providing for the legal recognition of the right of nature had immediate resonance because it was entirely consistent with the worldview of the indigenous peoples.

Since the adoption of the Ecuadorian constitution, defending the rights of Mother Earth has become a rallying cry for indigenous peoples and organizations concerned with stopping the terrible social and environmental destruction caused by industrial civilizations and globalisation.

On 22 April 2009 the United Nations General Assembly adopted a resolution proposed by Bolivia proclaiming 22 April as 'International Mother Earth Day'. In his speech to the General Assembly on that day, Bolivian President Evo Morales Ayma expressing the hope that, as the twentieth century had been called 'the century of human rights', the 21st Century would be known as 'the century of the rights of Mother Earth'. He called upon the member states to begin developing a 'Declaration on the Rights of Mother Earth' which, among other rights, would enshrine the right to life for all living things; the right for Mother Earth to live free of contamination and pollution; and the right to harmony and balance among and between all things.

The following month, on 21 May 2009, indigenous churches issued a joint declaration at the United Nations Permanent Forum on Indigenous Issues recommending that Forum recognize Mother Earth as a legal subject and expand human rights to include all forms of life. The declaration stated:

> "We recognize that the right to life is comprised not only of human beings, but also of all forms of life as well as Mother Earth who, for us, is alive. Our spirituality allows us to live in an interconnected manner because we know that all we do can affect the world's delicate balance. We do not separate our profound spirituality from our political struggles."

This was followed on 17 October 2009 by a declaration of the nine countries of the Bolivarian Alliance for the Peoples of Our America (ALBA) supporting the call for the adoption of a Universal Declaration of Mother Earth Rights. The Declaration expresses the fundamental principles of Earth Jurisprudence with great clarity, stating:

> "1. In the 21st Century it is impossible to achieve full human rights protection if at the same time we do not recognize and defend the rights of the planet earth and nature. Only by guaranteeing the rights of Mother Earth we can guarantee the protection of human rights. The planet earth can exist without human life, but humans cannot exist without planet earth.

> 2. Just as World War II caused a serious humanity crisis that in 1948 led to the adoption of the Universal Declaration of Human rights, today we are suffering the enormous consequences of Climate Change making it essential to have a Universal Declaration of Mother Earth Rights.

> 3. The ecological crisis, which global warming is a part of, is showing so palpably an essential principle that has been argued for centuries by the native and indigenous peoples all over the world: that human beings are part of an interdependent system of plants, animals, hills, forests, oceans and air that require our respect and care. This system is what we call Mother Earth. "Earth does not

belong to man, but man belongs to earth." The Earth is not a group of things that we can appropriate of, but it is a group of natural beings with whom we must learn to live together in harmony and balance respecting their rights."

After the failure of the December 2009 Copenhagen meeting of the Conference of the Parties of the United Nations Framework Convention on Climate Change (COP15) to agree on an international legal instrument to tackle climate change, the Bolivian President announced that Bolivia would host a People's World Conference on Climate Change and Mother Earth's Rights in April 2010. The Conference was intended to provide a forum at which the project of a Universal Declaration of Mother Earth's Rights, an International Tribunal on Climate Justice, and strategies for action and mobilisation to defend Mother Earth's rights, could be discussed and agreed.

Many people registered online to attend the People's World Conference, and as many as 15,000 people were expected to attend. Days before the Conference, ash from a volcanic eruption in Iceland closed European airports, preventing almost all European and Asian delegates, as well as many from other parts of the world, from attending. Despite this, more than 35,000 people attended and on Mother Earth Day, 22 April 2010, adopted a 'People's Agreement' and proclaimed a Universal Declaration of the Rights of Mother Earth (reproduced in the Appendix).

The Universal Declaration of the Rights of Mother Earth was produced by one of the Conference's 17 working groups, based on earlier drafts which had been posted on the internet for comment and discussed at a pre-conference meeting of indigenous people's organizations in Cochabamba. As co-President of the working group I was amazed by the commitment and passion of the 300–400 people who participated for many hours in working group meetings. One after another they spoke of their love of Mother Earth, the urgent necessity to defend her and to preserve the Andean glaciers on which their water supplies depend, and of the economic and political systems that were responsible for the sustained assault on Mother Earth and life itself. These were people, ranging from farmers from rural areas to academics and professionals, who collaborated to find the words to express to their perspective in legal language which the international community could understand. Despite having been colonized almost five centuries ago by cultures that denied and repressed their cosmologies, the indigenous peoples of the region still spoke with the fierce passion of people absolutely committed to the defence of their beloved native land and Mother. Everyone spoke of the urgency of acting decisively to stop the systematic and intentional assaults on Earth and life.

The contrast between Cochabamba and Copenhagen was striking. The Copenhagen COP 15 meeting was dominated by technical arguments about the precise level of abuse that the atmosphere could sustain without triggering catastrophic climate change, and bargaining about much of the 'carbon budget' each of the powerful nations would get and how little they would pay as 'adaptation funds' to those who had contributed least to the problem and would suffer most from it. It was all about national advantage, power and money, and concluded (perhaps fittingly) with a small group of countries striking a back-room deal that resulted in the 'Copenhagen Accord' which if implemented would result in many small island states disappearing and millions of people becoming refugees as huge areas became uninhabitable. Meanwhile on the other side of the barricades around the official meetings, the police were beating back and arresting the people who had gathered from all over the world to urge the nations of the world to work together to agree on the decisive action that the situation demanded.

I went to the Copenhagen COP 15 to speak at a side event on the Rights of Mother Earth which had been convened by the Bolivian government. What I saw there convinced me that the arteries of the international community of nations are too narrowed by short-term economic self-interest and hardened by outdated world-views to permit the flow of fresh ideas and decisive action that is now required. The energy and commitment that brought people who care deeply for Earth to Copenhagen in a desperate attempt to influence the formal negotiations, needed to create new channels through which to express itself.

Four months later the People's World Conference in Bolivia began to do exactly that. Instead of barricades to keep the people out, anyone could participate, and people stood patiently in long queues in the dusty streets to be accredited. Hundreds of people attended each of the 17 official working groups, and they spoke from experience of the social and ecological destruction which has been caused by political, legal and economic systems designed to facilitate human exploitation of Earth. The Copenhagen protestors had chanted "System change not climate change!", and system change was exactly what the People's World Conference discussed. The talk at Cochabamba was of addressing root causes and achieving fundamental changes in how our species relates to the Earth Community. It was about how to restore health to Mother Earth, not about how best to continue exploitative practices and adapt to living on a sick planet. In just two and half days the working groups articulated a common perspective about the key issues and what needed to be done to address them. The perspective set out in the resolution adopted by the Conference was remarkably coherent, consistent and detailed given the practical constraints involved. In a reversal of traditional international processes, the presidents of the working-groups then presented their findings to the presidents and other representatives of the governments which attended.

The proclamation by the people of a Universal Declaration of the Rights of Mother Earth is central to the process now underway to bring about fundamental changes to the legal, political and economic systems that currently dominate the world. The Declaration recognises that Earth is an indivisible, living community of interrelated and interdependent beings with inherent rights. It recognises that all natural entities which exist as part of Mother Earth, including plants, animals, rivers and ecosystems, are subjects who have the inherent and inalienable right to exist and to play their role within the community of beings. Unlike the Universal Declaration of Human Rights, the Declaration also defines fundamental human responsibilities in relation to other beings and to the community as whole. These range from the fundamental responsibility of every human being to respect and live in harmony with Mother Earth, to wider social responsibilities such as to establish and apply effective norms and laws for the defence, protection and conservation of the rights of Mother Earth.

The Declaration reflects the understanding that contemporary governance systems are part of the problem. The People's Agreement adopted at the People's World Conference states: "In an interdependent system in which human beings are only one component, it is not possible to recognize rights only of the human part without provoking an imbalance in the system as a whole. To guarantee human rights and to restore harmony with nature, it is necessary to effectively recognize and apply the rights of Mother Earth."

EARTH JURISPRUDENCE
AT THE INTERNATIONAL LEVEL

Earth jurisprudence burst into the international political arena remarkably quickly. Since first becoming visible to the international community in September 2008 with the adoption of the Ecuadorian Constitution, it has taken less than two years to articulate and proclaim a Universal Declaration of the Rights of Mother Earth with significant – and rapidly growing – public support, and to put it on the agenda of the UN General Assembly. Although opposition within formal United Nations structures to adopting the Declaration must be expected, early indications are that as a people's document it has great potential to unite a wide range of existing networks and movements.

The Declaration provides a context and support for the demands of indigenous people's organisations, conservation organisations, human rights groups, land rights movements in India, the international water rights movements and the emerging climate justice movements. If these different kinds of civil society organizations begin collaborating on the basis of the worldview expressed in the Universal Declaration of the Rights of Mother Earth, the artificial divide between activists who work for just relationships between people and those working for just relationships between humans and nature, would begin to dissolve. The Declaration may yet become a manifesto which unites a broad coalition of people and organizations who share the understanding that we will not succeed in addressing the fundamental issues facing humanity unless we transform the core values and governance systems of industrial civilizations. As the marchers at Copenhagen chanted, we need "system change not climate change"!

The divide between social and environmental issues has already been eroded in Latin America. For example, the nine Caribbean and Latin American countries of ALBA argue that the reason why we have climate change and a host of other environmental and social issues is because most political systems (whether based on capitalism or socialism) are inherently destructive because they do not take account of the need to strike a balance between the interests of humans and those of other members of the Earth community. They point out that in the same way that a leaf will only flourish if it is part of a healthy plant growing in fertile, well-watered soil, so individual human well-being can only be sustained by building healthy communities within healthy ecological communities. This traditional wisdom is as valid today as it ever was. Human rights are meaningless and cannot be sustained if Earth has no rights. The right to life is an empty slogan without food and water, which can only be provided by Earth.

A GLOBAL MOVEMENT EMERGES

The People's Agreement also called for "the building of a Global People's Movement for Mother Earth, which should be based on the principles of complementarity and respect for the diversity of origin and visions among its members, constituting a broad and democratic space for coordination and joint worldwide actions". Although this global movement has not yet coalesced, the beginnings of this process are already evident. Less than five months after the Conference in Cochabamba, a group of people who had been actively involved in promoting the idea that the rights of nature should be legally recognized, met in Ecuador and established a Global Alliance for the Rights of Nature. The Alliance is intended to enable individuals and organizations to come together like tributaries flowing into a river, in order to form a more powerful and effective means of advancing the ideas embodied in the Universal Declaration of the Rights of Mother Earth.

Support for both the Alliance and the Declaration is growing, and respected leaders such as Archbishop Emeritus and Nobel Peace Prize laureate Desmond Tutu have called for people to work for the implementation of the Declaration. As he said:

> "... creating viable human communities that live harmoniously within the Earth community will require committed and concerted action. The Universal Declaration of the Rights of Mother Earth calls upon each of us to embrace our kinship with all the beings of the Earth community and to recognize, respect and defend the rights of all. Now is the time to answer that call."[6]

FUTURE PROSPECTS

In Latin America, "Defend the rights of Mother Earth" is a battle cry not only for environmental protection but also for social justice and freedom from destructive cultural imperialism. The challenge before us is not only to articulate and defend these rights, but to bring into being individual and collective ways of living that reflect a renewed commitment to wholehearted participation in the wonderful community we call 'Earth'. In April 2010 in Bolivia I saw a movement that is both ancient and emergent, beginning to stir and grow. This is a movement rooted in people's deep connection with land and love for Earth. It is moving now – animated and inspired by the human desire for life and impulse to seek intimacy with our fellow beings. Powerful forces motivated by fear and greed may resist it, but ultimately cannot stem the flow of communion that continues to shape the unfolding of the cosmos.

UNIVERSAL DECLARATION OF THE RIGHTS OF MOTHER EARTH

Preamble

We, the peoples and nations of Earth:

considering that we are all part of Mother Earth, an indivisible, living community of interrelated and interdependent beings with a common destiny;

gratefully acknowledging that Mother Earth is the source of life, nourishment and learning and provides everything we need to live well;

recognizing that the capitalist system and all forms of depredation, exploitation, abuse and contamination have caused great destruction, degradation and disruption of Mother Earth, putting life as we know it today at risk through phenomena such as climate change;

convinced that in an interdependent living community it is not possible to recognize the rights of only human beings without causing an imbalance within Mother Earth;

affirming that to guarantee human rights it is necessary to recognize and defend the rights of Mother Earth and all beings in her and that there are existing cultures, practices and laws that do so;

conscious of the urgency of taking decisive, collective action to transform structures and systems that cause climate change and other threats to Mother Earth;

proclaim this Universal Declaration of the Rights of Mother Earth, and call on the General Assembly of the United Nation to adopt it, as a common standard of achievement for all peoples and all nations of the world, and to the end that every individual and institution takes responsibility for promoting through teaching, education, and consciousness raising, respect for the rights recognized in this Declaration and ensure through prompt and progressive measures and mechanisms, national and international, their universal and effective recognition and observance among all peoples and States in the world.

Article 1. Mother Earth

1. Mother Earth is a living being.

2. Mother Earth is a unique, indivisible, self-regulating community of inter-related beings that sustains, contains and reproduces all beings.

3. Each being is defined by its relationships as an integral part of Mother Earth.

4. The inherent rights of Mother Earth are inalienable in that they arise from the same source as existence.

5. Mother Earth and all beings are entitled to all the inherent rights recognized in this Declaration without distinction of any kind, such as may be made between organic and inorganic beings, species, origin, use to human beings, or any other status.

6. Just as human beings have human rights, all other beings also have rights which are specific to their species or kind and appropriate for their role and function within the communities within which they exist.

7. The rights of each being are limited by the rights of other beings and any conflict between their rights must be resolved in a way that maintains the integrity, balance and health of Mother Earth.

Article 2. Inherent Rights of Mother Earth

1. Mother Earth and all beings of which she is composed have the following inherent rights:

(a) the right to life and to exist;

(b) the right to be respected;

(c) the right to continue their vital cycles and processes free from human disruptions;

(d) the right to maintain its identity and integrity as a distinct, self-regulating and interrelated being;

(e) the right to water as a source of life;

(f) the right to clean air;

(g) the right to integral health;

(h) the right to be free from contamination, pollution and toxic or radioactive waste;

(i) the right to not have its genetic structure modified or disrupted in a manner that threatens it integrity or vital and healthy functioning;

(j) the right to full and prompt restoration for the violation of the rights recognized in this Declaration caused by human activities;

2. Each being has the right to a place and to play its role in Mother Earth for her harmonious functioning.

3. Every being has the right to well-being and to live free from torture or cruel treatment by human beings.

Article 3. Obligations of human beings to Mother Earth

1. Every human being is responsible for respecting and living in harmony with Mother Earth.

2. Human beings, all States, and all public and private institutions must:

(a) act in accordance with the rights and obligations recognized in this Declaration;

(b) recognize and promote the full implementation and enforcement of the rights and obligations recognized in this Declaration;

(c) promote and participate in learning, analysis, interpretation and communication about how to live in harmony with Mother Earth in accordance with this Declaration;

(d) ensure that the pursuit of human well-being contributes to the well-being of Mother Earth, now and in the future;

(e) establish and apply effective norms and laws for the defence, protection and conservation of the rights of Mother Earth;

(f) respect, protect, conserve and where necessary, restore the integrity, of the vital ecological cycles, processes and balances of Mother Earth;

(g) guarantee that the damages caused by human violations of the inherent rights recognized in this Declaration are rectified and that those responsible are held accountable for restoring the integrity and health of Mother Earth;

(h) empower human beings and institutions to defend the rights of Mother Earth and of all beings;

(i) establish precautionary and restrictive measures to prevent human activities from causing species extinction, the destruction of ecosystems or the disruption of ecological cycles;

(j) guarantee peace and eliminate nuclear, chemical and biological weapons;

(k) promote and support practices of respect for Mother Earth and all beings, in accordance with their own cultures, traditions and customs;

(l) promote economic systems that are in harmony with Mother Earth and in accordance with the rights recognized in this Declaration.

Definitions

1. The term "being" includes ecosystems, natural communities, species and all other natural entities which exist as part of Mother Earth.

2. Nothing in this Declaration restricts the recognition of other inherent rights of all beings or specified beings.

References

Chapter 1: Anthills and aardvarks
1. UN GA RES 37/7.
2. Brown's book, *Religion, Law, and the Land*. Native Americans and the Judicial Interpretation of Sacred Land focuses on discussions of the Supreme Court's ruling in *Lyng v Northwest Indian Cemetery Protective Association*, 485 U.S. 439, 99 L. Ed. 2d 534, 108 S. Ct. 1319 (1988) and the decisions in *Sequoyah v Tennessee Valley Authority*, 620 F.2d 1159 (1980); *Bandoni v Higginson* 638 F.2d 172 (1980), *Wilson v Block* 708 F.2d 735 (1983); *Frank Fools Crow et al v Tony Gullet et al*, 541 F Supp. 785 (1982).

Chapter 2: The illusion of independence
1. GEO-4 was prepared by about 390 experts and reviewed by more than 1,000 others across the world and at the date of publication of this edition was the most comprehensive United Nations report on the environment available.
2. In 20 years the global human population grew from about 5 billion people in 1987 to more than 6.7 billion by 2007.
3. Brown, Lester, *Eco-Economy: Building an Economy for the Earth*, New York, WW Norton & Co, 2001, pp.7-8.
4. Millennium Ecosystem Assessment, 2005. *Ecosystems and Human Well-being: Synthesis*. Island Press, Washington, DC., p.1.
5. Ibid p.1.
6. Ibid p.35.
7. Ibid p.2.
8. Ibid p.vi.
9. Ibid p.5, figure 4.
10. GEO-3, p 9.
11. WHO Factsheet No 313, 'Air Quality and Health' (updated August 2008).
12. Millennium Ecosystem Assessment, 2005. *Ecosystems and Human Well-being: Synthesis*. Island Press, Washington, DC, p.2.
13. Millennium Ecosystem Assessment, 2005. *Ecosystems and Human Well-being: Biodiversity Synthesis*. Island Press, Washington, DC., p.1.

Chapter 3: The myth of the master species
1. See Chapter 1, Note 2.
2. *The Ecology of Eden: Humans, Nature and Human Nature*, London, Picador, 2002.
3. Ibid p.286.
4. *Gaia: A New Look at Life on Earth*, Oxford: Oxford University Press, 1979.
5. *The Ecology of Eden*, p.288.
6. Ibid p.283.
7. Ibid p.285.

Chapter 4: Why law and jurisprudence matter
1. Allott, Philip, *Eunomia: New Order for a New World*, Oxford, Oxford University Press, 1990 p.298.
2. Kuhn, Thomas S., *The Structure of Scientific Revolutions*, University of Chicago Press, 1962.
3. Capra, Fritjof, *The Web of Life*, London, Flamingo 1997, p.5.

Chapter 5: The conceit of law

1. See 'The Origin, Differentiation and Role of Rights', which is quoted in Chapter Eight.
2. UNCTAD World Investment Report 2009: Transnational Corporations, Agricultural Production and Development.
3. Top 200, Institute of Policy Studies, 2000.
4. Bennett, D., 'Who's in Charge?', London, Programme on Corporations, Law and Democracy.
5. An Act for Limiting the Liability of Members of certain Joint Stock Companies.
6. *Bell Houses Limited v City Wall Properties Limited* [1966] 2 QB p.693.
7. Companies Act 1989 section 3A and section 35(1).
8. Harris, J. W., *Legal Philosophies* (2 ed), London, Butterworths, 1997 pp.12–16.
9. Liebes, Sahtouris and Swimme, *A Walk Through Time: from Stardust to Us*, New York, John Wiley and Sons, Inc., 1998.

Chapter 6: Respecting the Great Law

1. Swimme, Brian and Berry, Thomas, *The Universe Story: From the Primordial Flaring Forth to the Ecozoic Era—A Celebration of the Unfolding of the Cosmos*, HarperCollins, San Francisco 1992, pp.73–75.
2. Smuts, J., *Holism and Evolution*, 1926, quoted in Pepper, D, *Modern Environmentalism: An Introduction*, London, Routledge, 1996.
3. See Lovelock, J. E., *Gaia: A New Look at Life on Earth*, Oxford, Oxford University Press, 1979.
4. Lovelock, J. E., *Gaia: The Practical Science of Planetary Medicine*, London, Gaia Books, 1991, p.23.
5. Bohm, David 'Wholeness and the Implicate Order' in Bloom, William (ed), *The Penguin Book of New Age and Holistic Writing*, London, Penguin, 2001.
6. *The Awakening Earth*, London, Routledge & Kegan Paul (Ark paperback editions 1984).
7. See for example Margulis, Lynn and Dorion Sagan, *Microcosmos*, New York, Summit, 1986.
8. Goldsmith, E., *The Way: An Ecological World View*, London, Rider Books, 1992 (revised edition published by Green Books in 1996).
9. Berry, Thomas, *The Great Work: Our way into the future*, New York, Bell Tower, 1999.

Chapter 7: Remembering who we are

1. Diamond, Jared, *Guns, Germs and Steel: A Short History of Everybody for the Last 13,000 Years*, London, Vintage, 1998.
2. Diamond, 1998, p.109.
3. Eisenberg, 1988, p.124.
4. 'Cosmology as Ecological Analysis . . . A view from the Rain Forest', *Ecologist*, Vol. 7 No.1, p.5.
5. Ibid p.11.

Chapter 8: The question of rights

1. Stone, C. D., *Should Trees Have Standing? And other essays on law, morals and the environment*, New York, Oceana 1996, see introduction.
2. 405 U.S. 727 (1972).
3. *Fisher v Lowe*, No. 60732 (Mich. CA), 69 A.B.A.J., 436 (1983).
4. Stone C. D., *Should Trees Have Standing? And other essays on law, morals and the environment*, New York, Oceana 1996, p.viii.
5. Hohfeld, W. N., *Fundamental Legal Conceptions as Applied in Judicial Reasoning* (1946), which was based on two earlier articles published in 1913 and 1917.

6. This document was presented by Thomas Berry at the Airlie Center meeting (see p.11). A revised edition entitles 'Ten Principles for Jurisprudence Revision' appears asc Appendix 2 in *Evening Thoughts: Reflecting on Earth as Sacred Community.*

Chapter 9: Elements of Earth governance
1. Stone, C., *Earth and Other Ethics: The Case for Moral Pluralism*, New York, Harper and Row, 1987 p.60.
2. *Committee for Humane Legislation v Richardson*, 540 F.2d 1141, 1151, n.39 (C.A. D.C. 1976), quoted in Stone, 1987 p.60.
3. Leopold, Aldo, *A Sand County Almanac*, pp.224–25.
4. Berry, Thomas, *The Great Work*, p.13.
5. Stone, Christopher D., *Earth and Other Ethics. The Case for Moral Pluralism*, New York, York, Harper and Row, 1987.
6. Shiva, Vandana, unpublished paper, July 2002. An edited version
of this paper appeared in *Resurgence* no. 214, September/October 2002, entitled 'Paradigm Shift: Earth Democracy. Rebuilding true security in an age of insecurity'.

Chapter 10: Seeking Earth Jurisprudence
1. Ecopsychology and the Deconstruction of Whiteness', in Roszak et al (1995), p.272.
2. "If the doors of perception were cleansed, everything would appear to man as it is, infinite." From *The Marriage of Heaven and Hell* by William Blake (1757–1827).

Chapter 11: The rhythms of life
1. Eisenberg, Evan, *The Ecology of Eden*, London, Picador, 2000, p.292.
2. Griffiths, J., *Pip Pip: A Sideways Look at Time*, London, Flamingo, 1999.
3. Ibid p.21.
4. Ibid p.274.
5. Eisenberg, Evan, *The Ecology of Eden*, London, Picador, 2000.
6. Ibid, p.294.

Chapter 12: The law of the land
1. The precise content of the speech made in response to overtures by the President of the United States to purchase land occupied by his people, is controversial. No verbatim transcript exists and there are several versions in existence. The first was published on 29 October 1887 in the *Seattle Sunday*, and poetic revisions have been made by, among others, William Arrowsmith in the 1960s and Ted Perry in the 1970s.

Chapter 13: A communion of communities
1. Koestler, Arthur, *Janus: A Summing Up*, London, Pan Books, 1978.
Quoted by Liebes, Sahtouris and Swimme, 1998.
2. Liebes, Sahtouris and Swimme, 1998 p.167.
3. In the case of Diamond v Chakrabarty 447 US. 303 (1980) the United States Supreme court held that it was permissible to patent organisms that were the product of human ingenuity but not those that occurred naturally. Accordingly the court upheld a patent claim for a distinctive bacterium that did not occur naturally and was potentially useful.
4. Convention on Biological Diversity, Preamble. The issue of benefit sharing is also dealt with in the objective of the Convention (article 1), and in the provisions dealing with: access to genetic resources (article 15), the transfer of relevant technologies (articles 16 and 19) and funding (articles 20 and 21).

Chapter 14: Transforming law and governance
1. *The Universe Story* (see Chapter 6, Note 1).
2. Macy, Joanna and Young-Brown, Molly, *Coming Back to Life: Practices to Reconnect Our Lives, Our World,* Gabriola Island, BC, Canada, New Society, 1998.
3. Shiva, Vandana, 'Paradigm Shift: Earth Democracy. Rebuilding true security in an age of insecurity', in *Resurgence* no. 214, September/October 2002.

Chapter 15: The mountain path
1. *The Universe Story* (see Chapter 6 Note 1), p.250.
2. Global Environment Outlook 3, p.14.
3. The United Nations Conference on Environment and Development
convened in Rio de Janeiro, Brazil.
4. 'Perspectives on Traditional Law: Interviewing Inuit Elders', Nunavat Arctic College, Iqaluit, Nunavat, 1999. Quoted by Mike Bell in his essay 'Thomas Berry and an Earth Jurisprudence'.

Postscript: The emergence of Wild Law
1. See http://www.gaiafoundation.org.
2. Shiva, Vandana, *Earth Democracy: Justice, Sustainability, and Peace* (South End Press, Cambridge, Massachusetts, 2005) p.1 and p.5. For a synopsis see Shiva, Vandana, 'Paradigm Shift: Earth Democracy. Rebuilding true security in an age of insecurity' in *Resurgence* magazine no. 214, September/October 2002.
3. Shiva, Vandana, 'Paradigm Shift: Earth Democracy. Rebuilding true security in an age of insecurity', *Resurgence* magazine no. 214, September/October 2002.
4. See www.navdanya.com (last accessed on 21 February 2011).
5. Mahatma Gandhi encouraging Indians to make their own salt as an act of non-violent resistance (satyagraha) to the unjust laws of the British Empire which had created a monopoly in salt manufacture. See www.navdanya.com (last accessed on 21 February 2011).
6. See the Center's website at www.earthjuris.org.
7. 'The Rights of Nature: The Case for a Universal Declaration of the Rights of Mother Earth'. Council of Canadians, 2011 (in press).

Bibliography

Allott, Philip, *Eunomia: New Order for a New World*, Oxford, Oxford University Press, 1990.

Bell, Mike, *Thomas Berry and an Earth Jurisprudence*, unpublished essay, 2001.

Berry, Thomas, *The Dream of the Earth*, San Francisco, Sierra Club Books, 1988.

Berry, Thomas, *Evening Thoughts: Reflecting on Earth as Sacred Community*, edited by Mary Evelyn Tucker, San Francisco, Sierra Club Books, 2006.

Berry, Thomas, *The Great Work: Our way into the future*, New York, Bell Tower, 1999.

Bloom, William (ed.), *The Penguin Book of New Age and Holistic Writing*, London, Penguin, 2001.

Brown, Brian Edward, *Religion, Law and the Land: Native Americans and the judicial interpretation of sacred land*, Eastport, Connecticut, Greenwood Press, 1999.

Brown, Lester R., *Eco-Economy. Building an Economy for the Earth*, New York, W. W. Norton & Co., 2001.

Capra, Fritjof, *The Turning Point: Science, Society and the Rising Culture*, London, Fontana, 1983.

Capra, Fritjof, *Uncommon Wisdom: Conversations with Remarkable People*, London, Fontana, 1989.

Capra, Fritjof, *The Tao of Physics*, Boston, Shambhala, 1975.

Capra, Fritjof, *The Web of Life: A New Synthesis of Mind and Matter*, London, Flamingo, 1997.

Diamond, Jared, *Guns, Germs and Steel: A Short History of Everybody for the Last 13,000 Years*, London, Vintage, 1998.

Eisenberg, Evan, *The Ecology of Eden*, London, Picador, 2000.

Finnis, John, *Natural Law and Natural Rights*, Oxford University Press, Oxford, 1979.

Fox, Warwick, *Towards a Transpersonal Ecology: Developing new foundations for environmentalism*, Boston and London, Shambhala, 1990.

Goldsmith, E., *The Way: An Ecological World View*, London, Rider Books, 1992 (revised edition published by Green Books in 1996).

Griffiths, J., *Pip Pip: A Sideways Look at Time*, London, Flamingo, 1999.

Harris, J. W., *Legal Philosophies* (2nd ed.), London, Butterworths, 1997.

Hohfeld, W. N., *Fundamental Legal Conceptions as Applied in Judicial Reasoning*, 1946.

Hubbard, Barbara Marx, *Conscious Evolution: Awakening the Power of Our Social Potential*, Novata, California, New World Library, 1998.

Jones, Shirley Anne (ed.), *Simply Living: The Spirit of the Indigenous People*, Novato, California, New World Library, 1999.

Kimbrell, Andrew, *The Human Body Shop. The Engineering and Marketing of Life and Engineering*, Penang, Third World Network, 1993.

Kuhn, Thomas S., *The Structure of Scientific Revolutions*, University of Chicago Press, 1962.

Leopold, Aldo, *A Sand County Almanac, and Sketches Here and There*, New York, Oxford 1949.

Liebes, Sidney, Sahtouris, Elisabet and Swimme, Brian, *A Walk Through Time. From Stardust to Us*, New York, John Wiley and Sons, Inc., 1998.

Lovelock, James, *Gaia: A New Look at Life on Earth*, Oxford, Oxford University Press, 1979.

Lovelock, James, *Gaia: The Practical Science of Planetary Medicine*, London, Gaia Books, 1991.

Macy, Joanna and Brown, Molly, *Coming Back to Life. Practices to Reconnect Our Lives, Our World*, Gabriola Island, BC, Canada, New Society Publishers, 1998.

Margulis, Lynn and Sagan, Dorion, *Microcosmos*, New York, Summit, 1986.

Millennium Ecosystem Assessment, Ecosystems and Human Well-being, Washington DC, Island Press, 2005.

O'Donohue, John, *Anam Cara: Spiritual Wisdom from the Celtic World*, London, Bantam Press, 1997.

Quinn, Daniel, *The Story of B*, New York, Bantam Press, 1996.

Reichel-Dolmatoff, Gerardo, *The Forest Within. The World View of the Tukano Amazonian Indians*, Totnes, Green Books, 1996.

Reichel-Dolmatoff, Gerardo, 'Cosmology as Ecological Analysis . . . A View From the Rain Forest', *Ecologist* Volume 7 No. 1

Roszak, Theodore, Gomes, Mary E. and Kanner, Allen D. (eds) *Ecopsychology: Restoring the Earth, Healing the Mind*, San Francisco, Sierra Club Books, 1995.

Russell, Peter, *The Awakening Earth*, London, Routledge & Kegan Paul 1982 (Ark paperback edition 1984).

Sachs, Wolfgang (ed.), 'The Jo-burg Memo: Fairness in a Fragile World', Memorandum for the World Summit on Sustainable Development, Heinrich Böll Foundation.

Shiva, Vandana 'Paradigm Shift: Earth Democracy. Rebuilding true security in an age of insecurity', in *Resurgence* no. 214, September/October 2002.

Somé, Malidoma Patrice, *The Healing Wisdom of Africa. Finding Life Purpose Through Nature, Ritual and Community*, London, Thorsons, 1999.

Stone, Christopher D., *Earth and Other Ethics. The Case for Moral Pluralism*, New York, York, Harper and Row, 1987.

Stone, Christopher D., *Should Trees Have Standing? And Other Essays on Law, Morals and the Environment*, New York, Oceana Publications, 1996.

Swimme, Brian and Berry, Thomas, *The Universe Story: From the Primordial Flaring Forth to the Ecozoic Era—A Celebration of the Unfolding of the Cosmos*, HarperCollins, San Francisco 1992.

United Nations Environment Programme *Global Environment Outlook 3*, Nairobi, UNEP 2002.

United Nations Environment Programme *Global Environment Outlook 4*, Nairobi, UNEP 2007.

Index

aardvarks 27
Acosta, Alberto 185
Africa 85, 181
  see also Namibia; South Africa
African Biodiversity Network 181
agriculture 37, 86–7, 145
ALBA (Bolivarian Alliance for the Peoples of
  Our America) 186
all beings, rights 96–7, 98
Allot, Philip 58
Amazonian Indians 89, 90–2, 111, 148
America see Latin America; United States
American Constitution 19
animal rights 58, 125, 160
Anthony, Carl 123
apartheid 50–1, 124, 151, 159, 164
Aquinas, St Thomas 69
Australia 183
autopoiesis 56, 79, 80
The Awakening Earth (Russell) 81

Bacon, Francis 44, 45, 46
balance 115
Bennett, Daniel 65
Berry, Thomas
  career 21
  on ethics 114–15
  influences on 125, 183
  The Origin, Differentiation and Role of
    Rights 96, 97, 103
  on rights 101
  on universe 126
  The Universe Story 28, 79
  on well-being 170
  on Western civilization 16–21
bills of rights 19, 31, 57
bio-prospecting 156
bio-regional approach 153
biocide 35, 67
biodiversity 35, 40
biotechnology 135
biotic communities 147
Bohm, David 80
Bohr, Niels 47, 60
Bolivarian Alliance for the Peoples of Our
  America (ALBA) 186

Boyle, Simon 183
Britain see United Kingdom
Brown, Brian 31
Brown, Lester 37
Burdon, Peter 183
businesses see corporations
Buthelezi, Mandla 121

Campbell, Colin and Niall 181
Capra, Fritjof 47, 48, 60, 147
Center for Earth Jurisprudence (CEJ) 183
change 158–9
China 49
Cicero 69, 116
civilization, Western 16
climate change 39, 40, 42, 179
Cochabamba talks (People's World
    Conference on Climate Change and
    Mother Earth's Rights) 187, 188
communion 79, 80, 83
communities 147–56, 184
  see also Earth Community
community ecological governance 181
Community Environmental Legal Defense
    Fund (CELDF) 183, 184, 185
companies see corporations
Conference of the Parties of the United
    Nations Framework Convention on
    Climate Change (COP15; Copenhagen)
    187–8
constitutions
  America 19, 56
  Ecuador 160, 184–5, 189
  founding 19
  Germany 31
  law 56, 57
  legislation 112
consumption 37, 42
Convention on Biological Diversity (CBD)
  156
conventional wisdom 123
Copenhagen Accord 188
Copenhagen COP15 meeting (Conference
    of the Parties of the United Nations
    Framework Convention on Climate
    Change) 187–8

Copernicus 46, 82
corporations 17, 64–6, 150, 166, 184
cosmology 44, 54, 89, 90
    see also worldviews
cultures
    dominant 48, 55, 58–9, 170–1
    earth-centred 160–1
customary law 181

Damtie, Melesse 181
The Dancing Wu Li Masters (Zukav) 48
decision-making 161–2, 166, 175
The Decline of the West (Spengler) 16
Dell, Bruce 121
democratic participation 163
Descartes, René 44, 46
development destruction 18
differentiation 79, 83, 148
diversity 79, 83, 148
dominant cultures 48, 55, 58–9, 170–1

Earth
    attitude towards 20–1
    deterioration of 36–41, 62, 170
    paradigm shift 60, 61
    rights 98, 100, 102, 108–9, 186, 187,
        188–9, 192–5
    well-being 100, 117, 180
    see also environment; land; nature
Earth and Other Ethics (Stone) 115
earth-centred cultures 160–1
Earth Community 147–9
    constitutions 19
    decision-making 161
    Earth governance 117
    Earth jurisprudence 170
    rights 97, 100, 101–2, 105
    well-being 43, 59, 73
    wild law 31
Earth Day, International Mother 186
Earth Democracy Movement 155, 163,
    181–2
Earth governance 110, 116–17, 172–4
Earth jurisprudence
    contribution of 180
    defined 78
    Earth Community 170
    elements of 110–17
    and Great Jurisprudence 82–4, 110
    international level 189–90
    need for 29

as path 176–7
practice of 174–5
principles 100, 186–7
rights 105, 108
seeking 121–30
wild law 30–1
Earth Justice Movement (EJM) 155
Eco-Economy (Brown, L.) 37
ecocide 67
ecological footprint 36, 37
ecological overshoot 36–7, 42
ecological thinking 124–30
The Ecology of Eden (Eisenberg) 53
economy, growth 37
ecopsychology 49
ecosystem services 38–9, 41
Ecuador 160, 184–5, 189
Eisenberg, Evan 53, 87, 131, 136
enclosures 149, 160–1
environment 17–20, 36–43, 173
    see also land; nature
environmental law 113–14, 160
equity, intergenerational 92
ethics 113–15
extinction 35, 39–41, 105

feudal systems 140
Finnis, John 71
food *see* agriculture
Fundacion Pachamama 185

Gaia Foundation 183
Gaia Theory 80, 159
Galiardi, Margaret 183
Galileo Galilei 44–5, 46
genetic engineering 134–5, 136, 150
genetic resources 149
GEO (Global Environmental Outlook)
    reports 36–7, 52
Germany 31, 160
Global Alliance for the Rights of Nature
    190
Global Environmental Outlook reports
    (GEO) 36–7, 52
global warming *see* climate change
globalisation 37, 38, 83, 148, 186
governance systems
    bio-regional approach 153
    changing 160, 170–2
    communities 147–8
    cosmology 90

dominant 48, 55, 59
failure of 72–3
false premises 44
Great Jurisprudence 112–13
organic structure 151–2
purpose of 29, 54, 173–4
relationships 99, 115
rights 108
self-regulation 54, 62
and soul 172–4
subject matter of 26–9
transforming 48
see also Earth jurisprudence
Great Jurisprudence 78–84, 105, 112–13
see also Earth jurisprudence
Greenway, Robert 121, 123
Griffiths, Jay 133, 135
Grotius, Hugo 69
growth, economic 37
growth, population 38

Hart, H. L. A. 71
Hawken, Paul 180
healed state 123–4
health *see* well-being
Heisenberg, Werner 46, 47, 60
Hildebrand, Martin von 89
history, human 85–7, 158
Hohfeld, Wesley Newcomb 96, 98
holarchies 146–7, 151
holons 146–7, 151
homosphere 51–3, 59, 63, 72, 170–1
The Human Body Shop (Kimbrell) 27
Hume, David 69, 70
hunters 116

independence, mythology of 44–6
India 181–2
indigenous peoples
Amazonian Indians 89, 90–2, 111, 148
   inspiration from 88–90, 181
   knowledge 149
   land 31, 181, 187
   laws 68
   learning from 93–4
   reciprocity 116
   regulatory mechanisms 165
   rights 102
   wisdom 88, 142, 154, 181
interconnectivity 48, 83, 126
intergenerational equity 92

Intergovernmental Panel on Climate Change
   (IPCC) 39
international community 153
International Mother Earth Day 186

jurisprudence
defined 68
dominant cultures 58–9
Great Jurisprudence 82, 112
homosphere 72
learning 128
objects 63
rights 97, 105, 116
self-regulation 162
see also Earth jurisprudence; Great
   Jurisprudence
justice systems 67

Kimbrell, Andrew 27
Koestler, Arthur 147
Kuhn, Thomas 59

land 138–45
connection with 191
Earth Democracy Movement 182
ecological footprint 37
enclosures 149, 160–1
healed state 123
indigenous peoples 31, 181, 187
land ethic 114
management systems 141
rights 98, 109, 139–40, 141–2
and soul 173
see also environment; nature
Latin America 184–9
see also Ecuador
law
anthropocentric worldview 63
customary 181
degrading 164
environmental 113–14, 160
idea of 57–9
legitimacy of 112
natural 68–71
patent 150
purpose of 29
role of 55–7
wildlife 27
see also jurisprudence; rights; wild law
learning 128–30
legal positivism 70

Leopold, Aldo 114, 129
Linzey, Thomas 183–4, 185
local communities 147–52, 184
Lovelock, James 53, 80, 81, 159

Macy, Joanna 160
Mandelbrot, Benoît 146–7
Margil, Mari 185
marginalised people 41
Margulis, Lynn 81, 159
Marine Mammals Protection Act 114
mass extinctions 35, 39–41
master species, myth of 50–4
mechanistic worldview 17, 60
Mesopotamia 87
Metzner, Ralph 49
Millennium Development Goals 41
Millennium Ecosystem Assessment (MA)
    38–9
Morales Ayma, Evo 186, 187
Mother Earth see Earth
mountains 77, 169
multinational corporations see corporations
music 131, 136

Namibia 27
native Americans 31
natural capital 37, 38, 170
natural law 68–71
Natural Law and Natural Rights (Finnis) 71
natural resources 36–7, 38
nature
    inspiration from 28
    laws of 71–2
    rights 160, 184, 185, 190
    separation from 44–6
    study of 28
    World Charter for Nature 29
    see also environment; land
Navdanya 182
Newton, Isaac 44, 46
non-humans, rights 96–7, 98
noncognitivism 69
North America see United States

oneness see interconnectivity
The Origin, Differentiation and Role of Rights
    (Berry) 96, 97, 103
over-consumption 37–8

paradigm shifts 59, 60, 61

participation, democratic 163
patent laws 150
Pelizzon, Alex 183
People's World Conference on Climate
    Change and Mother Earth's Rights
    (Cochabamba) 187, 188
philosophy 46, 48
physics, quantum 47–8
Pip Pip: A Sideways Look at Time (Griffiths)
    133
political structures 135–6
poorer people 41
population 37, 38, 42, 86
positivism, legal 70
power 140–1, 162
prejudices 124–6
progress 16, 37
property rights 109, 135, 139–40, 141–2
Puffendorf 69

quantum physics 47–8

radical approach 127–8
reciprocity 116
regulatory mechanisms 165, 166
Reichel-Dolmatoff, Gerardo 90, 91, 92,
    148
Reid, Donald 182
relationships 98–9, 115, 142–3
religion 19
resources see genetic resources; natural
    resources
respect 163–4
responsibilities 116, 144, 145
restorative justice 67
rights 63–5, 95–109
    all beings 96–7, 98
    animals 58, 125, 160
    bills of rights 19, 31, 57
    communities 149, 155–6
    Earth 98, 100, 102, 108–9, 186, 187,
        188–9, 192–5
    Earth Community 97, 100, 101–2, 105
    Earth jurisprudence 105, 108
    humans 104–7
    indigenous peoples 102
    justice 116
    land 98, 109, 139–40, 141–2
    legal subjects 99
    legitimacy of 112–13
    nature 160, 184, 185, 190

property 109, 135, 139–40, 141–2
relationships 98–9
responsibilities 116
rivers 106–7
term 96, 97–8
river rights 106–7
Rivers, Elizabeth 183
Russell, Peter 81

sacred land 138–9
sacred places 31
scale, communities 152–4
science 18, 44–8, 60, 130
seeds 110–11
self-regulation 54, 62, 81, 148, 162
separation from nature 44–6
Shiva, Vandana 181, 182
Siemen, Patricia 183, 184
Smuts, Jan 80
social governance 60–1
social movements 154–5, 163, 180
Somé, Malidoma 148, 152
soul (quality) 16–18, 172–4
South Africa 50–1, 124, 151, 159, 164
South America see Latin America
Spengler, Oswald 16
Stone, Christopher 95–6, 113, 115
Swimme, Brian 28, 79
Switzerland 160
systems thinking 47–8

The Tao of Physics (Capra) 47, 48
technologies
  development 16, 17
  incentives 67
  power of 19, 20
  as solutions 53, 159
Teilhard de Chardin, Pierre 81
termites 25–6, 147
Thiong'o, Ng'ang'a 181
time and timing 131–4, 137
traditional knowledge 149
  see also indigenous peoples
Treatise of Human Nature (Hume) 69
tribal communities see indigenous peoples
Tukano Indians 90–2, 111, 148
Tutu, Desmond 190–1

ultra vires 112
uncertainty principle 46, 47
United Democratic Front (UDF) 151

United Kingdom 65, 160–1, 182–3
United Kingdom Environmental Law
  Association (UKELA) 183
United Nations 19–20
United Nations Environment Programme
  (UNEP) 36–7
United States 56, 58, 114, 183–4
Universal Declaration of the Rights of
  Mother Earth 186, 187, 188–9, 192–5
universe 46–8
  see also Great Jurisprudence
The Universe Story (Swimme and Berry) 28,
  79

well-being
  Earth 100, 117, 180
  Earth Community 43, 59, 73
  humans 41, 117, 170
Western civilization 16
whole-maintaining principle 83, 105, 126
wild, term 29–30
wild law 30–1, 158, 170, 178–91
wild time 133–4
wild weekends 182–3
wilderness 30, 31–2
wildlife legislation 27
wildness 30, 31, 170
wisdom
  conventional 123
  governance systems 166, 175
  indigenous peoples 88, 142, 154, 181
  science 130
  timing 132
  wilderness 30
Wiser Earth 180
World Charter for Nature 29
World Summit on Sustainable Development
  40
World Trade Organisation (WTO) 165
worldviews 17, 60, 63
  see also cosmology

Young-Brown, Molly 160

zebras 106
Zeitgeist 179
Zukav, Gary 48

ECONOMICS UNMASKED

From power and greed
to compassion and the common good

Philip B. Smith and Manfred Max-Neef

Economics Unmasked presents a cogent critique of the dominant economic system, showing that it works mainly to bring about injustice, and is also responsible for the merciless onslaught on the global ecosystem. The book then outlines the foundations of a new economics – where justice, human dignity and reverence for life are the guiding values.

The authors: Philip Bartlett Smith (1923-2005) was a Dutch-American experimental physicist who after his retirement devoted himself to studying economics. Manfred Max-Neef is a renowned Chilean-German economist and environmentalist, and author of Human Scale Development.

ISBN 978 1 900322 70 6 £12.95 paperback

FLEEING VESUVIUS

Overcoming the risks of economic
and environmental collapse

Richard Douthwaite & Gillian Fallon (eds)

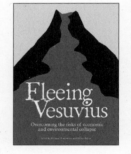

The financial crisis that has blighted the world's richest countries since 2008 is a turning point in human history. We now have to learn to live with economies that shrink rather than grow. Fleeing Vesuvius discusses the economic changes needed to cope with our new situation and how we must develop self-reliant local communities for the future. Contributors include Dmitry Orlov, Nate Hagens, Chris Vernon, David Korowicz, Brian Davey and Patrick Andrews.

The editors: Richard Douthwaite is an economist, author of *The Growth Illusion* and co-founder of The Foundation for the Economics of Sustainability (FEASTA). Gillian Fallon is a writer and journalist and a member of FEASTA's Executive Committee. See www.feasta.org.

ISBN 978 0 95450510 1 3 £17.50 paperback

For a complete list of all our books, please see www.greenbooks.co.uk